A New Form-Function Grammar of English

A New Form-Function Grammar of English

K. AARON SMITH

broadview press

BROADVIEW PRESS – www.broadviewpress.com
Peterborough, Ontario, Canada

Founded in 1985, Broadview Press remains a wholly independent publishing house. Broadview's focus is on academic publishing; our titles are accessible to university and college students as well as scholars and general readers. With over 800 titles in print, Broadview has become a leading international publisher in the humanities, with world-wide distribution. Broadview is committed to environmentally responsible publishing and fair business practices.

© 2023 K. Aaron Smith

All rights reserved. No part of this book may be reproduced, kept in an information storage and retrieval system, or transmitted in any form or by any means, electronic or mechanical, including photocopying, recording, or otherwise, except as expressly permitted by the applicable copyright laws or through written permission from the publisher.

Library and Archives Canada Cataloguing in Publication

Title: A new form-function grammar of English / K. Aaron Smith.
Names: Smith, K. Aaron (Kelly Aaron), 1965- author.
Description: Includes index.
Identifiers: Canadiana (print) 20220404127 | Canadiana (ebook) 20220404283 | ISBN 9781554815067 (softcover) | ISBN 9781770488632 (PDF) | ISBN 9781460407998 (EPUB)
Subjects: LCSH: English language—Grammar.
Classification: LCC PE1106 .S65 2022 | DDC 425—dc23

Broadview Press handles its own distribution in North America:
PO Box 1243, Peterborough, Ontario K9J 7H5, Canada
555 Riverwalk Parkway, Tonawanda, NY 14150, USA
Tel: (705) 743-8990; Fax: (705) 743-8353
email: customerservice@broadviewpress.com

For all territories outside of North America, distribution is handled by Eurospan Group.

Broadview Press acknowledges the financial support of the Government of Canada for our publishing activities.

Edited by Martin R. Boyne

Book design by Chris Rowat Design

PRINTED IN CANADA

Contents

Acknowledgments 13
Introduction 15

1 DOING GRAMMAR IN MODERN TIMES 17
Linguistic Description: Slipping Standards? 18
What Does Grammar Even Mean Now? 18
The Monolith Fallacy 20
A Note on the Prescriptive and Descriptive Approaches for Future Teachers 22

2 PARTS OF SPEECH: AN INTRODUCTION TO WORD CLASSES 27
Parts of Speech 27
    Lexical versus Grammatical Categories 28
    Word Classes Treated in This Book 28
    Word Classes and Productivity 29
    Lexical Word Classes 30
        Nouns 30
            Grammatical Pattern of Nouns: Occurrence with the Definite Article 31
            Grammatical Pattern of Nouns: Occurrence with the Plural Marker 32
        Verbs 33
        Adjectives 35
            Are Funner *and* Funnest *Correct?* 38
        Adverbs 39
    Grammatical Word Classes 42
        Pronouns 42
        Auxiliary Verbs 43
        Determiners 43
        Conjunctions 44
        Prepositions 44

3 UNITS OF GRAMMATICAL ANALYSIS 49
Word 49
Phrase 50
    Finite Verb 50
Clause 52
Sentence Types 52
    Declarative Sentences 53
    Yes/No Questions 53
    ***Wh*-Questions** 54
    Imperative Sentences 55
    Tag Questions 56
    Exclamative Sentences 56

4 THE BASIC SENTENCE 59
The Subject–Predicate Split 59
Language Is Like an Onion 60
Form versus Function 61
    Form–Function Diagrams 61
The Noun Phrase 62
    Potential Parts of the Noun Phrase 63
        Determiners 63
            The Definite Article 63
            The Indefinite Article 64
            The Demonstrative 65
            The Possessive Determiner 66
            Diagramming Noun Phrases with Determiners 66
        Adjectives 69
        Prepositional Phrases 70
    Review of Determiners within Noun Phrases 73

5 NOUNS AND PRONOUNS 77
Nouns 77
    Proper Nouns and Common Nouns 77
    Count and Non-Count Nouns 78
    Collective Nouns 80
    Pluralia Tantum and Similar Nouns 81
    Irregular Plurals 81
        Older English Plurals 82

Voicing Plurals 83
Foreign Plurals 83
   Latin 83
   Greek 84
   Hebrew 84

Pronouns 84
  Personal Pronouns 85
    Subject Pronouns 85
    Pronouns and Gender 86
    Object Pronouns 87
    Possessive Pronouns 88
    Compound Pronouns and Case 89
  Demonstrative Pronouns 91
  Indefinite Pronouns 92
  Impersonal Pronouns and Gender 93
  Reflexive/Reciprocal Pronouns 94
  Quantifier Expressions 95
  Relative and Interrogative Pronouns 95

6 FUNCTIONS OF THE NOUN PHRASE 97

Noun Phrase as Subject 97
  Dummy Subjects and Cleft Sentences 99
  Existential Constructions 101

Noun Phrase as Direct Object 102
  Transitivity 104

Noun Phrase as Subject Complement 104

Noun Phrase as Indirect Object 106

Noun Phrase as Object Complement 107

Diagramming Noun Phrases 108
  Noun Phrase as Direct Object 110
  Noun Phrase as Indirect Object 111
  Noun Phrase as Subject Complement 112
  Noun Phrase as Object Complement 114

Appositives 115

7 FUNCTIONS OF PREPOSITIONAL PHRASES 119

Adjuncts 119
  The Core of the Clause 120
  Attitudinal Adjuncts 121

Adverbial Adjuncts   123
Adverbial Complements   127
    Adverbial Complements Following Copulative Verbs   128
    Diagramming Adverbial Complements   128
    Completion of the Trajectory of a Verb   132
    Analyzing Sentences with Multiple Prepositional Phrases   133
    Prepositional Verbs   136
    Phrasal Verbs   137
        Intransitive Phrasal Verbs   137
        Transitive Phrasal Verbs   139
        Separable and Inseparable Phrasal Verbs   143
        Prepositional-Phrasal Verbs   145
    Adverbial Complements Following Adjectives   147

8   THE INFLECTION PHRASE   153

Tense versus Aspect   154
Verb Forms   155
    Notes on the Forms   155
    Synopsis of the English Verb   158
        Present Progressive   158
        Present Perfect   160
        Present-Perfect Progressive   161
        Past Progressive   161
        Past Perfect   161
        Past-Perfect Progressive   162
    Diagramming Verbs   162
        Be as the Only Verb in a Sentence   167

9   OTHER VERB FORMS   175

The Subjunctive Mood   175
    The First Subjunctive   175
    The Second Subjunctive   177
Modal Verbs   177
    Deontic Meaning   178
    Ability   179
    Epistemicity   179
    Future Time   179
    Quasi-Modals   181

        Modal Verbs in Combination with the Progressive and Perfect Verb Forms   181
        Diagramming Modals   182

10 NEGATION 193
Negation in the Predicate Phrase   193
    Not   193
    Near-Negatives   196
Negation in the Noun Phrase   196
    The Negative Determiner *No*   197
    Negative Indefinite Pronouns   198
    Any   199
Two Negatives Make a Positive?   201

11 ACTIVE AND PASSIVE VOICE 203
Semantic Roles   203
Passivization   204
    When to Use the Passive   205
    Passive Verb Forms   206
    Stative versus Inchoative Passive   207
    Diagramming Passive Sentences   207

12 QUESTION FORMATION 215
Types of Questions   215
    Yes/No Questions   216
    Wh-Questions   217
Who/Whom   219
Wh-Words as Objects of a Preposition: Pied-Piping versus Preposition Stranding   220
Echo Questions   221
Tag Questions   222
    Aren't I or *Am I Not?*   222
    Tag Questions with *There Is* and *There Are*   223

13 COORDINATION AND COMPOUND SENTENCES 227
Coordinating Conjunctions   227
    Lists and the Oxford Comma   228
    Parallel Structure   229
Correlative Conjunctions   230

False Coordination   230
Conjunctive Adverbs   232
Subordination versus Coordination   233
Simple, Compound, and Complex Sentences   234
Diagramming Coordinating Conjunctions   235

14 ADVERBIAL CLAUSES   245
Types of Adverbial Clauses   246
    Clauses of Time   246
    Clauses of Place   246
    Clauses of Concession   247
    Clauses of Adverseness   247
    Clauses of Cause   248
    Clauses of Result   248
    Clauses of Purpose   248
    Clauses of Similarity   249
    Clauses of Commentary   249
    Clauses of Condition   249
The Structure of Complementizers   249
The Second Subjunctive   251
    Subjunctive Verb Forms in Other Adverbial Clauses   254
    If I Were or If I Was?   254

15 RELATIVE CLAUSES   257
Restrictive versus Non-Restrictive Relative Clauses   258
    Restrictive Relative Clauses   260
        Who and *That* as Subjects and Direct Objects   260
        Ø-Relative   265
        Relative Pronouns as Object of the Preposition   266
            Pied-Piping versus Preposition Stranding   267
    Non-Restrictive Relative Clauses   269
Relative Determiner **Whose**   270
A Recap of Relative Pronoun Usage   272

16 NOUN CLAUSES   277
Type I Noun Clauses   278
Type II Noun Clauses   285

Type III Noun Clauses 289
Reported Speech and Tense Shifting 292

17 INFINITIVE AND PARTICIPLE PHRASES 299
Infinitives 299
    Forms of the Infinitive 299
Forms of the Participle 301
The Phrase-Clause Boundary 303
Participle Phrases and Gerunds 308
The Participle-Noun Continuum 311
Complements and Adjuncts in Infinitive and Participle Phrases 312
Compound Infinitives and Participles 315
Infinitives and Participles in Modifying Functions 316
Adverbial Function of Infinitives and Participles 320
A Final Note on Form-Function Trees 322

18 GRAMMAR MYTHS 327
Grammar Myth #1: Don't End a Sentence with a Preposition 327
Grammar Myth #2: Don't Start a Sentence with a Conjunction 329
Grammar Myth #3: People Who Don't Speak Correctly Are Lazy 329
Grammar Myth #4: People Who Don't Speak Correctly Are Stupid 330
Grammar Myth #5: Don't Use the Passive 332
Grammar Myth #6: Singular They Is Wrong 333
Grammar Myth #7: Use of Singular They Achieves Gender "Neutrality" 334
Grammar Myth #8: Two Negatives Make a Positive 335
Grammar Myth #9: People Used Better Language in the Past 336
Grammar Myth #10: Don't Split Infinitives 338
Grammar Myth #11: Ain't Ain't a Word 338

APPENDIX A: PREPOSITIONS 341
Single-Word Prepositions 341
Multi-Word Prepositions 342

APPENDIX B: LIST OF PHRASAL VERBS 343

Index 349

Acknowledgments

There are many people to acknowledge in the development of this book over the past several years. I am very grateful to Mijan Rahman and Allison Hauser, both of whom worked on designing the diagrams included in the chapters. I am also grateful to several teaching assistants over the years who have used a version of the book in their own classes on grammar: Reda Mohammed, Pouya Vakili, Amber Laquet, Allison Hauser, Mijan Rahman. Thanks are due to Allison Hauser and Reda Mohammed for their editing work at several points in the process. I also wish to express my gratitude to Joel Huether for his discussions and proofreading of the final manuscript. I wish also to acknowledge the editorial/production team at Broadview, not least Marjorie Mather, who showed great patience and support during the finalizing of the first draft, delayed because of the COVID pandemic and the stress it placed on everybody and every institution. My very special thanks go out to my copy editor at Broadview, Martin Boyne. His keen eye and deep engagement with the text and content have made this a better book.

Finally, I am very, very grateful to my many students over the years to whom I have taught grammar. Their excitement, insights, and humor have made my job one of the best I could have hoped for.

Introduction

Writing a grammar book for college coursework is a difficult task at any time, but I would argue that it is especially so in current times. Grammar curricula have atrophied so greatly in primary and secondary education that many students will enter into a college grammar class with very little previous knowledge. A book such as this attempts to teach many concepts and terms that might previously have been learned as part of every school child's education from grammar school through high school. Anxieties over whether the book covers enough or supplies too much information have been my constant companions during the preparation process. However, having used the book in several classes (as have several of my teaching assistants), I believe that the book strikes a good compromise and thus presents a firm knowledge of grammar up through an intermediate level. No book designed for use in a single semester of a college grammar class can be exhaustive; one of the most comprehensive grammars of the English language occupies some 1,779 pages![1] However, with the information from this book, a student will have a good grasp of the basics and a little beyond, since the book moves into more advanced areas and concepts in the final chapters. After having learned from this book, a student is well prepared to move on to more advanced topics in grammar and linguistics at either the undergraduate or beginning graduate level.

As I mentioned above, the study of grammar is out of curricular vogue in the American education system. And that's too bad. Arguments against the teaching of grammar often rely on the notion that grammar doesn't make students better writers. But whoever said that learning grammar was only for the sake of becoming a better writer? All human languages and varieties of those languages are structured, and the manner of describing that structure is learned from the study of the grammar of specific languages. Knowing about nouns, phrases, verb forms, and so on is what allows humans to investigate the nature of human language, and given that language is *the* quintessential human behavior, that endeavor is an academic pursuit of no small worth. Looked at in this way, grammar is not about stale drills to improve one's writing or even about "skills" to help students behave more correctly—in the verbal realm. It is about learning an apparatus that curious students can use to figure out why the word "funnest" sounds strange, or why some prepositions and verbs are the same word in an African language like Ewe.

---

[1] Randolph Quirk et al., *A Comprehensive Grammar of the English Language*, 2nd ed. (Longman, 1985).

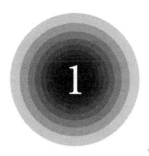

Doing Grammar in Modern Times

Nearly every college introduction to grammar begins with a section distinguishing prescriptive and descriptive approaches to the study of grammar. In the most general terms, grammar **prescription** is concerned with what is right and what is wrong, or what is correct and what is incorrect, with respect to language form. In this way of thinking about language, sentences like *He don't mean no harm* are "incorrect" because they violate some rules of grammar, specifically the prohibition of multiple or double negatives and the requirement of subject–verb agreement (*he don't* → *he doesn't*). Obviously such an approach may result in a list of rules that one might choose to follow in order to stay within the bounds of "Standard English."

On the other hand, grammar **description** attempts to describe what people actually do in language without evaluations of correctness. The fact of the matter is that many speakers of English do use multiple negation, and many speakers do generate subject verb pairings of the *he don't, she don't, and it don't* type.

It is often said of language description that it is objective (as opposed to subjective) and that this kind of objectivity in description is achievable through application of the scientific method to language study. In fact, linguistics is frequently defined as "the scientific study of language." Objectivity in language observation can be difficult to achieve, however, since language is so fundamental to that which defines us as humans and since the use of specific language forms is so intimately connected to our social identities. It is rarely the case that deviations from the prescriptive rules we may know can ever be simply observed without triggering some personal stirrings. Still, as heuristic constructs, prescription and description may and should be kept distinct.

LINGUISTIC DESCRIPTION: SLIPPING STANDARDS?

It is a curious phenomenon that upon learning the two general modes of language study, description and prescription, students of grammar and linguistics assume that acknowledgment of a descriptive approach precludes the need or reality of a prescriptive approach—as if recognition that people actually use multiple negation necessarily means that double negation must be acceptable in all contexts of language use; nothing could be further from the truth.

One of the major objectives of college-level study of grammar and linguistics is to develop a more sophisticated notion of language. Obviously such sophistication is possible only if students move beyond precepts of what one is supposed to do and begin to observe what people really do. Consider for instance a biologist who observes two cells dividing under a microscope but also notices something to have occurred in that division that they never witnessed before. That observer wouldn't be a very good biologist if they simply rejected the new observation as "incorrect." Similarly, simply dismissing any deviation from an idealized standard English as "incorrect" hardly gets to the heart of the nature of English (or any language) and certainly doesn't put a person in a position to make important and informed choices about language arts curricula, methods or approaches to teaching English, creative writing, linguistic study, and so forth. In other words, weighing language description against language prescription makes a person a better language practitioner, no matter what the purpose for learning grammar or linguistics is.

WHAT DOES GRAMMAR EVEN MEAN NOW?

As one develops a more sophisticated notion of language, particularly in terms of understanding prescriptive versus descriptive modes of language study, it becomes apparent that the term "grammar" itself has different meanings. From a prescriptive point of view, grammar refers to the set of rules that seeks to achieve good standard English. However, there are several complications concerning the notion of a "standard English" or any grammar of that variety.

First, it is important to recognize that there is no single, agreed upon standard English, and consequently, as one looks through different grammar books, one finds different rules. For example, traditionally sentences of the type *each student must bring their permission slip on Monday* have been condemned by grammarians. The problem is one of agreement; since *their* refers to *each student* and since *their* is plural and *each student* is singular, they do not agree in number. In fact, it is still easy to find grammar "authorities" condemning that use. However, increasingly one finds books that admit the use of *their* in such contexts.

Second, when talking about standard English, what do we mean? A standard for writing English? A standard for speaking English? In fact, if we were to accept the notion of a standard English for writing and speaking, we would have to understand that we would be dealing with very different grammatical apparatuses to regulate each medium. No one speaks like a book and no one writes completely in the way they speak; strictly speaking, neither is logically possible since the two media, speech and writing, are largely irreconcilable. For instance, people don't normally say "period" at the end of a sentence, or "semicolon," or "question mark," although they can and might do so for humor or emphasis: *I'm not going. Period!* Conversely, the written language is notoriously understaffed to express affectations such as sarcasm. (This lack of symbols for emotive language is one reason that emoticons, or emojis, have been so useful in media such as email and social networking, which rely on the written word but often with an immediacy or casualness akin to spoken genres.)

Along these lines, it should be noted that most grammars are designed to regulate writing. While there are certain uses of English in the spoken medium that would be viewed as offenses against the standard (cf. *he don't*), most usage that would violate the principles of good writing go unnoticed in speech. For example, in standard writing practice, one is taught to avoid the "impersonal you," as in *You can hardly afford to take a family vacation with gas prices so high*. (The standard would advise some other kind of construction, such as the impersonal *one: One can hardly afford...*) Yet even very accomplished writers use the impersonal *you* in speech to no great censure.

Third, it is not, as might be expected, that grammars of the standard tell you what to do; in fact, they just as often, or perhaps even more often, tell you what NOT to do. It is not a coincidence, then, that such grammars have been called "Mosaic grammars" because, like Moses' Ten Commandments, they strive to regulate behavior through a series of "Thou shalt not..." formulas. Consider how frequently, for example, standard grammars contain summary charts of the "Do's" and "Don'ts" of grammar (and how frequently the "Don'ts" list is longer!). Even when one is asked to state a grammar rule from memory, it is most likely that person will state one of the many grammar injunctions such as "Don't end a sentence with a preposition" or "Don't start a sentence with a conjunction."

Finally, and this may be the most surprising fact of all, there is no agreed upon method for determining what is "grammatical" from a prescriptive view, and in fact we see different criteria applied by different grammarians arriving at different judgments all the time. For instance, we have already seen the rule about the use of *their*, a rule that is not absolute but variable and allowing for choice. Sometimes prescriptive grammar rules give the impression of being based on sound logical principles, such as the rule that proscribes "double negatives" because they would cancel one another out. Of course, in certain situations this is sort of true, as in *I'm not unhappy* where the negative *not* cancels the negative prefix *un-*. But in most cases, no such cancellation takes place: *I don't have none* does not mean "I have some." Even in the case of *I'm not unhappy*, there is no true reversal since the sentence does not necessarily mean "I'm happy." Although language is largely systematic, it is not a system like numbers. Therefore glib applications of logic to language might sell a prescriptive rule but ultimately fall short of explaining the facts of language.

In other cases, a grammarian may make an appeal to conventions and histories of "usage" in order to recommend what people should do. While such an approach may seem quite democratic on the surface, the history of such appeals shows anything but egalitarianism. Historically, most forms selected as grammatically correct have been based on their use by the best speakers, the best writers, the best-educated segments of society, and so on. I'm sure it won't be too surprising to know that these "bests" did not include the working classes, people of color, women, or people from any disempowered segment of English-speaking society. It is then particularly under the criterion of "usage" that grammatical prescriptions and proscriptions reveal some of their greatest arbitrariness. However, as arbitrary as grammar rules might be from a linguistic point of view, they are certainly not arbitrary from a social or historical perspective!

In other moments, grammarians pushed to justify their strictures may resort to the last bastion of authority: *ipse dixit* justifications. *Ipse dixit* is basically the "because I said so" defense. These types of justifications often take the form of "Do X because it is more 'elegant/preferable/acceptable/etc.'" These kinds of justifications are circular and subjective; after all, how does one establish what is "elegant" or "preferable" without reference to the author's own sense of propriety, aesthetics, or tastes?

Again, these various grammar-writing justifications are ultimately linguistically arbitrary, and it should seem odd that language users would abdicate their right to question and criticize those who make and enforce laws of language use. However, instead of employing the kind of healthy debate and skepticism that we would direct toward other laws meant to govern us, people seem all too ready to accept grammatical strictures and even to suffer under them in some cases. If legislators in the United States and many other countries were to institute laws that were seen as arbitrary and socially unjust, they would face public outcry, denunciation, and perhaps even revolt. Grammar writers do not face the same public scrutiny even in the face of arbitrariness and outright social injustice. Given such a passive attitude toward language governance, it behooves us to ask why we are so accepting of grammar rules that essentially deny our rights to the languages and dialects we *really* speak.

THE MONOLITH FALLACY

The idea that there is one true language or one true language form is old. Most religions and mythological systems have accounts of the first person or persons to whom the "original language" is ascribed. In the Judeo-Christian tradition, it is Adam who is credited with creating the first language:

Genesis 2:19   And out of the ground, the Lord God formed every beast of the field, and every fowl of the air; and brought them unto Adam to see what he would call them and whatsoever Adam called every living creature, that was the name thereof.

Continuing in the Judeo-Christian tradition, apparently this single language continued until after the great flood that wiped out almost all of humanity, save Noah and his family:

Genesis 6:7   And the Lord said, I will destroy man whom I have created from the face of the earth, both man, and beast, and the creeping thing, and the fowls of the air; for it repenteth me that I have made them.

Genesis 6:8   But Noah found grace in the eyes of the Lord.

The result of having one family survive the flood was a single language, and even a single way of speech (perhaps a single dialect):

Genesis 11:1   And the whole earth was of one language, and of one speech.

The descendants of Noah then decided to reinforce their oneness by building a tower that would reach the heavens, a single structure that would transcend earthly existence:

Genesis 11:4   And they said, Go to, let us build a city and a tower, whose top may reach unto heaven and let us make us a name, lest we be scattered abroad upon the face of the whole earth.

However, God saw too much power and unrestrained behavior as a result of their sameness, linguistic and otherwise:

Genesis 11:6   And the Lord said Behold, the people is one, and they have all one language; and this they begin to do: and now nothing will be restrained from them, which they have imagined to do.

Thus as a means of restraining their potential, God "confounded" their language.

Genesis 11:7   Go to, let us go down and there confound their language, that they may not understand one another's speech.

The story of Noah is a good example of the belief that somehow, somewhere, at some time language in the past was more unified, and the metaphor of the single structure of Babel achieves two seemingly contradictory goals. On the one hand, its destruction is a penalty for the sins of humankind and imposes restraint on those very tendencies that may have caused God to have killed off humans from the Earth in the first place. Thus, diversity across languages and dialects is a constant reminder of our propensity toward sin. Ultimately, Babel reminds us about differences in language and that the inability to adhere to a single true form of language is due to our own moral shortcomings in some way.

On the other hand, the story of Noah and Babel offers a theoretical possibility of a linguistic sameness that existed in the dim past and a transcendence of humankind from the apparent conditions of this world. The contradiction is of course the desire for a state of language sameness that got us into trouble in the first place. That contradiction is resolvable since it was not linguistic unity and the potential of humankind per se that caused God's displeasure, but rather the inability of humans to restrain themselves despite such power (apparently there could be things one could achieve with the power of unity of language that wouldn't be offensive to God). Still, moments of linguistic unity like in the Garden of Eden or among the postdiluvian descendants of Noah are presented, at least for a time, as times of moral innocence, an innocence that is disrupted by humankind's propensity for wickedness.

That link between moral innocence and language unity has been reinscribed in several ways throughout history and among different peoples. Yule (2010) gives two accounts whereby children, who presumably have moral innocence like the first of humankind, were isolated from their speech communities in order to determine the original language. In one account passed down from the Greek historian Herodotus, the seventh-century Egyptian king Psammatichus attempted to discover the original language by having two children raised by a shepherd with no exposure to language in order to see what language the children would spontaneously use. They were reported to have uttered the Phrygian word *bekos*, meaning "bread." The children established, at least for Psammatichus, that Phyrigian must be the original language of humans.[1]

Within the Christian tradition, a similar experiment was attempted by James IV of Scotland. James's linguistically isolated subjects (again two children) were reported to have spontaneously spoken Hebrew—an exceedingly convenient outcome, particularly in a Judeo-Christian culture! The sad truth is that children raised without exposure to language actually acquire little to no language at all. Still, the belief in and search for the original, unified language of human innocence has been strong in many cultures and belief systems throughout history. Language prescription may be, at least in some sense, our modern search for language unity, and perhaps therefore moral rectitude.

Even today, most speakers/writers have the mistaken belief that English in the past was more unified and somehow more correct. The belief persists that English has atrophied by our inattention to correctness and that those speaking varieties furthest from the good old Standard are the worst offenders to this perceived historical correctness. Those speakers are accused of laziness, stupidity, and sometimes even more nefarious transgressions. However, for as much as we know of the history of languages and the history of English, there has never been a period of unity, and the notion of sameness through correctness, as we now think of it, is a rather modern construct.

As we have seen, a descriptive grammar on the other hand is an approach to studying language that takes into account how people really use language. Obviously such an approach is espoused by those working in the linguistic sciences since linguistics seeks to discover the nature of language in one way or another—either as a cognitive entity, a social phenomenon, or something else. Again, notions of "right" versus "wrong" are not part of the descriptive approach in linguistics.

Still, both our cultural belief in and desire for language unity and correctness are strong, and the very idea that there may be some way of thinking about language outside of the prescriptive paradigm strongly challenges those beliefs and desires. But again, it is very important to remember that prescription and description do different things; one is not absolutely better than the other. It is one's purpose or aim in studying language that will lead to the most appropriate approach or view.

A NOTE ON THE PRESCRIPTIVE AND DESCRIPTIVE APPROACHES FOR FUTURE TEACHERS

It may be falsely believed that teachers, especially English teachers, would have little use for language description since their job is to teach literacy in standard English. However, teachers especially stand to gain a lot by descriptive language experience. First, many students come to school speaking varieties of English that are structurally quite different from standard English. If a teacher is not sensitive to that variation, they can actually work as an agent to disenfranchise underrepresented student populations from school. Even some of the most well-intentioned comments can alienate linguisti-

---

1 George Yule, *The Study of Language*, 7th ed. (Cambridge UP, 2020).

cally diverse students. Imagine for instance a teacher saying, "we don't talk that way in school." The teacher, although quite unintentionally, is giving the student the message that they do not belong in the school environment. The aggregation of such comments over many years may encourage dropping out; the correlation between those who speak socially stigmatized dialects of English and drop-out rates among those same populations is probably not a coincidence. And in fact, a teacher who is well trained to understand the linguistically arbitrary nature of Standard English will be more effective in understanding that no single variety of English is really better than another; in other words, that teacher is equipped to teach Standard English as a rhetorical option, not as a moral imperative.

Furthermore, if a teacher is going to be effective in teaching students Standard English, they have to start from the structures that the students know. Students who generate sentences like *he don't* are not making an error in their (variety of) English. We don't teach that student *he doesn't* because it is absolutely right; we teach it because it is another variety of English that they can learn, and learning it allows that student more choices about language. *He doesn't* may well be rhetorically more effective in some contexts—but *he don't* is just as effective in others. In other words, it is not the job of the English teacher to eradicate language variation but instead to teach students how and why language varies, and to show them how to move among different varieties as a source of communicative power.

EXERCISES

A. While the distinction between language prescription and distinction seems straightforward, it requires some conscious thought if a person is to become aware of it naturally. Below you will find 10 statements. Identify each of them as being prescriptive or descriptive in tone and expectation.

1. Do not use *different than* but instead *different from*, as in *My new school is different than from my old one in several ways.*
2. *Bring* is used for conveyance toward the speaker and *take* is used for movement away from the speaker. (Hint: Many speakers of English say sentences like *I have to bring these books back to the library* even though the speaker is not at the library when they say it.)
3. Some speakers of English use the form *ain't* both as a copulative verb as in *He **ain't** from Illinois* and as the auxiliary verb in the perfect construction as in *I **ain't** seen him in many years.*
4. An independent clause should follow a semi-colon in writing.
5. Dialects of English in virtually every English-speaking country tolerate some degree of multiple negation, as in *We're not giving no donations to nobody.*
6. Wherever you can delete the word *that*, you should do so, as in *The Franklin Company has announced that its CEO will be stepping down from office next winter.*
7. There are varieties of English in which possessor nouns are not marked for possession as in *My daddy job is in the City.*
8. One should not start a sentence with a conjunction.
9. In contexts where the locational force of the utterance is clear, forms of the copulative verb *be* may be unexpressed, as in *Where you at?*

10. *Spoke* is the simple past form of the verb and therefore should be used only as a finite verb in the past. It should not be used after the auxiliary *have*, as in *Timothy has ~~spoke~~ spoken to his boss and can't get any days off.*

B. A problem of prescription is that it gives the impression of invariability, the idea that everyone uses prescribed forms, especially in formal contexts. Consider the following passages, all taken from university-press–published books (so we can't say that the writing is "informal" or so wrong that it wasn't accepted for publication!). In each, the author is not adhering to one of the prescriptive rules listed in A. What prescriptive rule in A above does the author seem not to be following?

1. "Is Globalization today really different than globalization a hundred years ago?"

    (Michael D. Bordo et al., NBER Working Paper No. 7195, June 1999)

2. "The world of the city and that of the kampung were indeed clearly different but they were not so divided. Becak (rickshaw) could then bring people to plazas, and kampung was accessible by any two-wheel vehicle." (p. 272)

    (Robbie Peters, *Surabaya, 1945–2010: Neighbourhood, State and Economy in Indonesia's City of Struggle* [NUS Press, 2013])

3. "The subsequent history of the area shows that Ethelwulf's primary motive was not to enrich himself, for only two estates…" (p. 120).

    (H.P.R. Finberg, *The Formation of English 550–1042* [Paladin Books, 1976])

4. "But William of Poitiers then goes on to make a virtue out of necessity, and says…" (p. 149).

    (T.A. Dorey, "William of Poitiers: 'Gesta Guillelmi Ducis,'" *Latin Biography*, edited by T.A. Dorey [Basic Books, 1967], 139–55)

C. Locate a favorite scene of yours from a movie or television show in which two or more people are having a conversation. Now attempt to transcribe into written English just two minutes of that conversation. What sorts of things about the conversation do not come across in writing?

Now, while speaking with friends or family, attempt to speak in only grammatically correct, full sentences. Even after a very short time, what was their reaction? Was it easy for you to maintain that mode of speaking? Would speaking in that way really be appropriate or effective for all situations?

Based on the kinds of experiments carried out above, is it possible or desirable for spoken and written language to be identical? To which medium does grammar prescription seem more applicable?

D. In your answer to C, you probably realized that writing and speaking generally have different domains and that at least for the two tasks described, the rules of prescription seemed more applicable to writing, rather than friendly conversation. However, not *all* writing requires a formal, prescriptive style and not *all* speaking is informal and prescriptively unregulated. Consider the following writing and speaking contexts. Which do you think call for more formality and attention to prescriptive rules? Why?

1. At work, speaking about a project you are directing with the regional manager, whom you are meeting for the first time
2. Talking to your mother about your sister's new boyfriend in the car
3. Writing a note for your husband/wife/partner explaining why you will be late
4. A term paper written in a university history class on the fall of Rome
5. An email to your boss regarding your willingness to work overtime
6. A social network comment on your best friend's page
7. Speaking to the customer service agent at the post office
8. Giving a lecture to a university class
9. Asking directions from a stranger at a baseball game
10. Writing comments in a customer satisfaction survey online

Parts of Speech
An Introduction to Word Classes

PARTS OF SPEECH

Traditionally, the categories of words that are necessary for the discussion of grammatical structure are referred to as **parts of speech**. While the actual catalogue of the parts of speech may vary among grammatical treatments, most grammars offer the following "top-level" set of categories:

noun
verb
adjective
adverb
conjunction
preposition
(and sometimes) interjection

I have referred to these as "top-level" categories because, in fact, the set presented is quite broad. In this book we will actually follow a more elaborate set of categories by recognizing other classes, some of which bear important syntactic resemblances to this top-level set of classifications. An important distinction that we make among groups of word classes is that between lexical and grammatical categories.

LEXICAL VERSUS GRAMMATICAL CATEGORIES
Consider the following sentence:

That **man** *has* **taken** *his* **sick cat** *to a* **vet** *and he is* **paying** *for* **unnecessary treatments**.

We can make a kind of basic cut between two types of words in the sentence, placing the italicized words *that*, *has*, *his*, *to*, *a*, *and*, *he*, *is*, and *for* into one list and the bolded words **man**, **taken**, **sick**, **cat**, **vet**, **paying**, **unnecessary**, and **treatments** into another. It is obvious from looking at the two lists that one major difference is specificity of meaning; the first list of words is more abstract and the second is more concrete. If you were playing a game in which you had to draw the words from this sentence and have your teammates guess the word from your drawing, the task would be much easier with words from the second list.

Another way of stating this difference is to recognize that the words from the second list provide the content of the sentence and the first list provides the functional or grammatical linkages between and among the content words. In fact, if you simply say the bolded words, a person could glean quite well the general intention of your message—not so, however, with the italicized words. In grammar we call the first set of words **grammatical** and the second set of words **lexical**. This basic division of word categories into grammatical and lexical is important because most of the broad word classes offered earlier—namely nouns, verbs, adjectives, and adverbs—may be related to smaller classes that are grammatical in nature. In this way, pronouns are similar in some ways to the larger category of nouns in that they can also fulfill noun functions, like subject, direct object, and so forth. However, while nouns are lexical, pronouns are grammatical. Similarly, verbs are lexical, but the related class of auxiliary verbs is grammatical. Adjectives are lexical but are syntactically similar to so-called determiners, which are grammatical. As you will see in the following list, I have placed prepositions between lexical and grammatical for reasons I will explain at the end of the chapter.

WORD CLASSES TREATED IN THIS BOOK
The word classes that will be treated in this book, divided into lexical and grammatical categories, are listed in Table 2.1.

TABLE 2.1 WORD CLASSES

Lexical	Grammatical
Noun	Pronoun
	Personal
	Subject
	Object
	Possessive
	Demonstrative
	Interrogative
	Relative
	Impersonal
	Reflexive
Verb	Auxiliary Verb
Adverb	
Adjective	Determiner
	Definite Article
	Indefinite Article
	Demonstrative
	Possessive
	Conjunction
	Coordinating
	Subordinating
	Preposition

Within many of the grammatical categories listed here, there are further subcategories. Pronouns have the following subcategories or types: personal, demonstrative, interrogative, relative, impersonal, and reflexive. And within the subcategory of personal pronouns, there are subject personal pronouns, object personal pronouns, and possessive personal pronouns. All of these categories and subcategories are treated in detail later in this chapter and in subsequent chapters of the book. Likewise, under the category of determiner, there are definite articles, indefinite articles, demonstrative determiners, and possessive determiners. And, under conjunctions, it is traditional to separate coordinating conjunctions from subordinating conjunctions. (Later we will see that those words that are often lumped together as subordinating conjunctions comprise a more complicated set of forms and functions.)

WORD CLASSES AND PRODUCTIVITY

There are several criteria for establishing a word class as lexical or grammatical, most of which we won't go into in this book. However, one important criterion is that of productivity. Simply put, languages are always changing, losing certain things but gaining others. Strictly speaking, addition and loss are not the only possibilities in language change since linguistic material can also just "shift" around. In terms of addition, it is generally faster and more frequent that a language will admit new lexical items into its repertoire of words. Remembering that nouns are a lexical category, it is fairly obvious to observe how often and quickly we acquire new nouns. It is perhaps in the domain of technology that we can see good examples of productivity at work: *nanotechnology, microcell, modem,* for example. Of course, given the rapidity of changes in technology itself, many of those new nouns have become or may become obsolete just as abruptly. Does anyone use a "CD changer" anymore?

Thus another term often used to discuss the lexical classes of noun, verb, and adjective (and some adverbs) is **open class**, open in the sense that those categories admit new members frequently and abruptly, although it would appear that some classes do not admit members as frequently as others. For example, the rate of new adjectives is slower than that of nouns and verbs.

The grammatical classes of words are often referred to as **closed class**, terminology which seems to suggest that those classes do not admit new members.

But obviously languages can and do acquire new grammatical words too; Modern English speakers/readers cannot make much sense out of Old English (450–1100 CE) without specialized training because the grammatical systems of Old English and Modern English differ greatly. For example, the auxiliary verb *will*, used now to show future time, as in *The house will be torn down next month*, began developing in Old English but was not primarily an auxiliary to show future; it originally expressed desire. It then continued to develop in the Middle English period (1100–1500), during which time it increasingly became a future auxiliary. It continues to develop even in Modern English (1500 to the present). The emergence of new grammatical items is studied under the framework of **grammaticalization** and constitutes a special subfield of historical linguistic study.

One interesting thing to note is that the appearance of new lexical items is frequently greeted with pleasure and even celebration; TV, radio, and internet news outlets frequently run stories on "new words." However, emergent grammatical patterns more often cause anxiety. The futurate auxiliary form *finna*, for instance, as in *My son is finna graduate next year*, is discussed not so much as the interesting novel auxiliary verb that it is but as a problem and even a potential threat to English. Obviously this kind of anxiety over new grammar is tied to the kinds of ingrained prescriptive thinking about language that we discussed in the last chapter.

LEXICAL WORD CLASSES

Nouns

In school (or on TV), you probably learned that "a noun is a person, place, or thing." Applying such a definition, *doctor* or *John* is a noun because each refers to a person; *playground* or *Springfield* is a noun because each refers to a place (although in some sense *playground* is a thing too); and *bed* or *carrot* is a noun because each refers to a thing (although *bed* can be thought of as a place too). Nouns that refer to abstract entities, like *freedom* or *unfairness*, although possibly thought of as things, have prompted the addition of "ideas" to the definition so that some give the definition of a noun as a "person, place, thing, or idea."

It is important to recognize that the definition of "person, place, thing, or idea" is a semantic one. Since NOUN[1] is a structural category, that is, a piece of the grammar of the language, such a semantic definition will be inapplicable and even confusing in certain circumstances. For example, what about the word "reintroduction"? While it may certainly be thought of as a "thing," particularly given that "thing" has such a broad meaning, it may also be thought of, and perhaps even primarily so, as a kind of action. However, an action is something we more often associate with verbs.

As it turns out, some semantic definitions are better than others, and the "person, place, thing, or idea" characterization works pretty well for defining nouns a lot of the time. However, again since NOUN is a structural category of the language, we can also define it through structural means, a kind of **structural definition**. A structural definition involves recognition of the kinds of grammatical patterns a given word can occur in.

Grammatical Pattern of Nouns: Occurrence with the Definite Article
The definite article in English is *the*. Nouns can occur with the definite article.

> *the doctor*
> *the playground*
> *the bed*
> *the carrot*
> *the freedom*
> *the unfairness*

Within the context of a specific sentence, this structural test will work very well for determining a noun. Out of context, however, its usefulness is limited. For example, if you were asked to say whether the word *love* is a noun, you might generate *the **love** I feel for you* and conclude that it is a noun. Of course, it may be a noun as in the phrase just given, but it is just as likely to be a verb, as in *They **love** baseball*. What is at issue is the flexibility of words in English, particularly nouns and verbs; nouns can frequently be used as verbs, and vice versa, without changing the form of the word. So the structural test of use with a definite article may be a good clue as to the use of a given word in a specific context, or it may tell us the possible uses of a given word.

In the above paragraph on the semantic definition of nouns, the examples included *doctor*, *John*, *playground*, *Springfield*, *bed*, *carrot*, *unfairness*, and *freedom*. While the definite article occurs very naturally with *doctor*, *playground*, *bed*, *carrot*, *unfairness*, and *freedom*, it may, upon first thought, seem odd with *John* or *Springfield*, since expressions like ?*the John*[2] or ?*the Springfield* are odd without further context. The reason for their oddity is that they are so-called proper nouns; that is, they are the names of specific people or places. Since the definite article often works to specify a noun (*the doctor* refers to a specific one, as opposed to *a doctor* or *any doctor*), the definite article is most often unnecessary with names of people, places, or things since the names already make the referent quite specific.

---

1 Word classes when referred to in the abstract will appear in small caps.
2 A question mark before a form indicates that it is questionable, in the sense that it will not be accepted by all speakers/writers.

Still, *John* and *Springfield* can be used with the definite article in the case that the name potentially refers to more than one noun with that name, that is, when it isn't specific:

No, no. I'm talking about John, the florist. The John you met last night is a teacher.
The Springfield in Oregon is the basis for the town on the TV show The Simpsons.

Of course, proper nouns may also become common nouns. *The john* can mean the toilet or bathroom, or the solicitor of financially arranged sexual services. Note that in writing, commonalized proper nouns are more likely to be written with a lower-case initial letter.

Grammatical Pattern of Nouns: Occurrence with the Plural Marker
Another grammatical pattern into which nouns enter involves their ability to take the plural marker. In English, the regular plural is *–s* (although it sometimes sounds like a *-z*, as in *beds*, or like *-es* as in *bushes*; in fact, we write *-es* after a noun that ends in letters such as *s*, *z*, *ch* and *sh*). Applying the plural marker test, we find that it works well with many of our examples of nouns:

doctors
playgrounds
beds
carrots

Like the definite article test, however, the plural works with proper nouns only in the case that we are using them in a common sense:

There are several Springfields in the United States.
There were three Johns at the meeting: John Smith, John Jones, and John Saito.

Abstract nouns often do not work very well with the plural marker because they denote non-countable entities. For example, *coldnesses[1] and ?*freedoms* may sound odd; *freedoms* could refer to types of freedoms, but *coldnesses is very difficult to create a context for.

Our many freedoms come with responsibilities.

While it is true that nearly every noun that can be made plural takes *-s*, there are of course some irregular noun plurals, such as *oxen, sheep, mice,* and *syllabi*. The topic of irregular plurals is taken up in Chapter 5.

---

1 An asterisk indicates that the form is unlikely to be produced by a fluent speaker/writer.

Verbs

Similar to the category NOUN, verbs are frequently defined semantically. When asked, most students of grammar, even those who have not had much grammar, will say that a "verb shows action." Some years ago, the US Department of Health and Human Services' Centers for Disease Control and Prevention, the CDC, launched a health awareness campaign with the slogan "Verb; it's what you do," thus invoking the widely-known semantic definition. However, while the CDC's campaign is certainly laudable as a social campaign, it is questionable from a grammatical perspective.

Consider the verbs in the following sentences (with the so-called base form given in parentheses after it):

*Yoko **drank** coffee.* (drink)
*Ahmed **saw** a movie.* (see)
*We **love** the weather.* (love)
*An accident **occurred** on Sycamore St.* (occur)

Of these verbs, only *drink* expresses a clear subject-initiated action; *saw* and *love* express something more like an experience and *occurred* expresses an event for which the subject has no causal role.

Therefore, if we wanted to provide a semantic definition for a verb, perhaps something like "a verb expresses an action, experience, or event" might be better, but still such a definition would not be wholly adequate. Consider the following expression:

the destruction of the city

In this expression there is clearly an activity (or action), but that activity is not being expressed by a verb at all but instead by a noun, *destruction*. (Note that *destruction* passes at least one of the two noun tests we gave above: the availability of the use of the definite article, *the destruction*.)

Again, since VERB is a structural category in the grammar of English, a structural definition will yield more consistent results. In fact, the structural test for verbs is the easiest to apply and requires the fewest sub-rules or corollary explanations. Simply put, verbs can express tense, distinguishing for example the present from the past. That distinction is made clear by placing a verb into the following form-generating matrices:

Every day [Subject] _____.
                  [VERB]
Yesterday [Subject] _____.
                  [VERB]

Above we established a list of verbs for example purposes. They were: *drink, see, love, occur*. From a semantic point of view, these verbs were quite disparate, but each of them works perfectly in terms of the tense-test:

*Every day Yoko **drinks** coffee.*
*Yesterday Yoko **drank** coffee.*

*Every day Ahmed **sees** a movie.*
*Yesterday Ahmed **saw** a movie.*

*Every day we **love** the weather.*
*Yesterday we **loved** the weather.*

*Every day an accident **occurs** on Sycamore St.*
*Yesterday an accident **occurred** on Sycamore St.*

Obviously, as with nouns, it is necessary to recognize that we have in English both regular and irregular types of verbs. Regular verbs are those that take an *-ed* to show past tense (although that *-ed* may sound like a *-d*, as in *loved*, or it may sound like a *-t*, as in *picked*, or it may sometimes sound like *-ed*, as in *mended*). The vast majority of verbs in English are regular. Irregular verbs show various patterns in the past tense. The stem vowel may change (*speak~spoke*), there may be no change (*hit~hit*), or the past tense marker may be a *-t* (*feel~felt*); and there are others too. So for the vast majority of verbs in English, the tense-test will show a difference in form between the present and past matrices given above:

*Every day Mack **speaks** to the office.*
*Yesterday Mack **spoke** to the office.*

*Every day the children **spell** their vocabulary words.*
*Yesterday the children **spelled** their vocabulary words.* (*spelt* is also possible and more likely in UK English)

Obviously, for the small set of verbs like *hit* (and *put*, *cast*, and a few others), there may be no difference in form:

*Every day the students **hit** the books.*
*Yesterday the students **hit** the books.*

However, one can still sense that the two instances of *hit* are not the same and that there is a tense distinction. Of course in the 3rd singular, a formal difference can be seen:

Every day Bill hits the books.
Yesterday Bill hit the books.

Chapter 8 will have more details on regular/irregular verbs and on tense and other verb forms.

Adjectives

Functionally, adjectives are said to "modify or describe a noun." This formulation is similar to a semantic definition and it is very often true:

*The fugitive drove a **red** car.*
*The car was **red**.*

In the above examples, *red* modifies or describes the noun *car*. In fact, the two examples show the two most common ways in which adjectives work to modify nouns, either directly before the noun or after a linking verb, like *be*. The fact that the word *red* in the two sentences above or *flat* in the two sentences below can appear in these two positions is the first structural test of adjectives. The first position is called the **attributive** position and the second the **predicative** position (consequently the types are sometimes called attributive or predicative adjectives).[1]

*A **flat** pavement makes for the smoothest driving.* (attributive)
*The pavement was **flat**.* (predicative)

*The victim drank the **poisonous** coffee.* (attributive)
*The coffee was **poisonous**.* (predicative)

Due to the historical way in which certain adjectives developed, it is not the case, however, that every adjective can occur in both attributive and predicative positions. For example, *alive* can occur only in predicative position (and also *ashamed, asleep, loath, suspect, glad*, and others, although present-day English speakers may show variation as to which of these are limited to predicative position):

*The spider remained **alive***
the **alive spider*

Lone, on the other hand, can only occur attributively, as can *polar, vehicular, orthopedic*, etc.:

*A **lone** wolf*
The wolf was **lone.*

***Vehicular** manslaughter*
The manslaughter was **vehicular.*

---

1 Another position may be identified as postpositive, where the adjective follows its head. For example, this is the required position of the adjective when it follows an indefinite pronoun like *someone, nobody*, etc. (see Chapter 5).

He's nobody special.
Anyone sane can see that the current regulations are not enough.

It is also possible in English that the same adjective can have different meanings in attributive and predicative positions. For example, the adjective *poor* in attributive position has two possible interpretations:

*The **poor** man*

One interpretation is that the man has little wealth (inherent meaning). The other is that he is unfortunate (noninherent meaning). However, in predicative position, the only interpretation is the inherent meaning:

*The man is **poor**.*

While the functional definition of an adjective stating that they modify or describe a noun captures well what they do, there are other words that can modify nouns. For example, nouns can modify other nouns in compound noun constructions. In the compound noun *coffee cup*, the noun *coffee* modifies the noun *cup*.

Some traditional grammar approaches have explained this noun-modifying relationship by stating that the noun *coffee* is acting like an adjective, "acting" capturing its function. But that is a very different thing from saying that the noun "becomes" an adjective. The confusion can be cleared up by appealing to the difference between the form of a word and its function (a central organizing theme of this book and a topic treated extensively in the next chapter). Briefly, if we say that a noun like *coffee* in *coffee cup* is acting like an adjective in so far as it modifies another noun, we are simply making a statement about its function. However, to say that it now has become an adjective would be to claim that it had changed its word class from noun to adjective—something that clearly hasn't happened.

In order to define the structural category of ADJECTIVE in a way that avoids confusing semantic or functional definitions, we again turn to a structural means of defining word categories. The structural test of syntactic position for adjective in either the predicative or attributive positions was mentioned above, and a second structural test involves the fact that adjectives express comparative and superlative degrees, often through the addition of the endings *–er* and *–est*, respectively.

red, redder, reddest
flat, flatter, flattest

However, the adjective *poisonous* does not admit this pattern; **poisonouser* isn't a word.

In fact, there are two comparative- and superlative-making strategies in English. While some adjectives add *–er* and *–est*, others express comparative and superlative with *more* and *most*. Thus, while we can say *flatter* and *flattest*, we have to say *more poisonous* and *most poisonous*. However, there is a pattern. Adjectives of one syllable take the *–er/-est* endings, and adjectives of three or more syllables take *more/most*.[1]

---

1 There are a few one-syllable adjectives, however, that do not take *-er/-est*: e.g., *right, wrong, real, fake,* etc.

One-syllable adjectives	Three (or more)-syllable adjectives
big–bigger–biggest	*beautiful–more beautiful–most beautiful*
short–shorter–shortest	*terrible–more terrible–most terrible*
close–closer–closest	*reasonable–more reasonable–most reasonable*

The difficult adjectives are those of two syllables because some pattern with the *-er/-est* type and others with *more/most*. Traditionally, the prescriptive rule has been that adjectives of two syllables ending in *-y*, *-er*, *-le*, or *-some* should occur with *-er/-est* in the comparative and superlative. And in fact, examples of those adjectives ending in *-y* sound natural enough (of course with the accompanying change of <y> → <i> in writing):

sunny–sunnier–sunniest
happy–happier–happiest
tacky–tackier–tackiest

However, the others sound archaic or otherwise non-idiomatic to most present-day English speakers:

tender–tenderer–tenderest
humble–humbler–humblest
able–abler–ablest
handsome–handsomer–handsomest

For most English speakers/writers, *more* and *most* probably sound more natural with such adjectives:

more tender, most tender
more humble, most humble
more able, most able
more handsome, most handsome

It is even rather easy to find examples of *more* and *most* used with two-syllable adjectives, including those ending in *-y*, as any internet search of something like "more sunny" will uncover. In fact, it isn't terribly difficult to find examples of *more* and *most* used even with one-syllable adjectives. (Try an internet search for *more glad*, for example.)

A good practice in light of these variations would be to use *-er/-est* for adjectives of one syllable and adjectives of two syllables ending in *-y*. For all others, use the *more/most* pattern.

In order for adjectives to be comparable, they need to have the quality of gradability, meaning that the nouns they describe can be expressed as having more or less of their quality. *Big* is not an absolute quality. A thing can have variable amounts of the quality of "big," so *big* is said to be a gradable adjective. Other adjectives are not really gradable (except perhaps for humorous or ironic effect) in the same way; they are called non-gradable adjectives. *Dead* for instance is an either-or proposition, and one isn't usually *deader*, nor would it make sense to refer to one thing or person being *deader* than another.

To return now to the idea that *coffee* in *coffee cup* "has become an adjective," we are able to reject that notion on structural grounds. There is no way that *coffee* can be put into a comparative or superlative form:

*a coffee-ier cup
*a more coffee cup

Nor can it occur in predicate position:

*The cup is coffee.

Coffee is not an adjective even in compound structures where it functions to modify or describe a noun because it cannot behave like an adjective.

Are *Funner* and *Funnest* Correct?
A hotly debated issue in present-day English concerns the grammatical legitimacy of *funner* and *funnest*. Certainly examples are not hard to find, and some years ago the Apple corporation marketed one of its popular products with the slogan "The Funnest iPod Ever!"

The question of the legitimacy of *funner* and *funnest*, as with all grammar questions, should be considered through both prescriptive and descriptive lenses. Prescriptively, the answer is simple: *funner* and *funnest* are highly stigmatized forms and should not be used as one approaches more formal and academically disseminated writing. Descriptively, the answer is more interesting.

Historically the word *fun* is a noun, and the adjective form of the noun has been *funny* (like *sun* and *sunny*). *Funny*, as an adjective, can occur easily in the comparative and superlative form:

funnier, funniest

And it can occur as a predicate or attributive adjective:

the funny clown ~ The clown is funny.

To return to the noun *fun*, it has appeared over the years in a number of compound nouns:

fun times
fun house
fun guy
fun game

In such compounds, the first noun modifies the second, just as we said earlier of such compounds like *coffee cup*. The modifying function of *fun* in so many compounds has caused a reanalysis in the minds of English speakers moving *fun* away from the category of noun and toward that of adjective. Put more simply, *fun* has largely become an adjective in present-day English. As an adjective of one syllable, then, it follows the expected *-er/-est* rule.

The grammatical purist today will continue to reject *funner* and *funnest* as solecisms, using the time-worn prescriptivists' techniques of sneering, deriding, and impugning the moral character of would-be offenders. Those of more liberal grammatical leanings might adopt the slogan "Language changes; deal with it."

Adverbs

The category traditionally referred to as "adverb" presents some problems for grammar because the kinds of words that have been called adverbs hardly constitute a coherent group. Additionally, as we will see shortly, ADVERB has been described almost completely in terms of function; there are few structural tests for the category and the various types of adverbs, but the question of whether we should consider them a single class of words presents problems for the lexical/grammatical division described earlier.

Traditionally, an adverb has been described as a word that modifies or describes the following:

1. A verb

   *Jane ran **quickly** past the guards.*

   Quickly tells us how Jane ran—it describes the verb.

2. An adjective

   *The tree grew **really** tall.*

   Really tells us the degree of tallness the tree grew into—it describes or qualifies the adjective *tall*.

3. Another adverb

   *Jane ran **very** quickly.*

   Very tells us about the degree of quickness—it modifies the adverb *quickly*.

4. An entire sentence

   ***Unfortunately**, Mary didn't win the prize.*

   Unfortunately comments on the entire sentence, or more accurately positions the entire sentence within the domain of the speaker's/writer's opinion or attitude.

Adverbs of the first type listed above are often derived from adjectives, often through the addition of the suffix -*ly*. Of course, not all words that end in -*ly* are adverbs—*friendly* is an adjective, for example—and some adverbs, like *fast*, do not take -*ly*.

*Casper, the **friendly** ghost*
*He drove **fast**.*

For many speakers, the -*ly* is not included on adverbs in natural/casual speech:

Jane ran quick.
Drive safe!

While the non-*ly* forms in the sentences above are condemned by prescriptive grammars, they usually go unnoticed in everyday language use, especially in informal speech.

It was mentioned above that the category traditionally referred to as ADVERB challenges the distinction between the lexical and grammatical division among word classes. The difficulty stems from the fact that certain adverbs, as catalogued above, behave more like open-class items, while others behave more like closed-class items. For example, the type of adverb that is derived from an adjective by adding -*ly* is as open as the category adjective. So if a new adjective is added to the English lexicon, then a new adverb may be as well:

Bootylicious → *bootyliciously*

However, adverbs that are said to modify an adjective or another adverb, like *very*, do not so easily add new members to the category, and presumably we could make a finite list: *very, quite, terribly, awfully, truly,* etc.

Adverbs give information about the structures they modify in terms of various things:

1. Manner (often an adjective form with the suffix -*ly*)

*Jason **silently** closed the box.*

Silently tells us how, or the manner in which, Jason closed the box. These are the adverbs most commonly derived from adjectives by the addition of -*ly*.

2. Place or direction (*home, here, there, away, north, outside,* etc.)

*The travelers headed **home**.*

Home tells us the direction the travelers headed.

3. Indefinite time (*soon, recently, lately*, etc.)

   *I will see you **soon**.*

4. Sequencing (*next, first, last[ly], second[ly]*, etc.)

   ***First**, place the flour in the bowl.*

5. Frequency (*often, sometimes, rarely, never*, etc.)

   *The Nguyens **often** travel to San Francisco in May.*

6. Degree (*really, very, exceedingly, completely, terribly*, etc.)

   *The house was **completely** destroyed.*

7. Limit (*only, merely, almost*, etc.)

   *The publisher read **only** the first two pages of the manuscript.*

Adverbs that modify an entire sentence can be placed into two types:

1. **Adjuncts**. These adverbs situate the entire sentence in the attitude, opinion, or other subjective state of a speaker's/writer's mind. They include adverbs like *obviously, sadly, unfortunately, honestly, typically*, etc.

Adjuncts are obvious because one can paraphrase them as

It is _____ that [rest of sentence].

So for example, the sentence

Fortunately, Jamie found her lost key.

can be paraphrased as

It is fortunate that Jamie found her lost key.

Note that in the case of a manner adverb, such a paraphrase doesn't work. So the sentence

Randomly, Jennifer chose her seat for the lecture.

cannot be paraphrased as

**It was random that Jennifer chose her seat for the lecture.*

Random does not describe the attitude of the speaker concerning the entire proposition of Jennifer's choosing her seat; it is not an adjunct.

2. **Conjunctive Adverbs**. Conjunctive adverbs are treated in more detail in Chapter 13. For now, they are introduced as a type of adverb that serves to connect (or disconnect) the content of one sentence with another. For example,

The team lost their last game. **However**, *they still made it into the playoffs.*

The conjunctive adverb *however* links up the adversative fact that the team still made it into the playoffs despite their having lost the last game. As another example,

Mariam worked on Saturday. **Otherwise**, *she would have had to work on Sunday.*

In this instance, the conjunctive adverb *otherwise* creates disjunction, an either/or proposition. Mariam either worked on Saturday or she would have worked on Sunday.

Because adverbs do such disparate things and because they do not constitute a category that resides easily in the lexical or grammatical realm, but in both, they are treated in a number of places in the rest of this book. Ultimately, it is not the form category of ADVERB that is of much usefulness in grammatical analysis but instead the function ADVERBIAL that will merit most of our attention. And, as we will see, adverbial functions can be achieved by a number of language structures, not merely adverbs alone.

GRAMMATICAL WORD CLASSES

In this chapter, various grammatical word classes are introduced, but only in a very general way. The grammatical word classes are treated in more detail in subsequent chapters.

Pronouns

A pronoun is a word in a closed class that has a function typical of nouns. However, since NOUN is a lexical category, the possible set of nouns that could act as the subject (a typical noun function) in the following sentence is determined by what actually happened or what referent the speaker/writer has in mind:

_____ *fell over the wall.*

The noun here could be *Mary, the elephant, an egg*—really almost anything depending on the situation. Likewise, a pronoun can also function as a subject; we could fill the slot in this sentence with *he*, *she*, or *it*. The use of *he*, *she,* or *it*, however, is chosen through a relationship between the pronoun and some noun previously introduced into the context:

> *Mary fell over the wall.* **She** *wasn't seriously hurt, however.*

Note that the choice of *she* as the subject in the second sentence is not a free choice. Once *Mary* has been established as the referent in this scene, the only possible subject in the second sentence is *she*; the choice was obligatory; *he* or *it* is not a possible subject in that case, assuming Mary uses the pronouns *she/her*.[1] This kind of obligatoriness is the nature of grammar and of grammatical word categories. Details concerning pronouns are treated more fully in Chapter 5.

Auxiliary Verbs

Lexical verbs, which were discussed above, constitute an open class. Typical of open-class items, the one to be used in a given sentence or utterance has to do with what actually happened in the real world or in the world in the mind of the speaker/writer. In the following sentence, numerous lexical verbs are possible:

> *Matt and Jacob* _____ *in the hallway yesterday.*

Danced, shouted, kissed, etc. are all possibilities. Now consider the following sentence:

> *Matt and Jacob* _____ *talking in the hallway now.*

The only possible verb that one could put in this spot is *are*; the choice is obligatory. As you saw above, obligatoriness is the hallmark of a grammatical system. The grammatical system that *are* belongs to is that of auxiliary verbs. An auxiliary verb is a verb form from a closed-class system that works in conjunction with a lexical verb to build specific types of meaning. For example, the use of *are* with the *-ing* form of the verb builds the so-called **progressive form**, the meaning of which is to denote that a given action is ongoing; in this case we understand from *are talking* that Matt and Jacob are doing the action of talking in an ongoing manner *now*.

The English verb system depends a lot on auxiliary verbs, and appropriately they are taken up in more detail in Chapters 8 and 9.

Determiners

Determiners are closed-class, grammatical words that occur with nouns and help to establish the referent of the noun. Some determiners limit the potential referents of a noun. For example, for any given noun, say, *car*, the list of possible referents is virtually limitless. However, if I say *the car*, then it becomes apparent that there must be a specific car in mind. *The* is one type of determiner, a so-called

---

1 Increasingly in present-day English people might choose the gender non-specifying use of *them/them/their*. The matter is addressed in more detail in Chapter 18.

definite article, and its function is to limit the possible referents of the noun *car* to one previously mentioned, or somehow specified in the shared experience of the speaker/writer and hearer/reader.

There are several subclasses of determiners in English and they are treated in detail in Chapter 4.

Conjunctions

A conjunction is a word that connects pieces of a sentence or utterance into specific relationships.

*The copies were blurred **and** the font sizes were irregular.*

In this sentence, the conjunction *and* serves to connect the first and second parts of the sentence in an **additive** sense. Conjunctions can also be **adversative**:

*Mary can sing **but** refuses to do so.*

Or **conversative**:

*You can meet me in the building **or** outside on the sidewalk.*

Traditionally, conjunctions are **coordinating**, as in the examples above, or **subordinating**. Coordinating conjunctions are treated in more detail in Chapter 13, and subordinating conjunctions are discussed in Chapters 14 and 16.

Prepositions

Prepositions are a closed-class set of words, usually quite short, that express various spatial and temporal relationships among nouns in a sentence.[1]

*Jerry lives **on** Maple Ave.*

Here *on* expresses the place where Jerry lives.

*I will meet you **at** 9:00pm.*

Here *at* expresses the time when I will meet you.

In addition to time and place, prepositions may be used to express a large set of meanings for nouns in an utterance/sentence. Prepositions are treated in detail in Chapter 7.

You will remember from the first part of this chapter that I placed prepositions in an intermediary position between lexical and grammatical status. On the one hand they constitute a closed class, but one that has admitted the most new members over the history of English among the closed-class items; their closed-class status, however, makes them seem more grammatical in nature. On the other hand, they serve to build major syntactic structures and they are more contentful than other gram-

---

[1] Note, however, that adverbs may also be the object of a preposition, as in *over here, from below*, etc.

matical classes, facts that make them seem lexical. Ultimately, whether a given grammar approach considers them grammatical or lexical may have to do with the aims of the approach at hand, or the theoretical context of that approach.

EXERCISES

A. Despite what some may say, terminology in grammar (and language study) is important. Terms have definitions, and those definitions, if learned and practiced, become routines of thinking and classification. It is shocking to a linguist to hear that students are sometimes recommended by some teachers to "do" grammar without "being burdened" by learning the terms. Imagine trying to learn biology without learning what photosynthesis means.

In this exercise, you should work to commit to memory the terms of the parts of speech and their general definitions, both semantic and structural. Grammar is a complex topic, and you should not expect definitions to be simple, one- or two-word statements but rather elaborated arguments.

1. Noun
   a. Semantic Definition

   _____
   _____
   _____

   b. Structural Definition
   i.

   _____
   _____
   _____

   ii.

   _____
   _____
   _____

2. Verb
   a. Semantic Definition

   _____
   _____
   _____

   b. Structural Definition

   _____
   _____
   _____

3. Adjective
   a. Functional/semantic Definition
   _____
   _____
   _____

   b. Structural Definition
   i.
   _____
   _____
   _____

   ii.
   _____
   _____
   _____

B. Below you will find several words about which you will be asked to evaluate whether they can be the part of speech indicated through the application of the structural tests for that category.

   Example: *key* (noun?)

   1. Can it be pluralized? *key~keys*. Yes.
   2. Can it occur with the definite article? *The key.* Yes.

   Based on its passing the two structural tests for nouns, the word *key* may be a noun. (Remember we can only say "may" because it is only in actual use or context that we would know if a specific word were being used as a particular part of speech. In fact as you well know, *key* can be a verb, as in *to key someone's car*, meaning to scratch the paint by swiping a key over the body of a car.)

   Example: *through* (verb?)

   Can it show present and past tense distinction? **He throughs every day/*He throughed yesterday.* No.

   Based on its not being able to show present- and past-tense distinctions, *through* would not be used regularly as a verb. (We say "would not...regularly" because word categories in English are porous, and items that normally belong in one category can be squeezed into another, often quite easily. Under the so-called poetic functions of language, for example, one could feasibly say or write *The deer throughed the thicket of trees and stood before the road.*)

1. band (adjective?)
2. friend (verb?)
3. hand (noun?)
4. religion (verb?)
5. plump (adjective?)
6. lounge (verb?)
7. after (adjective?)
8. grass (adjective?)
9. representation (noun?)
10. seem (verb?)

C. As you learned in this chapter, one of the structural tests for adjectives is their ability to occur in attributive (before the noun it modifies) or predicative (after a linking verb) positions. For this exercise, change the position from an attributive position to a predicative position, or vice versa. In those instances where you cannot change the adjective, note that it may be only attributive or predicative. If the position of the adjective changes meaning, indicate that change.

Example: *The book is long.* → *the long book*
the expensive vacation → *The vacation is expensive.*

1. The grass is green.
2. the utter truth
3. an old friend
4. The students are abroad.
5. my entire family
6. This cake is wonderful.
7. The teacher is aware.
8. The cat is asleep.
9. a misty mountain
10. The candidate is wrong.

D. In this chapter you have learned that adjectives may be made comparative or superlative in two ways: some take the endings *-er/-est*, and others are preceded by *more/most*. Which of the two patterns would you use for the following adjectives and why? If an adjective is non-gradable, state so.

1. large
2. windy
3. cumbersome
4. pregnant
5. black
6. communicative

7. fuzzy
8. atomic
9. high
10. nimble

E. In this chapter you have learned that traditionally an adverb is said to modify a verb, an adjective, another adverb, or an entire sentence. For each of the sentences below, determine what structure the adverb in bold is modifying.

1. **Quickly**, Jason ran into the building and saved the helpless kitten.
2. **Unfortunately**, you can't park there.
3. That vase seems **entirely** fragile.
4. I will **surely** notify you if there is any problem.
5. The car sped down the highway **extremely** fast.
6. **Happily**, the law was overturned by the Supreme Court.
7. **Happily** the lovers strolled down the lane.
8. The exam was **really** easier than most students had expected.
9. The baby spilled the **overly** full glass of milk.
10. Jane answered the question **honestly**.

Units of Grammatical Analysis

In this chapter we will consider the various levels of analysis, in terms of both form and function, that we will make reference to in carrying out grammatical analysis.

WORD

For the purposes of this book, a word may be defined simply as a group of letters that has space on either side. This is clearly a definition for the written word, and in fact defining "word" in the spoken language is sometimes difficult even though we have a strong intuitive sense about just what constitutes a word. Still, while such easy definitions and/or intuitions might work fine for the purposes of doing grammar in this book, it should be noted that the actual question of what constitutes a word is a bit more complicated. For example, the expression *a lot* is still considered two separate words in formal writing, although many people in casual writing put them together as a single word, *alot*. This frequent writing pattern would suggest already that for some speakers/writers of English, *a lot* has become a single word.

The tendency to write *a lot* as a single word is motivated by certain linguistic facts. For example, between the word *a* and a noun, a speaker/writer can usually place any number of adjectives: *a **big/red/happy** clown*. However, this kind of flexibility isn't available between *a* and *lot*, when the meaning is "great degree."

> *I love you a lot.*
> *I love you a **whole** lot.*
> *?I love you a **really** lot.*

*I love you a **big** lot.
*I love you a **red** lot.[1]

While I might accept *a whole lot* and marginally *a really lot*, I cannot say **a big lot* or **a red lot*. This sort of evidence suggests that the "space" between *a* and *lot* is closing up and that they are becoming one word (i.e., they are "univerbating"). The evidence also suggests that *a lot* is not a noun construction any longer. While *really*, a degree adverb, may modify an adjective or adverb, it does not modify a noun, **a really book*. The fact that *really* can modify *lot*, at least for some speakers, suggests that the entire phrase has become adverbial to a large extent.

For another potentially unclear case of what exactly constitutes a word, consider *gonna*. From a prescriptive point of view, the form is not to be written as a single word, but of course people say it as a single word all of the time and certainly write it in informal situations. Most of us know, of course, that it is "really" *going to*, as in *I am going to (gonna) shop for new jeans next week*. However, given that young children have to be taught that *gonna* is two words and that many of them are surprised to learn so, we can assume that it is largely because of literacy and the slowing effects of prescription in literacy that *gonna* has remained divisible as "two words."

PHRASE

In traditional grammar terms, a phrase is defined as a group of words that cluster together without a finite verb, for example, *in the house, the very big dog, with his last breath*. Obviously, understanding this definition depends on understanding what is meant by a finite verb.

FINITE VERB

Succinctly put, a finite verb in English is one that has a grammatical subject and expresses tense.[2] Consider the following sentences:

A. Roger **carried** the papers in an envelope to his secret meeting.
B. **Carrying** the papers in an envelope, Roger left for his secret meeting.

Both sentences A and B contain a form of the verb *carry*. However, note that in sentence A the form *carried* has a grammatical subject, *Roger*. Sentence B, however, has no grammatical subject for the form *carrying*; in that sentence the grammatical subject *Roger* is the subject for the verb *left*. Furthermore, we know the verb *carried* in sentence A happened in the past because of the form of the verb, while *carrying* in sentence B does not establish when the verb takes place; instead we get that information from the simple past verb *left* in that sentence. Note that if I had a different form of the verb *leave* than the past-tense form *left*, it would change the time of *carrying*:

---

1 Remember that a question mark before a form indicates that it is questionable whether fluent speakers of English would accept the expression and an asterisk means it is very unlikely that the expression would be acceptable.
2 We will limit this definition to English, although it clearly works for many other languages, like Spanish discussed in this section. It is not clear that the definition or concept is necessary for the description of all languages, however.

Carrying the papers in an envelope, Roger **left** for his secret meeting at 3pm yesterday.
Carrying the papers in an envelope, Roger **leaves** for his secret meeting every afternoon at 3pm.

We say *carried* is a finite verb form because it has a grammatical subject and expresses tense, while we refer to *carrying* as a non-finite verb form because it does not have a grammatical subject and does not express tense independently.

Let's take a moment to observe the properties of a grammatical subject. In languages like English, the relationship between the grammatical subject and the verb is often apparent in **agreement** patterns, a principle by which the ending on the verb is selected by the subject, also sometimes called **concord**. Agreement is easier to illustrate in a language like Spanish in which one learns to change the ending on the verb, depending on the subject. Thus, the paradigm for a Spanish *-ar* verb in the present tense is this:

*yo habl**o**</br>
tú habla**s**</br>
él* or *ella habla*

*nosotros habla**mos**</br>
vosotros hablá**is**</br>
ellos* or *ellas habla**n***

The selection of *-o, -s,* Ø, *-mos, -ís,* or *-n* depends on the subject: *yo* (*I*), *tú* (*you* singular), *él* or *ella* (*he* or *she*), *nosotros* (*we*), *vosotros* (*you* [plural]), or *ellos* or *ellas* (*they* [masculine or feminine]). So a finite verb, at least traditionally, is one that is bound to its subject by these kinds of agreement patterns.

Spanish, and some other languages, shows agreement well because of the pervasive variation in endings throughout its verbal paradigms.[1] Similar agreement patterns appear in most European languages, including French, German, Latin, Russian, etc. but not in all languages of the world; no such agreement principle is found, for example, in Japanese or Chinese, in which the concept of "grammatical subject" has to be defined differently.[2] English used to have more variation in verb endings but no longer shows agreement-induced changes so extensively. Thus a verb in the simple present paradigm in present-day English is as follows:

*I speak</br>
You speak</br>
He, she,* or *it speak**s***

*We speak</br>
You speak* (dialects: *y'all, y'uns, youse,* etc.)</br>
They speak

The only agreement marker in the present tense for verbs in English is the *-s* that occurs when *he, she,* or *it* (or any singular noun, like *Roger, the cat, my mother,* etc.) is the subject (although not in all dialects of English). Still, it can be recognized, even if abstractly, that the same kind of relationship exists between the subject *they* and the verb form *speak* in a sentence like

They speak French very well.

In Chapter 8, the matter of finite and non-finite is revisited.

---

1 A paradigm is a pattern for displaying the various forms of a word.
2 In Japanese, for example, the finite subject of the verb will be marked with the suffix *-ga*: *Taro-ga sushi-o tabemasita* (*Taro-*subject, *sushi-*object *ate*) 'Taro ate sushi.'

CLAUSE

Traditionally, a clause is defined as a group of words that has a subject and a finite verb. Also traditionally, clauses have been divided into independent and dependent types. An independent clause is often defined as a clause that can stand alone as a sentence. But, there are problems with this definition. First, it presupposes knowledge of what can and cannot be a sentence in prescriptive terms, and second, sentences that would most often be prescriptively incomplete are used often in actual writing. For example, it is not very uncommon to find sentences like these:

> *The ship was ready to set sail on a cloudy March morning. "All aboard." The sailors shuffled up the gangway, each racing to his destiny or his demise.*

All aboard is not a complete sentence by any prescriptive measure, but its use is clearly effective within the development of this particular scene.

Ultimately, we should have some way of conceiving of an **independent clause** that explains it on its own terms—linguistic terms, to be exact. However, this might not be as satisfying as it first sounds, because an independent clause is probably best defined negatively. That is, an independent clause is best defined as not being a dependent clause.

A **dependent clause** (also called a **subordinate clause**) is one that is embedded within another clause or dependent on material within another clause, meaning that the dependent clause serves some kind of function in the main clause. Consider the following sentences:

> *The notebook **that you left in the room** has been found.*
> *I can meet you **when the moon is full**.*

In these sentences, *that you left in the room* and *when the moon is full* are both dependent clauses because they serve functions in the main clause. *That you left in the room* is a **relative** (or **adjective**) **clause** that modifies the noun *notebook*, which is the subject inside the main clause. *When the moon is full* is an **adverbial clause** that tells the time when I can meet you; it modifies the verb *meet* in the main clause.

Having defined the dependent clauses in the sentences, what's left are the independent clauses: *The notebook has been found./I can meet you.* Identification of the independent clause is often best determined by eliminating dependent clause material, and this method of locating an independent clause is what is meant when saying that independent clauses are sometimes more easily defined negatively.

Chapters 14–16 treat subordinate clauses in detail.

SENTENCE TYPES

Throughout this book, we will need to make reference to a number of sentence types, and those are defined in this section. The list of types could be augmented, but those discussed here are the major ones.

DECLARATIVE SENTENCES

A declarative sentence is one that makes a statement; it says something about something or someone. It is the basic sentence type, and in fact other types of sentences are often conceived of as being derived from that basic type:

The Texas live oak sheds its leaves in March.
Our porch needs to be repaired.
That car was driving too fast.
The cat has gotten out of the house and we can't find her.

In writing, declarative sentences are marked for completion with a period (called "a full stop" in the United Kingdom). In speech, declarative sentences have a slight rising and then falling intonation at their end (see Figure 3.1).

FIGURE 3.1

That car was driving too fast.

YES/NO QUESTIONS

A yes/no question (sometimes referred to as a "closed interrogative") is a question for which the appropriate response is typically "yes," "no," or "maybe."

Is he working at the pool again this summer?
Did the Senator speak about the bill?
Are the children going to take a field trip again this year?
Can I get another cup of coffee?

In writing, a yes/no question is completed by a question mark (?). In speech, yes/no questions are completed with a rather dramatic rising intonation (see Figure 3.2).

FIGURE 3.2

Can I get another cup of coffee?

In fact, that rising intonation is so definitive of a yes/no question that speakers can use declarative sentence word order with the rising intonation and hearers will respond appropriately as if it were a question (see Figure 3.3).

FIGURE 3.3

He still lives with his mother?

Sometimes speakers are criticized for "speaking every sentence as if it were a question." What people mean is that some speakers show a rising intonation on the end of many or all declarative sentences, something called "up-speak," a phenomenon you have likely experienced. An unfortunate criticism of such speakers is that they sound "insecure" or "ditzy." Accusations of insecurity or ditziness may be motivated more so socially than linguistically, because another way of interpreting such patterns is to recognize that in those cultures where young women might be prone to such intonational patterns, they have been acculturated to focus on group consensus. Consider the kinds of toys or games that female and male children have traditionally been assigned. While boys' games traditionally underscore individual achievement and even maverick-ism (cowboy, policeman, sports), girls' games have focused on group cooperation (nurse, teacher, jumping rope that depends on members of the group to twirl the rope, etc.). Thought of in this way, it isn't surprising that young females typically would use the rising intonation characteristic of yes/no questions, not because they don't know what they mean or they are insecure, but because they are interested in group input. Not a bad thing at all!

WH-QUESTIONS

*Wh-*questions (sometimes called open interrogatives) are those questions that seek information. They begin with an **interrogative word** (also called a "*wh*-word"):

what
who
where
when
why
how

Or any number of question phrases:

how much
how often
what time

Examples of this type of question are:

Where did he move?
How can I get to Monroe St. from here?

Who wrote the Book of Love?
What are we to do in such times of travail?

Again, in writing, *wh*-questions are punctuated by a question mark, while in speech, they have a falling intonation, without the slight rise first that characterizes the declarative sentence (see Figure 3.4).

FIGURE 3.4

Where did he move?

IMPERATIVE SENTENCES

Imperative sentences are those which issue a command.

Give me a little space!
Help your brother in the yard!
Take two of these pills and call me in the morning.
Always have patience with your loved ones.

Commands can, of course, be more or less forceful. In the case that a command is given with greater force, it is common to punctuate the imperative sentence with an exclamation point. However, when the force is not so strong, a period is generally used.

A remarkable thing about imperative sentences is that they appear with the subject suppressed; traditionally, students learn this as an "understood *you* subject." In the examples given above, the subject of the sentences is understood to be second person (either singular or plural), and in fact it is also possible to express imperative sentences with *you*.

You get over here now!
You leave that child alone!

However, it is probably better to analyze the use of *you* in such sentences not as the subject, but as a **vocative**, that is, an utterance to get the attention of the person being addressed. Note, for example, how *you* in such sentences often creates a different kind of intonation contour and includes a pause between *you* and the verb. Compare these two sentences:

You have been selected as the winner of the prize. (*you* as subject)
You, bring me my mead! (*you* as a vocative in a command)

When *you* is the vocative in a command, a comma may be placed after it as in the example above.

Obviously, imperative sentences can be socially problematic because they are demonstrations of power played out in the linguistic realm. Therefore, speakers/writers will sometimes downplay the force of a command by not choosing the form of an imperative. Instead, the form of a **hortative** may be used, which has a characteristic "let us/let's" formula:

Let us begin to retrace our steps.
Let's not fight.

TAG QUESTIONS

Tag questions are treated more fully in Chapter 12. For now, tag questions can be thought of as a question added to the end of a sentence, usually a declarative one, that seeks to build communicative cohesion by checking for information, building consensus and solidarity, and so forth:

You already spoke to Erin about the role, didn't you?
The Watsons have rented that cabin by Lake Jason, haven't they?
We didn't need to read that whole book after all, did we?

Note that even though such tag questions appear to be seeking information, the speaker/writer already has some assumption that what they are asking is already true. If the speaker/writer really didn't know the answer, they would be more likely to use a simple yes/no question:

Did we need to read that whole book?

EXCLAMATIVE SENTENCES

A final type of sentence for us to consider is the exclamative. An exclamative sentence is one that is meant to show emotion or some visceral reaction/involvement:

They cut down all the trees!
He is a total jerk!

In the written language, exclamatives are most often completed with an exclamation point (!), sometimes in tandem with a question mark, when the exclamation is also a question:

Where do you get off?!

Because exclamations are about expressing an emotion, and emotions are not meant to be "thought out" into complete sentences, they often appear as non-independent structures, some of which are traditionally called interjections:

Of all things!
No way!
My ass!

Wow!
Neato!

In this book, we will focus on the grammar of declarative and interrogative types of sentences.

EXERCISES

A. Consider the following bolded forms and discuss whether we are dealing with a single word or multiple words. Why is the matter confusing in these cases? What might that confusion indicate?

1. I wish he **woulda** called.
2. Mariam didn't speak up **even though** she knew the man was wrong.
3. We didn't think it was going to, but it rained on Monday **after all**.
4. I love it when I can wear my **everyday** clothes to work.

B. Indicate whether the bolded verb form is finite or non-finite based on the principle of agreement.

1. **Clogged** by pet hair, the window fan stopped working during one of the most severe heatwaves of the season.
2. Jamie **stepped** out onto the veranda to find her brother.
3. We all want **to see** improved bipartisan cooperation in Washington, but our hopes are beginning to fade.
4. Iceland **is** located in the North Atlantic Ocean adjacent to the Arctic Sea.
5. **Roasting** coffee at home, while popular before the twentieth century, has seen a revival in practice in recent years.
6. Many US states **had** established land-grant universities before 1900, originally with the aim of focusing on more practical courses of study rather than the liberal arts.
7. **Having** pled the Fifth Amendment for the third time in the trial, the witness clearly was not going to be of much use for the prosecution.
8. The snow **was** melting slowly due to the rather extensive ice pack that had developed on the ground in the coldest days of January.
9. The contractors were dismissed by the architects after **arriving** more than two weeks late.
10. Because of the low energy use, LCD displays **can** be generated by battery, as they are in a number of handheld electronic devices.

C. Identify whether the bolded group of words is a phrase or a clause in traditional grammar terms.

1. The computer **in the lab** has a larger storage disk than the one in my office.
2. The florist charged me more than the advertised price **because I wanted to add lilacs to the arrangement.**

3. If you don't hear from Charlie about the plan before Tuesday, **you may proceed with your own employees**.
4. **Because of so many interruptions due to weather**, completion of the new bridge will be delayed for two weeks.
5. Marilyn has worked **beyond the number of hours required for full-time employees** and must be given overtime pay.
6. The word *fabric* is commonly used as a synonym for *textile*; however, in the trade of textile production **there are subtle differences between the two terms**.
7. Japan is first mentioned **in first-century Chinese writings**.
8. Daylight Saving Time, or DST, was originally proposed to limit evening use of electric lighting **and thus to save energy**.
9. The skill of candle making is one **that was apparently created independently by several different peoples in history**.
10. William Faulkner's *Absalom, Absalom!* has been called **the best Southern novel of all time** by some critics.

D. Identify the independent clause by removing the dependent clause.

1. *Sanitation* refers to the removal of wastes from the physical environment in which humans reside.
2. The term *Iron Curtain*, which is no longer applicable in modern political times, was used to refer to the physical and ideological boundary between the communist East and capitalist West in Europe during the twentieth century.
3. Although lemon juice is called for in this particular recipe, the rind of the fruit may be substituted.
4. The word *television* can be thought of as an etymological hybrid, since *tele-* is from Greek, meaning 'far,' and *-vision* is from Latin, meaning 'seeing.'
5. Domestic cats are descended from African wildcats that lived about 10,000 years ago.

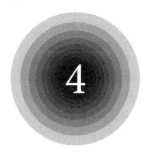

The Basic Sentence

In the last chapter, the declarative sentence was given as the basic sentence type. In this chapter, we will look at some of the core pieces of a declarative sentence, specifically the subject–predicate split.

THE SUBJECT-PREDICATE SPLIT

The first division that we can make in a clause is between the subject and the predicate. In the most general terms, we can say that the predicate expresses some verbal notion about an action, event, state, existence, etc., and that the subject of the clause is the person, place, or thing which that verbal notion is said about.

Minnie carried the pie into the kitchen.
My grass has been growing.
The females of the species choose their mating partners from a pool of over 50,000 candidates.

In this set of sentences, the subjects are

Minnie
My grass
The females of the species

The predicates are

> *carried the pie into the kitchen*
> *has been growing*
> *choose their mating partners from a pool of over 50,000 candidates*

If you apply the definition given above, the predicates all express a verbal notion, and the subject is what they say it about. The string of words *carried the pie into the kitchen* expresses a verbal action, and *Minnie* is who it is said about in terms of her doing that action.

In fact, students with little to no experience in grammar are quite successful in identifying the subject–predicate split.

LANGUAGE IS LIKE AN ONION

Notice how the subjects in the above examples can sometimes be a single word, like *Minnie*, but they can also consist of many words that belong together such that they constitute a phrase, like *my grass* or *the female of the species* (see again Chapter 3 on the definition of a phrase in traditional grammar). This fact may raise the question of what exactly is the subject of a sentence such as *My grass has been growing*. Is it the whole phrase, *my grass*? Or merely the noun, *grass*?

The answer is both!

In the last chapter, a phrase was defined as a group of words that belong together without a subject and a finite verb. However, all words in a given phrase are not equal; at least one of them is the **headword**. For our purposes, a headword can be thought of as the most important or central word in the phrase. It is the word around which the other words cluster. For example, given the set of phrases below, what word would a person most likely indicate as the "most important" or "most central" word?

> *The red chair*
> *A babbling brook on the mountainside*
> *Our decrepit grandfather*

It's likely that *chair*, *brook*, and *grandfather* would emerge as the headwords in these phrases. Note that each of these words has in common the fact that they are nouns. The phrases for which they are heads are called **noun phrases**, or **NPs** for short.

In assessing functions of a sentence, we are concerned with those functions on multiple layers at once—at the level of the word and at the level of the phrase and clause too. These layers of structure and analysis are the chief motivation behind the metaphor that language is "like an onion," since onions, too, have several layers that constitute its whole.

FORM VERSUS FUNCTION

When analyzing language, there are two equally important areas of analysis to consider—one is form and the other is function, and no small amount of confusion for learners of grammar has arisen because all too often the two areas of analysis are conflated. Thus, in analyzing a sentence like *My grass has been growing*, we can note that *my grass* is a noun phrase and that *grass* is the head noun. But so far we have identified only their **form**.

We could also say of *my grass* (and its head noun *grass*) that it is the subject of the sentence. **Subject** is its **function**.

Maintaining the distinction between form and function is key to doing grammatical analysis—and to making sense out of grammar generally.

FORM-FUNCTION DIAGRAMS

In order to illustrate the importance of both levels of analysis, form and function, we will employ a schematic representation of sentences, referred to as **form–function trees**, that show both levels of analysis.[1] In these diagrams, functions will be underlined and labeled under the words, phrases, and clauses, while forms will be represented as branching nodes in a hierarchically arranged structure above the words. These kinds of tree diagrams have been used in linguistics for many decades, but mostly to show structure only. The tree diagram in Figure 4.1 shows the basic subject–predicate split in the sentence *My grass has been growing*.

FIGURE 4.1

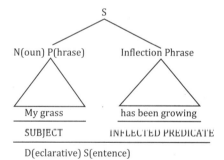

The diagram indicates to us that the entire group of words is a clause (S) and that the group of words *my grass* within the clause is a noun phrase (NP) in terms of its form, but a subject in terms of its function. Meanwhile *has been growing* is an **inflection phrase**, the function of which is **inflected**

---

1 To my knowledge, Paul Hopper developed the general form–function diagram. The form–function trees used in this book are similar, but they differ in some significant ways. Perhaps the biggest difference is that the diagrams in this book include more detail in the predicate, on both the formal level (Inflection Phrase) and the function level (INFLECTED PREDICATE), and the diagrams have been extended to include non-finite clauses, as in Chapter 17.

predicate. Note, too, that the entire clause is underlined below the functions of subject and inflected predicate (which appear all in caps for a reason that will be apparent later in this book). The entire underlined clause has the function **declarative sentence** (DS). In fact, the diagram in Figure 4.1 lacks a lot of detail because, as we will soon see, each word in the sentence has a form and a function, and groups containing those words have a form and function, and groups of words containing those groups of words have a form and function, and so on. In other words, the use of triangles here is a way to avoid giving details about the more specific structure in this sentence. For now, we turn to the details of the noun phrase.

THE NOUN PHRASE

A noun phrase is a group of words that belong together in which the head word is a noun or a pronoun, as in the following examples:

> Marcus
> a telephone
> our rusty car
> that really tall skyscraper
> she
> they

As the examples show, a noun phrase can range from being a single word, for example, the noun *Marcus* or the pronouns *she* and *they*, to longer and longer groupings of words. In each case, however, there is a noun (or a pronoun) serving as head: *Marcus, telephone, car, skyscraper, she,* and *they*, respectively. After identifying that the headword is a noun in each, we can identify that the other words in the multi-word noun phrases **depend** on the noun, or we might think of them as "satellites" of the noun.

The term *depend* is actually a more complex grammatical notion than the word implies. Essentially, dependent linguistic items **modify** or **complement** a head item. In the case of the noun phrase *our rusty car, rusty* is an adjective and it modifies *car* in the sense that it limits the number of possible referents *car* can have to at least those that are rusty. Dependent linguistic material can also complement a headword. For example, if a sentence consisted only of **Jane is*, it would be incomplete. While *is* is a verb, it wouldn't be a complete predicate without a noun or an adjective following it: *Jane is a teacher* or *Jane is tall*. Thus the noun phrase *a teacher* or the adjective *tall* completes or complements the verb *is*. Complementation comes up again in future chapters of this book, as does modification. In the section that follows, we look at several modifying structures of the noun.

The head–dependent relationship is also apparent in that dependent linguistic material moves around with the head in certain syntactically derived constructions. For example, the noun-adjective pair *green flower* appears in that same order in the sentence *Jack placed the green flower on the pillow*. And that pairing also stays together when the noun is moved to a different position in the sentence, as in *It was the green flower that Jack placed on the pillow*. It would not be possible to move only the noun: **It was the flower that Jack placed green on the pillow*. This propensity to cluster together even under conditions of movement is what was meant in the earlier definition of a phrase or a clause as a group of words "that belong together." In other grammatical terminology, such a grouping of words is called a **constituent**.

We might also note that in the type of dependency relationship that exists between *green* and *flower*—that is, modification of a noun by an adjective—the dependent modifier is grammatically optional while the head is not: *Jack placed the flower on the pillow* is grammatically allowable, but **Jack placed the green on the pillow* is not. While it is true that we can use adjectives so that they might appear without an expressed noun, as in *the rich get richer*, a head noun is implied by the modifier, something like *the rich people*. The fact that the modifier implies the presence of a head underscores the relative grammatical primacy of the head in the first place.

POTENTIAL PARTS OF THE NOUN PHRASE

The possible dependents of the noun phrase include adjectives, determiners, prepositional phrases, and relative clauses. Adjectives, determiners, and prepositional phrases will be discussed in this section; relative clauses are treated in Chapter 15.

Determiners

Determiners precede noun phrases and give some information about them in terms of specificity, definiteness, general location, or possession of the noun. Determiners include the definite article (*the*), the indefinite article (*a/an*), demonstratives (*this, that, these, those*), and the possessive forms: *my, your, his, her, its, our, their*.

The Definite Article

The definite article in English is the invariable form *the*. Its principal use is to make the noun it precedes definite. Definiteness means that the speaker/writer and hearer/reader have the same noun in mind. Having the same noun in mind may result from shared physical environment, previous reference, or shared world knowledge:

The trees are late in blooming this year. (said of trees in our shared environment)

We need a new mayor, and after we elect the mayor, we need to hold them accountable for their fiscal policies. (*the mayor* follows the introduction of that noun in the earlier part of the sentence)

The Taj Mahal is in Agra, India. (*Taj Mahal* is known to both of us because of our shared world knowledge)

In reality, article usage in English, and other languages too, is a very complex matter. For example, even though the central purpose of the definite article is to make nouns definite, one use of it is to refer to generic, unspecified groups:

The domestic cat is a good house pet.

In this case, *the* does not refer to any specific *domestic cat* but to the entire class of *domestic cats*. The complexity of use of the definite article (and the indefinite article) is the reason that speakers of English as a second language generally have difficulties with article usage, even after acquiring very fluent and communicatively successful English.

The Indefinite Article

The indefinite article in English is *a/an*. Its use is to mark a noun as indefinite or non-specific (i.e., no certain one in mind).

>*We need a hammer.* (indefinite and non-specific—we could be referring to any possible hammer)

>*A hammer was sitting on the shelf just a minute ago.* (indefinite and specific—we know the hammer in question exists, but we do not share knowledge of it)

The indefinite article has the form *a* before words that begin with a consonant sound, and *an* before those beginning with a vowel sound:

>*a sweater*
>*an instance*

It is important to state the rule for the use for *a* and *an* in terms of the initial sound of the next word and not the letter. For example, we say *an hour*, even though *hour* begins with a consonant letter, because that consonant letter is silent. On the other hand, we say *a university* because even though *university* begins with a vowel, that vowel makes a consonant sound.

In present-day English, there is some variation among English speakers between those who say ***a*** *historical view* versus ***an*** *historical view*. The rule for such variation seems to depend on the placement of stress in words derived from *history*. If the word has stress on the first syllable, *a* is preferred by most speakers:

>*a hístory of French*

But if the stress falls on a syllable other than the first, some speakers will use *an*:

>*an histórical view*

Such variation probably has to do with both the weakness of the h-sound and the general uncertainty of whether it is to be pronounced at all. Speakers who prefer *an historical* do not necessarily prefer *an* for other words beginning with *h* and containing multiple syllables with non-initial stress. Thus, even a speaker or writer, like me, who might use *an historical*, would be less likely to produce

>**an hierarchical structure*

Sometimes such a speaker might say something like

?an habitual problem

However, that use of *an*, and others similar to it, is avoided in edited, written English. In modern usage, *an historical* is somewhat tolerated, both in spoken and written English, but no other use of *an* followed by a word beginning with the *h*-sound is. The facts considering the indefinite article form *an* with words beginning with *h*- is another prime example of the arbitrary nature of language prescription, in which some speakers' practices are elevated to "acceptable" while those of others are not.

The Demonstrative

The demonstratives include forms along the dimensions of singular/plural and proximal/distal. **Proximal** refers to nouns that are close to the speaker (physically, temporally, or psychologically), and **distal** refers to those that are farther away from the speaker (again physically, temporally, or psychologically).

	Singular	**Plural**
Proximal	this	these
Distal	that	those

For example:

this book versus *that* book (*this* = right here, *that* = over there)

these problems versus *those* problems (*these* = current problems, *those* = past problems)

When studying other Indo-European languages, learners have to become used to the notion that determiners have to agree with the nouns they modify. In Spanish, for example, one uses the definite article *el* when a noun is singular and masculine: *el libro*. But one uses *los* when the masculine noun is plural: *los libros*. Similarly, one uses *la* when the noun is singular and feminine: *la pluma*, but *las* when the feminine noun is plural: *las plumas*. Similar kinds of agreement have to be considered for other Indo-European languages, too, including German, French, and Italian.

English, as an Indo-European language, used to work very much like Spanish, or its closer relative German, but it lost that kind of agreement between a determiner and a noun during its history such that our definite article is now the invariable form *the*. However, note that it is in the use of demonstratives that agreement between the determiner and the noun remains since one has to decide between singular and plural forms based on the number of the noun: *this/that book, these/those books*.

The Possessive Determiner

Possessive determiners indicate a relationship between a noun and a possessor, although possession in this sense must sometimes be understood abstractly, as we will see in a moment.

Possessive determiners are akin to pronouns, since they reference a noun (or noun phrase) that has been established in the discourse through previous mention or shared experience. Thus in the expression *my house*, *my* refers to the speaker, similar to the way in which *I* would refer to the speaker in *I live in that house*.

The forms of the possessive determiner are arranged in a **paradigm**, distinguishing singular and plural, and first, second, or third person:

		Singular	Plural
First		my	our
Second		your	your
Third	masc.	his	their
	fem.	her	
	neut.	its	

As indicated above, "possession" has to be understood in a somewhat abstract way, because while we certainly use possessive determiners to indicate possession in the traditional sense of the word, we also use it for abstract senses of possession. Thus, *my book* is about ownership, but *my mother* is not about ownership but about a relationship referred to more often as "source." *Our judgment* is not about ownership but about the judgment of something/someone.

Diagramming Noun Phrases with Determiners

In the tree diagram earlier in this chapter, we were concentrating on the level of phrase and ignoring the internal structure of those phrases by using triangles in order to group words together without indicating the form and function of the various words in the group. Now, however, we are prepared to consider the internal structure of at least one type of phrase, the noun phrase, which we will consistently abbreviate as NP.

A very important concept to grasp in grammatical analysis as one moves from the phrase level to the word level is that a single word can constitute an entire phrase. Therefore, if we simply have a single noun that we wish to diagram, we do not omit the level of NP for it. Thus, the noun *whales* would be diagrammed as shown in Figure 4.2.

FIGURE 4.2

That is, the NP consists of a single noun (N). Placing the actual word under the N is the **lexical entry**, that is, the word of the phrase and clause. So far we have not indicated any function for the NP because it is not anchored in a clause. However, if we were to diagram *whales* in the sentence *Whales give birth to live young*, as in Figure 4.3, the NP would then have the function of subject in the sentence. (NP functions, such as subject, are discussed in Chapter 6.) While SUBJECT is spelled out in this example, it will be abbreviated from now on as SUBJ.

FIGURE 4.3

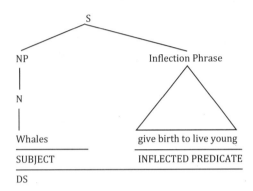

Since the NP *whales* is the subject, we indicate so by underlining all of the words that comprise that NP and label it as subject. Recall from our discussion above that when we consider what is the subject of a sentence, we can answer that question on the level of phrase or word. This point can be a little confusing in examples such as *Whales give birth to live young*, because *whales* is both the NP and N. However, consider a sentence like *A whale has entered the river delta*. Now we are presented with an NP that has two words, *a* + *whale*, and only one of those words is a noun or N, *whale*. In order to diagram *a whale*, we will have two lines extending from the NP, one of which will lead to a node called "Ind. Art." for indefinite article and the other to the node N for the noun (see Figure 4.4).

FIGURE 4.4

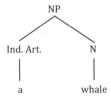

Now if we were to diagram the NP *a whale* in the sentence *A whale has entered the river delta*, as in Figure 4.5, we can see that it is necessary to label the function of the parts of the NP as well as the NP itself.

FIGURE 4.5

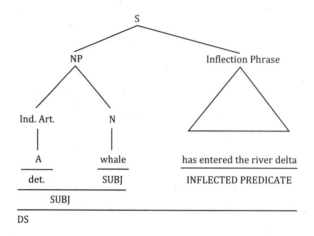

Obviously the N *whale* is the subject, and the function of definite articles, indefinite articles, demonstrative determiners, and possessive determiners is always determiner (det.), as indicated in the tree. Also, all of the words that comprise the NP *a whale* are underlined as a group, with its function given. In this case, the NP also has the function subject, as it did in the earlier example when the NP was just a single word. Another very important concept to grasp is that the head of a phrase and the phrase for which it serves as head always have the same function. So if the N that is the head of the NP is a subject, then the whole NP will also be subject, and vice versa.

In the case that the NP is a single pronoun like *she*, its analysis will look very much like those cases in which the NP is a single noun, except that the branch coming off of the NP will be labeled "Pro" for pronoun (see Figure 4.6).

FIGURE 4.6

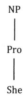

If we place *she* in a sentence like *She is the mayor*, then we underline *she* and label its function as subject (see Figure 4.7).

FIGURE 4.7

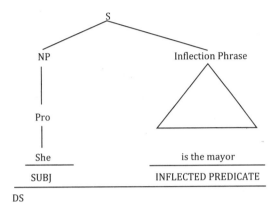

Adjectives

Adjectives as a word class were treated in some detail in Chapter 2, so here the focus is more on their function within a noun phrase (so-called attributive adjectives). As was already stated in Chapter 2, essentially adjectives modify nouns, as did *rusty* in the example *our rusty car*. In analyzing a noun phrase with an adjective, we simply place the adjective in the NP, as in the diagram in Figure 4.8 for the sentence *Our rusty car has broken down*. Note that *our* is labeled as Possessive (Poss.); its function is determiner (det.).

FIGURE 4.8

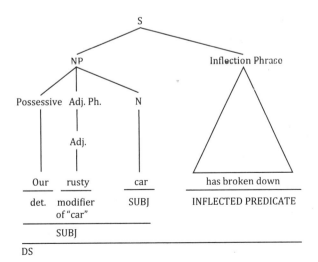

Note first that the function of the adjective (Adj.) is *modifier of "car."* Also notice that in the same way that a single noun could comprise an NP, so too can a single adjective comprise an Adjective Phrase (Adj. Ph.). Therefore in the tree we do not proceed directly from NP to Adj. but insert an intervening level of Adj. Ph. every time an adjective is present.

We do this because the adjective itself may have a modifier, as it does in the example *our really rusty car*. *Really* is traditionally assigned to the class of words known as adverbs, which were treated in some detail in Chapter 2. For now, we can simply call *really* an adverb and note that it modifies the adjective *rusty* by stating some degree of rustiness—in this case, a lot of rustiness.

In this way, *really rusty* itself constitutes a group of words that belong together, since *really* modifies *rusty* and since *rusty* is the headword in that phrase; in other words, the adjective is the head of the adjective phrase. Note that *really* does not modify *car*, as it would not be grammatical to have *really* without the adjective *rusty*, *the *really car*. Thus, *really rusty* is an adjective phrase, as in the diagram for the NP *the really rusty car* (see Figure 4.9).

FIGURE 4.9

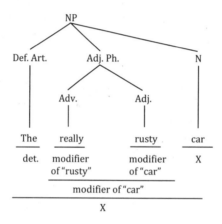

In this phrase, *the* has been used. Its form in the tree is labeled Def. Art. and its function is det. The function of the N and the entire NP has been labeled X since the NP is not in a clause and therefore we cannot know what its precise function would be. Note that at the word level, *really* is a *modifier of "rusty"* and *rusty* is a *modifier of "car."* However, when underlined as an adjective phrase, *really rusty* as a group also has the function of *modifier of "car."* Again, heads and their phrases always have the same function. If the adjective functions as the modifier for the noun, then so does the adjective phrase.

Prepositional Phrases

Prepositional phrases are often understood by students on an intuitive level, perhaps because prepositional phrases are the one piece of grammar that seems to find its way into pre-college classroom grammar instruction. Many a student has spent time "circling the preposition" and "underlining the object of the preposition" in school. And although the ability to identify and analyze prepositional phrases is, certainly in a grammarian's view, a respectable skill, most pre-college instruction does not treat the use or function of prepositional phrases with much detail at all. One use (but note just *one* use) of the prepositional phrase is to modify a noun phrase; there are many other uses, as will soon be clear.

Imagine, for instance, two people standing in front of a display of birds at a zoo and one saying, "Look at that bird!" Of course, unless there just happens to be a single bird in the display, there may well be some confusion as to the specific bird referred to. In the case that there are multiple birds, however, the other person is likely to ask, "Which bird?" The answer may be "The bird with the multi-colored tail." *With the multi-colored tail* is a prepositional phrase, and its role is to give more detail about the noun referred to in order to make the reference clearer; that is, the prepositional phrase *with the multi-colored tail* modifies the noun. The following list gives more examples of nouns modified by prepositional phrases:

the man **with glasses**
a message **for you**
his house **on the lake**
the snake **in the grass**
our class **at noon**
that kid **on the bike**

There are many prepositions in English, and a list appears in Appendix A.

When diagramming a prepositional phrase, abbreviated PP, we add another layer into the tree, as see in Figure 4.10.

FIGURE 4.10

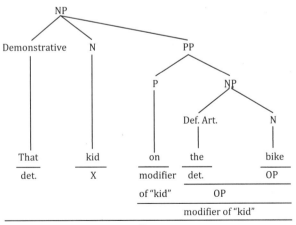

In that diagram, we start with the uppermost phrase level, which comprises all of the words *that kid on the bike*. It is an NP off of which we have a demonstrative, serving the determiner function, and the head N, *kid*. Also coming off of the NP is a PP. Inside the PP we have the NP *the bike*. Note that it is never possible to have a determiner or noun coming directly off of the PP; there will always be an intervening layer of NP. The structure of the NP is similar to those we have already seen. The function of an NP inside a PP is always object of the preposition (OP). Since the function of the NP is OP, we also know that the function of the individual N within that NP will also be OP. Again note the function of the head of the prepositional phrase, the preposition *on*, is the same as the entire prepositional phrase; both function as *modifier of "kid."*

Again the head N, *kid*, and the entire NP are labeled X since the NP does not occur in a clause and so we cannot name its function. However, if we were to put *that kid on the bike* into a sentence like *That kid on the bike wore a jean jacket*, we could then assign the function of subject to the noun *kid* and likewise to the entire NP, *that kid on the bike* (see Figure 4.11). Note that demonstrative has now been abbreviated as Dem.

FIGURE 4.11

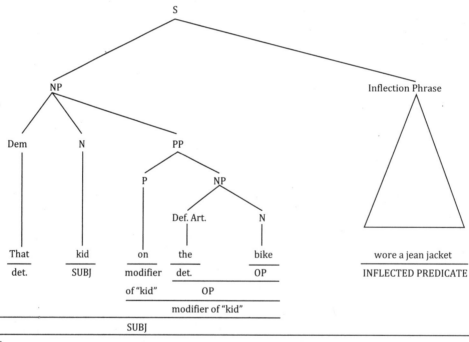

REVIEW OF DETERMINERS WITHIN NOUN PHRASES

In this chapter we have seen four classes of words that can serve a determiner function within the NP:

1. Definite Article (Def. Art.)

FIGURE 4.12

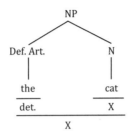

2. Indefinite Article (Ind. Art.)

FIGURE 4.13

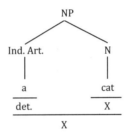

3. Possessive Determiner (Poss.)

FIGURE 4.14

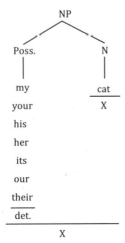

4. Demonstrative Determiner (Dem)

FIGURE 4.15

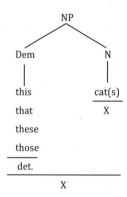

EXERCISES

A. Indicate where the subject–predicate split is in the following sentences.

1. The cat was sleeping on the bed during the night.
2. A warm breeze flowed in off the sea and through the window.
3. Painting is offered in the art department.
4. We hired contractors to pour the cement for our patio.
5. The picture on the wall depicts the building of the pyramids in ancient Egypt.
6. Our new clock from Italy didn't work on our electric current.
7. It will be over 70 degrees on Monday.
8. Simon tried to bake a cake for his friend's birthday.
9. The flowers from the florist have remained fresh for more than two days.
10. My sister is leaving for Spain next week.

B. Make form–function trees with triangles for the subject–predicate splits in A.

C. Change the following singular demonstratives to plural demonstratives. Do not forget to change the number of the noun, verb, and any other parts of the sentences too, as necessary.

1. This manufacturer has sent the wrong order to that company.
2. The guests won't be able to follow this itinerary for long.
3. That sheep lost its way and wandered into this field.
4. This road was under construction for most of the summer.

5. The professor handed out this syllabus to all of the students on the first day of class.
6. I have had significant pain in this tooth for several days.
7. Our students have benefited greatly from that mentorship program offered through the community center's after-school program.

D. Draw form–function trees for the following noun phrases with determiners. In each case, the noun phrase functions as a subject and should be labeled as such.

1. The clock stood still for more than three hours.
2. These peanuts were roasted over an open flame for just the right taste.
3. Your appeal was quite convincing to the members of the selection committee.
4. A defect was pointed out in the procedure for removing excess tissue.
5. My resolution is to treat all members equally but fairly.

E. Draw form–function trees for the following noun phrases with determiners and adjective phrases. Note that not all of the noun phrases will contain determiners. If there is no determiner, do not include it in the tree. In each case, the noun phrase functions as a subject and should be labeled as such.

1. The black silhouette was seen striding along the beach in the dead of night.
2. That overly ripe apple will not taste good in the salad.
3. Our really costly bill has risen even more this winter because of the hike in oil prices.
4. Very necessary repairs will be contracted out this summer.
5. An exquisite diamond is on display at the museum this week.

F. Draw form–function trees for the following noun phrases with determiners, adjective phrases, and prepositional phrases. Note that not all sentences will contain determiners or adjective phrases. If there is no determiner or adjective phrase, do not include them in the tree. In each case, the noun phrase functions as a subject and should be labeled as such.

1. A package of seeds costs about $2.50.
2. These unnecessary interruptions from the audience will extend the meeting for several hours.
3. Their recipe for spicy tomatoes is delicious.
4. Knives with really dull blades will not work for cutting even slices of bread.
5. The cold water from the tap overfilled the sink.

Nouns and Pronouns

NOUNS

There are several subclassifications of nouns in English. The various classifications are important because they capture certain grammatical patterns that nouns become involved in.

PROPER NOUNS AND COMMON NOUNS

Proper nouns are names of specific nouns, like *Jason, Lady Liberty, Illinois State University, Michigan*, and so on. They are written with an initial capital letter. Common nouns, on the other hand, are generic; they refer to a class of items, like *bed, trailer, teacher,* and *tree*. Of course, in many actual sentences, common nouns are not generic because they in fact refer to a specifically intended referent. In the sentence *The tree was cut down*, the speaker/writer and the hearer/reader both know the specific tree being referred to. That specifying function is achieved through the use of the definite article with the noun (see again Chapter 4). In other instances, however, the noun *tree* might be non-specific, as in *We need to plant a tree in this spot*. *A tree* may refer to any tree that exists or can grow from a seed.

Proper nouns are usually specific; *Lady Liberty*, with no other contextual information, refers to the one and only Statue of Liberty. However as discussed in Chapter 2, nouns that are proper in one context may be common in another. Imagine, for instance, that there was a play with several actors dressed up as Lady Liberty. The director might say, "*Would all of the Lady Liberties please stand over here!*" Earlier, the point was made that if a proper noun becomes highly conventionalized as a common noun, like the use of *john* to refer to the toilet, it will usually no longer appear with a capital letter. *Lady Liberty* used as a common noun in the example just given, however, is probably not so conventionalized and should be capitalized.

COUNT AND NON-COUNT NOUNS

A count noun is one that is divisible from other nouns with the same or a similar referent and therefore is also easily countable. For example, the noun *table* refers to a flat surface with four legs. If there are two items that have a flat surface and four legs, I would speak of two *tables*. *Table* is singular; *tables* is plural.

On the other hand, consider a noun like *sugar* in its prototypical sense of an aggregate collection of white grains. *Sugar* in this sense is not divisible in the same sense that the noun *table~tables* is. In the prototypical sense of a mass of white grains, *sugar* is not countable; we don't count the grains as **one sugar,* **two sugars,* **three sugars,* etc. Some other typical non-count nouns include *water, wood, flour, dirt, rice,* and so on.

Although we do not count *sugar* in the prototypical sense of a mass of white grains as reiterative instances of the same or similar noun, the form *sugar* can appear with a plural marker; *sugars* does exist in English. At a diner, one may ask for *two sugars*. However, in this sense (and in this context) *sugar* does not refer to a mass of white grains but instead to the normal packaging of sugar for diner use—a packet of sugar. In this case, one would even have to say that *sugar* in the first sense and *sugar* in the second are different words, the second being a count noun, and a good dictionary would list them as separate words. Other prototypically non-count nouns that have count-noun derivatives that refer to packaged quantities in this way include *waters* (bottles of water), *coffees* (cups of coffee), and *puddings* (two servings of pudding). In other cases, the pluralized form of an otherwise non-count noun will refer to types or species of that noun. For example, in the sentence *The Christmas Sampler includes five different teas*, the word *teas* refers to types of teas.

One of the important reasons to know the difference between count and non-count nouns has to do with the type of quantifier word or expression used with each. In some cases, the same quantifier is used with either:

*There is **a lot of** sugar in this particular recipe.* (non-count)
*There are **a lot of** reasons you should go back to school.* (count)

*We really need **some** rain!* (non-count)
***Some** insurance plans include protection in case of flood.* (count)

It is important to note that with quantifying expressions that denote more of the noun, like *a lot*, count nouns are plural and non-count nouns remain singular. Thus, we have a difference in the singular versus the plural verb in the sentences *there **is** a lot of sugar~there **are** a lot of reasons*.

Quantifying words used with count and non-count nouns are given below:

Count	Non-Count
many	much
a lot of	a lot of
a few (fewer)	less
a	some
another	
one, two, etc.	
some	

In present-day English, people seem to be especially concerned with the use of *few* (*fewer/fewest*) and *less* with regard to count and non-count nouns. While in casual speech or unedited writing we regularly hear sentences such as *there are less clouds in the sky today than there were yesterday*, prescriptivists would be quick to point out that according to the rules of usage, *fewer clouds* is preferred since *cloud* is a count noun. It is perhaps in grocery stores especially that people like to point out the prescribed error in signage announcing that a given check-out lane is limited to *12 items or less*. Of course, those with a prescriptive bent would like to see *12 items or fewer* since *items* is a plural count noun. The distinction between *few* and *less* is becoming a shibboleth of good usage among some, although insistence on observing the distinction everywhere is somewhat pedantic.

We have already learned *a* as an indefinite article. *A* derives historically from the numeral *one*, and it continues on as a kind of quantifying word, since it still signals *one*. Therefore, it occurs with singular, count nouns:

a desk
a man
a board
a truck

It does not occur with non-count nouns in (in their non-count sense):

*a sugar
*a flour

In some grammar traditions, *some*, in its use with non-count nouns, is considered to be the plural indefinite article:

some sugar
some flour

Thus, at least for some grammarians, the use of *some* as in *I need some water* is like the use of *a* in the sentence *I need a pen*; neither the *water* nor the *pen* is definite. However, unlike a singular count noun, which almost always occurs with a determiner in American English,[1] non-count nouns may appear without a determiner, in which case the meaning is non-specific as well.

I need water.

COLLECTIVE NOUNS

Collective nouns are those that refer to a group of individuals. Examples of collective nouns include *cattle, crew, family, team,* and *herd.* The tricky thing about collective nouns is that they are semantically plural but singular in form. However, one can pluralize some collective nouns, for example *crews* or *families,* but not others, such as **cattles.*

In American English, collective nouns are generally regarded as singular count nouns in the sense that they occur with a singular verb:

The crew has worked into the night.

And they occur with the same quantifying expressions used for count nouns:

The foreman sent in another crew to finish the job.

The exception to this usage is *cattle,* which is considered plural everywhere:

The cattle are allowed to graze in those two fields during the day.

In British English, collective nouns are more frequently plural:

His family are on holiday in Norway.

However, even in American English, one can sometimes find a plural verb used with a collective noun. For example, there is a rule in traditional grammar that the singular verb is used with collective nouns when they are said to be acting as a whole, or in unison. However, when the members of the collective are acting in divergent ways, the plural is preferred.

The committee has agreed upon a proposal to send to the governor's office.
The committee have disbanded and formed several different splinter groups.

---

1 In certain expressions, singular count nouns may appear without any determiner: *in bed, at school, on task,* etc., but *in the hospital* (contrast British English *in hospital*), *at the gym,* etc. Such expressions are best thought of as idiomatic, that is, pre-packaged chunks that may defy grammatical or semantic explanation.

PLURALIA TANTUM AND SIMILAR NOUNS

There are in English some nouns that end with an *-s*, which, at least historically, was a plural marker. However, in present-day English, these nouns always appear with the *-s*, and sometimes that *-s* does not signal plural at all. For instance, the noun *news* (derived from making the adjective *new* plural—an odd thing to do for an English adjective!) is semantically like a non-count noun; note, for example, its use with a singular verb:

*The news **is** not good.*

Other examples of nouns that have a plural marker but are singular in meaning (and agreement with the verb) include various words in the following categories:

Games—*cards, checkers, tiddlywinks, hearts*

Diseases—*measles, mumps, herpes*

Disciplines/fields of study—*linguistics, mathematics, acrobatics, physics, humanities*

The one thing that such nouns have in common is that there is no corresponding singular, at least not in the normal sense. Thus a single game of checkers is not **checker*.

There is also a group of nouns that are in some sense a pairing of two connected parts, such as *scissors, clippers, binoculars,* and *tongs*. These nouns are commonly used as plural nouns, but one sometimes hears them being used as if they were singular, although such uses are pedantic:

Please pass me a scissors. (where the singular determiner *a* is used)

Or a singular is back-formed from the normally occurring plural:

I like the pant, but the blouse is atrocious.

Yet another similar set of nouns are those called **pluralia tantum**, that is, nouns that occur in the plural: goods, guts, dregs, funds, accommodations, amends, annals, arms, brains, clothes, congratulations, dues, looks (as in good looks), outskirts, premises, savings, surroundings, tropics, and so forth. These nouns have no singular counterpart and always trigger plural agreement:

The accommodations were most satisfactory.

IRREGULAR PLURALS

There are in English several nouns that retain an irregular plural, even against the fierce regularity of the plural marker *-s/-es*. These irregular plurals have their origins either in older English or in plural forms borrowed from other languages.

Older English Plurals

The first set of older English plurals is called **umlaut plurals**. Umlaut, sometimes called *i-mutation* in Old English handbooks, is the changing of a vowel in the stem of the word based on the addition of a suffix with a high vowel ([i] or [y]). The suffix that originally caused the change and the original vowels involved in the umlauting process have long been lost or obscured by subsequent kinds of changes in this small set of nouns. Still the effect of this older process is that some nouns have a different vowel in the stem in the singular and plural:

mouse~mice
louse~lice
man~men
woman~women
foot~feet

Another set of irregular plurals, again a very small group, has a suffix in *-(r)en*; there are only three such nouns, the last of which in the list below is fairly obsolete or at least very highly specialized in meaning:

ox~oxen
child~children
brother~brethren

Such nouns constituted a much larger group in older stages of English, in which they are known as weak nouns (actually neither *child* nor *brother* were originally **weak nouns** but came to have the *-n* plural later). Even as late as Shakespeare, several nouns had retained the Old English weak-noun plural form. For example, Shakespeare could use *shoen* for *shoes* and *eyen* for *eyes*.

Another native Old English plural is actually the absence of a plural marker, known as a Ø-**plural** (pronounced "zero-plural"), for example *one deer* and *two deer*. The Ø-plural was regular for a certain class of nouns in Old English (so-called long-stem neuter nouns) which used to be a larger group; the plural of *word* was, in Old English, *word*. Perhaps based on analogy with the noun *deer*, several other animal groups, particularly game animals, now take a Ø-plural:

antelope~antelope
buffalo~buffalo
bear~bear (as in *we went hunting bear*, although *bears* is possible too)
fish~fish

The noun *fish*, which now most often takes a Ø-plural, took the regular *-s/-es* plural in older English. Even today one hears the plural *fishes*, but *fish* is more common.

Irregularity may be inconvenient, particularly from the perspective of learning English as a second language, but it is interesting because it often leads to further discovery about the nature of human language. For example, we might ask the question why these particular irregular plurals survive despite the regularization of the plural with the *-s/-es*, which accounted for only about 45 percent of all nouns in Old English. Notice that the kinds of words that have kept an irregular plural are those that are quite likely to occur in the plural. In other words, we have just as much opportunity to talk about *lice* as we do a single *louse*, perhaps even more.[1] The frequent use of the plural forms against the frequency of use of the singular form may well have to do with the maintenance of irregularity among these nouns.

Voicing Plurals

There are in English a number of nouns that end in *-f* (or *-fe*) for which the corresponding plural is *-ves*: *wife~wives, life~lives, calf~calves, half~halves, thief~thieves, shelf~shelves*, and so on. Unfortunately, the pattern does not hold for every word that ends in *–f*. The plural of the word *sheriff*, for example, is *sheriffs*, and we also have *beliefs*, *cliffs*, and *safes*.

While f~v shows an alternation in the spelling between the singular and the plural, the alternation also manifests on the level of pronunciation in the spoken language. The letter <f>, placed in angle brackets to show that we are talking about the letter, represents a voiceless sound [f], placed in straight brackets to show the phonetic value of the actual sound; sometimes the phonetic symbol and the alphabetic letter coincide, and [f] sounds like the first letter in the word *fat*. <v> represents a voiced sound, [v], like the first sound in the word *vat*. A voiceless sound is one made without vibration of the vocal folds in the larynx, while a voiced sound involves such vibration. The difference can be felt by placing the hand on the larynx, also called the Adam's apple or voice box, and pronouncing an <f> as in *fat* and a <v> as in *vat*. During the articulation of <f> there is no vibration in the larynx, but there is during the <v>.

This same tendency for voicing in the plural extends to several, but not all, words ending in <th>. Voicing normally occurs in plurals such as *mouths, paths, bath*s, but not in *deaths* and *faiths*. At any rate, voicing causes no change in spelling in these cases since both the voiced and voiceless variants are consistently spelled with <th>.

Foreign Plurals

During the course of its history, English has borrowed many words from many different languages. Words borrowed before 1500 tended to be nativized and act like English words in terms of how they would come to be pluralized. However, many words borrowed after 1500 appear to have been consciously kept in their foreign plural patterns—Early Modern borrowers were proud of their foreign-language knowledge. Many of these foreign plurals continue today, the chief among them coming from Latin, Greek, and Hebrew. There are also a few foreign plurals from French and Italian.

Latin

There are four Latin plural patterns of note:

Singular in *-us*, plural in *-i*: *stimulus~stimuli, alumnus~alumni*, etc.

---

[1] See Peter Meijes Tiersma, "Local and General Markedness," *Language*, vol. 58, no. 4, Dec. 1982, pp. 832–49.

Singular in -*a*, plural in -*ae*: *fauna~faunae, larva~larvae,* etc.

Singular in -*um*, plural in -*a*: *stratum~strata, erratum~errata,* etc.

Singular in -*ix/-ex* plural in -*ices*: *index~indices, vortex~vortices,* etc.

The more a word is used in English, the more likely it is to become nativized. Therefore, some Latin words have become so anglicized that the foreign plural would be impossible: *area~areas, campus~campuses,* and not **areae* or **campi*. With some borrowed nouns, there is a choice between the foreign plural and the regular English plural: *syllabus ~ syllabi* or *syllabuses*.

Greek
There are two Greek plural patterns of note:

Singular in -*is*, plural in -*es*: *synopsis~synopses, diagnosis~diagnoses,* etc.

Singular in -*on*, plural in -*a*: *phenomenon~phenomena, criterion~criteria,* etc.

Hebrew
There is one Hebrew plural of note:

A few words of Hebrew origin take the plural in -*im*: *seraph~seraphim, cherub~cherubim,* etc.

For all foreign plurals, consultation with an authoritative dictionary is the best way to determine accepted usage, which again will sometimes involve speaker/writer choice.

PRONOUNS

A pronoun is often defined as taking the place of a noun, but in fact, if we wanted to say that it takes the place of anything, we would have to say it takes the place of an entire noun phrase. For example, in the sentence *The proud father brought his daughter with him,* the pronoun *him* refers back to the entire noun phrase *the proud father* and not just the noun *father*; notice that we cannot say **the proud he*. Additionally, "takes the place of" is an inaccurate characterization of what a pronoun does. When one uses *I* or *you*, the pronoun hasn't taken the place of any noun phrase; it refers to a discourse participant. Even when the pronoun refers to a noun phrase, to say that it takes the place of the noun phrase is at least a gross oversimplification of the nature of that relationship.

In fact, a noun and a pronoun are bound together in a referring relationship. One such referring relationship can be seen in the following example:

> <u>Our oldest living relative</u> has just recently passed away. <u>She</u> was an avid dog lover and left her life's savings to the ASPCA.

In this instance, the pronoun *she* refers back to a noun phrase previously mentioned in the discourse; this sort of relationship in which a pronoun "looks back" to find its referent is called **anaphoric** reference. The noun in this relationship is called the **antecedent** to the pronoun.

In some other cases, a pronoun may "look forward" to find its noun phrase referent, as in the following example:

> <u>It</u> flew from the tree into the sky, its terrible black wings silhouetting the late-day sun. <u>The black raven</u> had returned and was on the hunt.

Here the pronoun *it* anticipates the noun phrase it refers to, *the black raven*. This direction of reference is **cataphoric**, and, strictly speaking, the noun phrase is a **postcedent** of the pronoun.

PERSONAL PRONOUNS

Personal pronouns distinguish number, case, and gender; they constitute one of the grammatically oldest systems in English. Pronouns are modeled in a paradigm distinguishing first, second, and third person as well as singular and plural. There are three sets of these paradigms, each presenting a different **case** of the pronouns. Case, while formerly an important grammatical system for all noun phrases in English, has largely been lost except among personal pronouns. Case is a system in which the form of a noun phrase (or some parts of the noun phrase) changes according to syntactic function. For example, a noun phrase functioning as subject would have a different form, in whole or in part, from a noun phrase functioning as a direct object (Chapter 6 treats the various functions of the noun phrase). Remember from Chapter 4 that a single pronoun may function as a noun phrase.

Subject Pronouns

Subject pronouns are those that serve as the subject of the sentence (see Chapter 6 for a definition of subject).

The forms of the subject personal pronouns are as follows:

		Singular		**Plural**
First person		I		we
Second person		you		you
Third person	masc.	he	all genders	they
	fem.	she		
	neut.	it		

Whereas the third-person pronouns, either singular or plural, often refer to a noun based on an anaphoric or cataphoric relationship as discussed above, first and second person pronouns refer to the speaker/writer or hearer/reader. That is, first- and second-person pronouns refer contextually to actual participants in the discourse, as stated earlier.

Even though we refer to the pronoun *we* as the plural of *I*, that characterization isn't true in the same sense that *cats* is the plural of *cat*. *We* is not "more of I" but a group that includes "I." However, it is important to note that "we" can have different meanings; it may include the hearer/reader, as in

> *We will need to work all night, so you had better call your family and let them know you won't be home.*

Or it may exclude the hearer/reader, as in

> *We sure had a great time last night at Ryan's birthday party; it's a shame you couldn't be there.*

Some languages distinguish between such uses of "we" by having different forms of the pronouns, called inclusive and exclusive forms. In English that distinction is left to context.

In the prescriptive tradition of English, subject pronouns are also preferred when the pronoun is a subject complement, that is, following a copulative or linking verb like *be* (and see Chapter 6):

> A: *(on the phone) May I speak with Azha?*
> B: *This is she.*
>
> *It was I who thwarted their evil plan.*

For most speakers the object pronouns sound more natural, and their use in the subject complement function is widespread enough to license that use:

> *This is her.*
>
> *It was me who thwarted their evil plan.*

Pronouns and Gender

Anyone who has studied a language like Spanish, French, German, or any one of many other European languages knows that in those languages one has to take care to learn the gender of every noun. For example, the word for *table* in Spanish, *mesa*, is a feminine noun, while the word for *book*, *libro*, is masculine. English speakers, whose language does not show gender of nouns in this way, sometimes try to figure out what is womanly about tables or manly about books to make them feminine or masculine. Of course, such an endeavor is ridiculous; grammatical gender, like that in Spanish, is a noun-classifying system of the language and is, at least from the perspective of learning or using the language, arbitrary. If there were something womanly about tables in Spain, why wouldn't they also be womanly in Germany? The German word for *table*, *Tisch*, is in fact masculine.

English used to have a system of grammatical gender like that in other languages, but that system eroded away in the transition from Old English to Middle English as we lost most of our noun endings, or inflections.[1] What we are left with in English is what is often called "natural gender." That is, animate objects, particularly higher animate objects—so people, pets, mammals, but probably not insects—are typically gendered when referring to them with pronouns. In fact, when referring to singular third-person referents, we will often divulge the gender of the referent through pronoun selection; the language puts pressure on us to do so:

Terry was biking on Constitution Trail this morning when she ran into Bryan.

The gender of the noun referred to by *Terry* is revealed to be feminine by the use of the pronoun *she*. As we will see later, sometimes speakers of English do attempt to avoid such gender revelations, although at a grammatical cost, as discussed below.

Finally notice that in the paradigm given above, the forms of the singular and plural second-person pronouns are identical: *you*. Like most other European languages, English used to have distinct forms for second-person singular and plural forms, *thou* and *ye*, but this distinction was also lost. While this leveling of distinction is true in prescribed standard or academic English, most varieties of spoken English have developed a distinct second-person pronoun: *y'all, y'uns, yinz, all y'all*, for example. On the one hand, forms like these show the ingenuity of speakers who, for whatever reason, feel the need to augment the pronominal system to distinguish between singular and plural second-person reference. On the other hand, the continuing stigma against such forms attests to the suppressing tyranny of language prescription, its idiosyncrasy, and its effect of denying legitimate linguistic practices—at least in certain domains.

Object Pronouns

Object pronouns are those that serve as the direct object, indirect object, or object of preposition of the sentence (see Chapter 6 on the syntactic functions of the noun/noun phrase).

The forms of the object personal pronouns are as follows:

		Singular		**Plural**
First person		me		us
Second person		you		you
Third person	masc.	him	all genders	them
	fem.	her		
	neut.	it		

---

1 It is interesting to note that speakers of some varieties of English use *he/him/his* and *she/her* to refer to inanimate objects, and that usage is probably the source for the stereotyped expression "git 'r done," in which the *'r* is the feminine singular object pronoun *her*.

Among object pronouns we see again gender distinction in the third-person singular and conflation of the singular and plural second-person forms. In fact, we could note that the object forms of the second-person pronoun are identical to the subject forms. The subject and object forms of the second person pronoun, both singular and plural, used to be distinct in older varieties of English (perhaps familiar from Shakespeare or the Bible):

Subject

Second person	**Singular**	**Plural**
	thou	ye

Object

Second person	**Singular**	**Plural**
	thee	you

These forms, however, have collapsed with the older second-person plural object form *you* for all instances of the pronoun, whether singular or plural, subject or object.

Possessive Pronouns

Possessive pronouns are those that refer to the possessed noun by identifying the possessor.

The forms of the possessive pronouns are as follows:

		Singular		**Plural**
First person		mine		ours
Second person		yours		yours
Third Person	masc.	his	all genders	theirs
	fem.	hers		
	neut.	its		

In the case of possessive pronouns, note how they are similar, both in terms of form and function, to possessive determiners (see again Chapter 4). However, the key to understanding the difference between possessive pronouns and possessive determiners is the designation *determiner*. Determiners, as discussed in Chapter 4, are grammatical words that "fine-tune" the reference of a noun in terms of definiteness, indefiniteness, and, in the case of possessive determiners, possession. While denoting possession is also true of possessive pronouns, possessive determiners occur with a noun in a noun phrase, as *my* occurs with *pen* in the following example:

I don't have my pen.

A possessive pronoun refers to a noun phrase antecedent but identifies the possessor of the noun phrase with a unique pronoun form:

I don't have mine. (referring to *my pen*)

In some grammar treatments, possessive determiners are referred to as **dependent possessive pronouns** and possessive pronouns as **independent possessive pronouns**. Possessive determiners are also sometimes called possessive adjectives. In this book we will continue to use the terms possessive determiner and contrast that word class with possessive pronouns.

Compound Pronouns and Case

As mentioned above, case used to be a more pervasive grammatical system that affected all noun phrases. However, that system was largely lost and remains in present-day English only in limited form among pronouns. Given that case is no longer a strong feature of English grammar, it is perhaps not surprising to find that there is confusion in case among pronouns in certain contexts.

Most varieties of English maintain a strict division between subject and object case in the following kinds of sentences:

***I** saw the new play last week.*
*Sadie told **me** the sad news.*

That is, speakers are not likely to say (or write)

*Me saw...

Or:

*Sadie told I the sad news.

There are, however, languages known as pidgins and creoles, some of which are largely based on English vocabulary words, but with their own grammar, and in those languages, pronouns may be based on English object-pronoun forms, yielding sentences like the following in Jamaican Creole, in which the first-person singular pronoun in the subject role is based on the English object-pronoun form *me*:

Mi nuh nyam "I don't eat"   mi = I, nuh = no, nyam = eat

There are also certain dialects of English in which object pronouns might show up as subjects. For example, Alice Walker in her book *The Color Purple* represents the speech of her character Celie with structures such as

Us was poor.

The character Celie is a poor, African American woman in the South around 1930, and Walker's choice of language for the character is meant to represent the speech-ways of speakers who were immediately descended from enslaved Africans from the century before.

However, even though most speakers of most varieties of English would not generate sentences with singular object pronouns as subjects or singular subject pronouns as objects, most will use object forms with a subject function in compound pronoun situations, at least in informal speech. For instance, it is not rare at all to hear a speaker of American English say the following:

Me and Yuri are on the same team this year.

Prescriptively speaking, *me*, which is an object pronoun, should be in the subject case, *I*, since it is functioning as the subject of the sentence along with the conjoined noun *Yuri*. This tendency is quite old in English, and for several hundred years speakers have been told by various authorities, "don't say 'me and X'; say 'X and I.'" (Note that the recommended order of putting the first person last in the compound is stylistic, not grammatical.)

Now consider the following sentence:

Please ask the office to send the results to Yuri and me as soon as they have reached a decision.

In the above sentence, the conjoined nouns *Yuri and me* (here following the stylistic form of having the first-person pronoun, *me*, last) is correct from a prescriptive view because the conjoined nouns *Yuri and me* function as the object of the preposition *to*, a function somewhat familiar from Chapter 4 and one that appears again in Chapter 6. In the section above in which object pronouns were introduced, they were said to be the form used when the pronoun was the direct object, indirect object, or object of a preposition. However, because speakers of English have become so accustomed to being corrected when they use object pronouns like *me* in compound noun situations, the momentum of being corrected comes to take on a life of its own, and speakers begin to "correct" themselves in areas where nothing was wrong in the first place, as in the following sentence:

Please ask the office to send the results to Yuri and I as soon as they have reached a decision.

Yuri and me was not wrong, but the "correction" to *Yuri and I* creates a new error, at least from a prescriptive standpoint. This is called **hypercorrection**, and because of hypercorrection toward the use of subject case pronouns in conjoined nouns, the determinant for using subject pronouns for some speakers appears to be more about an attempt to sound more formal and, ironically, more correct.

DEMONSTRATIVE PRONOUNS

Demonstrative pronouns are the familiar proximal and distal forms from Chapter 4:

	Singular	**Plural**
Proximal	this	these
Distal	that	those

In this chapter, note carefully that they are being presented as pronouns, meaning that they function as noun phrases and refer to some linguistic material already mentioned. In the situation of the personal pronouns, we talked about how first- and second-person pronoun forms referred to discourse participants, *I* and *you*, and how third-person pronouns referred to nouns that had already been introduced into the discourse, or will be introduced in the case of cataphoric reference. Demonstrative pronouns can refer to nouns cataphorically or anaphorically, as in this example in which *these* refers back (anaphorically) to the two vials mentioned in the first sentence:

There are two vials before you. These contain samples of the deadliest virus known to humankind.

However, just as frequently, demonstratives, especially the singular *this* and *that*, refer to entire propositions or sentences.

Two paths diverged in the mall, and I took the one with less expensive stores. This has made all the fashion savings difference in the world.

In this case, the demonstrative pronoun *this* stands for the entire proposition expressed in the first sentence, i.e., that I took the hall with less expensive stores. Thus, demonstrative pronouns aren't pronouns because they "take the place of a noun" but because they serve noun functions in the way that *this* is the subject in the above sentence, and in this case, *this* took the place of an entire clause.

Having an identical set of forms for the demonstrative determiners and demonstrative pronouns is a good opportunity to reflect on the form/function distinction. In certain cases, a given form can have only one function, a relatively rare link between the form and function levels. For example, *the* is always a definite article in terms of form and always a determiner in terms of function. But most forms can have any number of different functions. *That* can be a demonstrative by form, but now, as we have seen, it can be a determiner when used with a noun, or a pronoun when it stands alone and refers to other linguistic material, as in the contrasting pair below, in which the first is a demonstrative determiner and the second a demonstrative pronoun.

That awful man showed up again last night. (determiner of the noun *man*)
That is a bald-faced lie! (pronoun referring to something previously said)

INDEFINITE PRONOUNS

The central set of indefinite pronouns includes compounds of *any-*, *some-*, *no-*, *every-*, and (more limitedly) *each*, with *-body*, *-one*, and *-thing*. These combinations yield the following forms:

anyone	everyone
anybody	everybody
anything	everything
someone	each one
somebody	
something	each thing
no one	
nobody	
nothing	

The indefinite pronouns given above refer to a person or a thing that is not known or has not previously been deployed in the discourse.

Anyone can do it.

In this sentence, *anyone* refers to no one particular person but to any one person who might attempt to do it.

In some instances, *anywhere* (or *anyplace*) may also serve as an indefinite pronoun:

Just put the tent down! Anywhere is fine.

In the above sentence, *anywhere* refers to an indefinite location and is the subject of the predicate *is fine*.

The form *one* is also an indefinite pronoun by itself:

Kennedy served only three years in office, but his legacy is so strong that one gets the impression he was president for many years.

One is, in fact, the only pronoun that allows the various kinds of noun phrase modification that we saw in the last chapter. It may occur with determiners:

The one who guesses correctly wins the prize.

Or with an adjective:

The bigger one will probably be more comfortable.

Or with a prepositional phrase:

The one with the glasses probably knows the answer.

The uses of *one* with an adjective or a prepositional phrase verge more on instances of quantification and even definiteness. For me to say *the one with glasses* must mean that I have a definite person in mind and that the person has already been deployed in the discourse context. We can also note that the indefinite *one* can also be pluralized, as in *these ones/those ones*, although some do not accept such forms in formal, edited English.

IMPERSONAL PRONOUNS AND GENDER

Indefinite pronouns pose a special problem for English grammar when one wants to refer back to those indefinite referents. Since indefinite pronouns do not require antecedents (or postcedents), as personal pronouns do, we aren't always sure exactly what we are referring to. Consider the following example:

Anyone is welcome to join the club if _____ pays the dues.

What precisely should I put in the blank? The answer to that question will depend on how I interpret *anyone*. Logically, *anyone* can be multiple persons, in fact as many people as are willing to pay the dues and want to join the club. This logical plurality has drawn English speakers to the third-person plural forms of pronouns and possessive determiners, *they, them, their,* and *theirs*.

*Anyone is welcome to join the club if **they** pay the dues.*

This tendency is quite old, the first instance of which being found as early as the tenth century. However, grammarians over the years have made much ado about the fact that *anyone* and *they/them/their/theirs* do not agree in number; *anyone* is singular, as evidenced by the singular verb *is*, while *they/them/their/theirs* is plural.

Historically, the prescriptive grammarian's solution was to require the singular, masculine pronoun forms *he/him/his* in such environments:

*Anyone is welcome to join the club if **he** pays the dues.*

In fact, in 1852 the English Parliament passed an edict prescribing just this solution! Happily, such usage nowadays offends our sense of gender equality. Obviously, the solution of *they/them/their/theirs* is a good one in order to avoid *he/him/his*, and one can find handbooks in modern times that admit usage of *they/them/their/theirs*.

But the pull of prescriptive grammar has been too strong for some, and the apparent grammatical imperative for singular agreement has brought about several stylistic options, ranging from the use of *he/she* (or *him/her*, etc.):

*Anyone is welcome to join the club if **he/she** pays the dues.*

to *he or she*:

> *Anyone is welcome to join the club if **he or she** pays the dues.*

or *(s)he*, where possible:

> *Anyone is welcome to join the club if **(s)he** pays the dues.*

or just the feminine forms:

> *Anyone is welcome to join the club if **she** pays the dues.*

This latter practice may represent an attempt to "make up" for the years of preference in the direction of masculine reference and perhaps to raise attention to issues of gender (in)equality. (For more on this point, see the section on "gender neutral language" in Chapter 18.)

REFLEXIVE/RECIPROCAL PRONOUNS

The forms of the reflexive pronouns are presented in the familiar paradigm of first, second, and third persons as well as singular and plural:

		Singular	**Plural**
First person		myself	ourselves
Second person		yourself	yourselves
Third person	masc.	himself	themselves
	fem.	herself	
	neut.	itself	

It is interesting to note that it is only among the reflexive pronouns that the second person singular and plural have distinct forms because of the plural form *-selves*.

A reflexive pronoun is one that refers back to a noun or a pronoun in the same clause:

Jack saw himself in the mirror.
I must be true to myself.
Yoshiko gave herself a party to celebrate her birthday.

In each of these expressions, the reflexive pronoun refers back to the subject, serving as the direct object in the first sentence, an object of the preposition in the second sentence, and the indirect object in the third.

Reflexive pronouns sometimes serve other functions that can be thought of more as intensifying pronouns used to emphasize a noun/pronoun. The more precise grammatical function of such uses would be "appositive":

I myself will see to it that no one ever does that again.
Tyrell and Adam made the float for the parade themselves. (meaning without help)

English also has what some refer to as a set of reciprocal pronouns, *each other* and *one another*. A reciprocal pronoun is one that expresses an equal back-and-forth between multiple referents:

*Ahmed and Ji Yeong gave **each other** a knowing look.*
*The players knew that they would always support **one another**.*

QUANTIFIER EXPRESSIONS

In addition to the categories of pronouns we have seen in this chapter, many expressions of quantity can serve pronoun functions:

*Alan and Cybil applied for the scholarship, and **both** received it.*
***Many** have tried; **many** have failed.*
*You will need to take these three medications twice a day for one week. **All** should be taken with a meal.*

In the above sentences, the quantifier expressions *both*, *many*, and *all* are pronouns in that they refer to entities already in the discourse, or indefinite entities in the case of *many*.

RELATIVE AND INTERROGATIVE PRONOUNS

There are yet two other categories of pronouns referred to as relative pronouns and interrogative pronouns. Relative pronouns are used to introduce a relative clause, and they are treated in Chapter 15. Interrogative pronouns are used to make certain kinds of *wh*-questions; they are taken up in Chapter 12.

EXERCISES

A. Indicate the type of noun given as count, non-count, or collective. Indicate whether it involves singular or plural verb agreement.

1. lotion
2. leaf
3. tar
4. bark (of a tree)
5. pack (of wolves)
6. building
7. corner
8. mail
9. clergy

10. gang
11. history
12. intruder
13. climate
14. homework
15. thesis

B. Give the irregular plural and indicate what type of plural it is, e.g., umlaut, Ø-plural, Greek plural, etc.

1. wife
2. sheep
3. ox
4. goose
5. syllabus
6. flora
7. curriculum
8. codex
9. crisis
10. ganglion
11. axis
12. kibbutz

C. How might the following sentences be edited for standard written English? In your response, indicate the original linguistic structure and the changes you made.

Example: *Me and Jackie left on a hot summer's day.* → *Jackie and I left on a hot summer's day.*

In the original, the compound subject *me and Jackie* contained an object pronoun, *me*, which was changed to the subject pronoun *I* to accord with the subject function.

1. Terry and I's flight was delayed for over two hours in Philadelphia.
2. Ilona will bring the books next time because unfortunately the book sellers sent the wrong edition to Brian and she last week.
3. Anyone forgetting his book will not be excused from the assignment.
4. Him, Alan, Andrew, and Perry formed a band and actually got a couple of jobs playing music during wedding receptions.
5. We decided to stop at the store and buy some chocolate for Amy and Ron's anniversary.
6. You ran into Sherry and I just last week. Have you forgotten?
7. The fund is available to anyone as long as his gross annual income is below $20,000.

Functions of the Noun Phrase

In Chapter 4, noun phrases were introduced informally in their function as **subject** of a clause, as in *My grass has been growing*. In that chapter too, noun phrases in their function as **object of a preposition** were informally introduced, as in *the kid on the bike*. However, noun phrases can also fill various other functions within a sentence, among them **direct object**, **indirect object**, **subject complement**, and **object complement**. In this chapter, these various functions of nouns are treated in detail.

NOUN PHRASE AS SUBJECT

Noun phrases fill the function of subject in the following sentences:

> *Margaret* always forgets the keys.
> *Our friends* have warned us of the dangers.
> *That problem* is getting bigger by the day.

In Chapter 2, we saw that lexical classes of words like noun or verb could be defined semantically, by trying to define what the class of words meant, or we could define various lexical classes structurally by indicating the different morphological or syntactic patterns they enter into. For instance, a noun could be defined semantically as a person, place, or thing, or it could be defined as a part of speech that shows number, usually by the addition of the regular *-s* inflection for plural.

When defining the functions of nouns, such as subject, we can also do so semantically or structurally. Semantically, if we consider the basic division of a clause into subject and predicate, then the subject is what or whom is being predicated on. Therefore, in the example sentences listed above, *always forgets the keys* is being said of *Margaret*, which is the subject. *Have warned us of the dangers* is what *our friends*, the subject, did, and it is *that problem*, the subject, that *is getting bigger by the day*.

This kind of semantic definition is most easily identified when the predicate expresses some kind of overt action caused by an animate subject, as in *Jack kicked the ball* or *The firefighter from Unit 34 quenched the blaze*. In such cases the subject is the entity that performs the action of the predicate, *Jack* or *the firefighter* in these sentences. It is this basic subject–predicate relationship that people have in mind when they say that "the subject *does* the verb" and thereby offer a semantic definition for a subject. However, such a definition is really inadequate for identifying the subject consistently because not all subject–predicate relationships are based on the subject doing an action. In the sentence *That problem is getting bigger by the day*, the subject, *the problem*, is not doing any action.

In a structural definition, on the other hand, we make reference to the property of agreement to define a subject, a topic brought up first in order to define the concept of a finite verb in Chapter 3. You will recall that agreement accounted for why there were different endings on verbs in certain languages, like Spanish, French, German, or Russian. Since the matter is so important for understanding the structural definition of subject, it is a good idea to review agreement again, this time with an example from Latin. In Latin, the present tense of the infinitive *laudare* 'to praise,' will take different endings to indicate various subjects. In fact, the ending on the verb is often the only indication of the intended subject because the pronoun or noun that would be the subject is frequently not expressed (as in Spanish or Italian).[1] For that reason, the pronoun subject that would be expressed is placed in parentheses in the following paradigm to indicate it is not obligatory.

(ego) laud**o**	(nos) lauda**mus**	I praise	we praise
(tu) lauda**s**	(vos) lauda**tis**	you (sg.) praise	you (pl.) praise
(is) lauda**t**	(ei) lauda**nt**	he praises	they praise

In this paradigm, agreement can be seen in that -*o* appears on the verb when *ego*, the first-person singular ("I"), is the subject. The suffix -*s* appears in the second-person singular, -*t* in the third person, and so on.

As mentioned in Chapter 3, English used to show much more of this kind of agreement, but most of the agreement markers have been lost and replaced by other grammatical means of showing noun-phrase function. Still, English does maintain some markers of agreement. Take, for instance, the example sentence from above *Margaret always forgets the keys*. Note that the form of the verb in that sentence is ***forgets***. However, what if we changed the subject from *Margaret* (third-person singular) to *Margaret and Philippe*? Then the sentence would become *Margaret and Philippe always **forget** the keys*. In other words, the verb changed from *forgets* to *forget* because the subject changed from the third-person singular to the third-person plural. (In the Latin example above, that would be like the difference between *laudat* and *laudant*.)

---

[1] It should not be thought, however, that having a distinct form of the verb is what allows the subject to go unexpressed. In German, for example, there is a different verb form for the first person singular, *ich glaube* 'I believe,' versus second person singular, *du glaubst* 'you think.' However, the subject must be expressed in German. Contrastively, in Japanese, there is no difference in the verb form for person and yet the subject can be dropped if it is obvious from the context, e.g., *Sensei desu* '(she) is the teacher.'

In our other examples, *Our friends have warned us of the dangers* and *That problem is getting bigger by the day*, the verbs (actually verb phrases) are *have warned* and *is getting* respectively. We can also see agreement in these sentences:

*Our friends **have** warned...* (third plural *friends* induces the form *have*)
*Our friend **has** warned...* (third singular *friend* induces the form *has*)

*That problem **is** getting...* (third singular *problem* induces the form *is*)
*Those problems **are** getting...* (third plural *problems* induces the form *are*)

It is the verb *be* that shows agreement the most, with three different forms in the present:

*I **am***	*we **are***
*you **are***	*you **are***
*he, she, it **is***	*they **are***

Given the very high frequency of *be*, agreement occurs more often than one might think in English. Still, subject-verb agreement does not occur in many grammatical contexts in English. For example, agreement never occurs in the past tense other than with the verb *be*: *I was~you were~he/she/it was*:

I liked	*we liked*
you liked	*you liked*
he, she, it liked	*they liked*

Finally, we can note that in present-day English, there is a very strong tendency for the subject to occur before the predicate. And although that order is not obligatory, it is so regular in present-day English that variations of the subject–predicate order are likely to sound archaic, poetic, or stylistically marked (dramatic):

From out of the sewer far below the metropolis emerged the monster.

In this case, *the monster* is what is being predicated on; it is the subject.

DUMMY SUBJECTS AND CLEFT SENTENCES

It was mentioned above that in some languages like Latin (but also in Spanish, Italian, and others) the subject can at times be left unexpressed, particularly when it is contextually redundant, as for instance it often is when it is a pronoun. English, on the other hand, cannot generally omit the subject, but it does so in certain exchanges of this type:

A: *You can't climb that pole.*
B: *Can so!* (i.e., ***I** can so.*)

Generally, however, English must fill the subject position of a clause (especially in standard written English), even in those cases where the subject has no real meaning. In those cases, the subject will be *it*, and because *it* is often just a prop for the subject without any real reference, it is called an "expletive" *it*, or even a "dummy subject" or "dummy *it*."

> *It is raining.*
> *It sure is nice today.*

While it may be possible to argue that "it" in the sentences refers to "the weather" or some such noun, there is no need to establish that noun in the discourse before using "it" in such contexts, as would be the case with most pronouns used as the subject. Consider, for instance, the difference in the meaning of *it* in a sentence like *It is on the table*; in this case, we have to have some knowledge of what *it* refers to in order to make sense of its use.

Expletive *it* also appears in sentence types known as **cleft sentences**. Consider this sentence:

> *The butler killed the guest.*

The subject in this sentence is a rather straightforward matter: *the butler* did it. However, there is an alternative way to express this sentence in the case that the speaker/writer wants to focus more attention on the noun phrase *the butler*:

> *It was the butler who killed the guest.*

This sentence is an example of a cleft sentence in which the subject is placed after the verb *be* and followed by a relative clause. Relative clauses like *who killed the guest* will be taken up in Chapter 15, but for now it can be seen that the noun phrase *the butler* appears after the verb *was* (a form of *be*) and is followed by *who killed the guest*. Notice, too, that the expletive *it* has filled the subject slot. In some grammatical treatments *the butler* would be considered the logical subject, but there is no debate that *it* is the grammatical subject: even if the logical subject is plural, the form of the verb *be* remains singular to agree with the expletive *it* subject:

> *It was the butler and his lover that killed the guest.*

Expletive *it* also occurs frequently in English in the case that the real subject is very long, as for instance an infinitive phrase (Chapter 17) or a noun clause (Chapter 17).

> *It was nice **for him to bring extra chairs**.* (= ***For him to bring extra chairs*** *was nice.*)
> *It has been unfortunate **that so many young people have turned to drugs in order to escape the problems of the modern world**.* (= ***That so many young people have turned to drugs to escape the problems of the modern world*** *has been unfortunate.*)

*It appeared obvious **that someone had forgotten to close the gate**.* (= ***That someone had forgotten to close the gate** appeared obvious.*)

*It seems logical **to consult a dictionary before assuming the origin of a word**.* (= ***To consult a dictionary before assuming the origin of a word** seems logical.*)

*It drove her crazy **that he always brought up his exes**.* (= ***That he always brought up his exes** drove her crazy.*)

In each of these sentences, a long subject has been **extraposed** to the end of the sentence and replaced by the dummy subject *it*. In some grammars, this particular *it* is called **anticipatory it**, since it "anticipates" the longer subject that was extraposed.[1]

EXISTENTIAL CONSTRUCTIONS

In order to make the predication that something exists in English, we use the construction *there is* or *there are*. In such constructions, it is the noun phrase after the verb *be* that is the subject, as is obvious through agreement patterns:

*There **is an apple** on the desk.*
*There **are some apples** on the desk.*

In casual English, agreement with the post-verbal noun phrase is sometimes not followed, and it is not uncommon to hear (and even to see in informal, written contexts)

There's some apples on the desk.

One reason for the tendency toward an invariable *there's* is likely because of the overwhelming tendency for the subject to precede the verb, and since "there" is always the same form, the verb has come to always be the same form. In other words, the following noun phrase, *apples*, which is the real subject, has lost control over the verb form.

Some grammarians group existential *there* together with *here*, as used in

Here's your receipt.

In such a treatment, *here* and *there* are grouped together as "presentational" constructions. At least for some speakers, presentational *here* also tends toward invariability with the singular form of *be*:

(server speaking to a table of patrons) *Here's your beers. Enjoy!*

---

1 Anticipatory *it* can also fill in the place of a postposed "long" object, as in

I find it hard to believe that she took his car without asking.

In this sentence, the "real" object is the clause *that she took his car without asking* (and see Chapter 16). But since it is so long, it is extraposed to the end of the sentence and an anticipatory *it* is placed in the object position to fill its place.

NOUN PHRASE AS DIRECT OBJECT

Noun phrases can also fulfill the function of direct object. Like many grammatical concepts, direct objects can be defined semantically or structurally. Semantically, a direct object is said to be the noun phrase that is affected by the verb. Consider the following examples of direct objects:

*Harry drank **a cup of coffee**.*
*The voters elected **Min-Ju Kim**.*
*My sister carried **the wood** inside.*
*Networks broadcast **those shows** only late at night.*

In each of these cases, it can be said that the bolded noun phrase (*a cup of coffee, Min-Ju Kim, the wood, those shows*) is affected by the verb (*drank, elected, carried,* and *broadcast*). The affectedness is sometimes captured by asking *whom* or *what* about the action of a verb. For example, *What did Harry drink?* Answer: *A cup of coffee.* However with some other verbs, affectedness might not be so apparent:

The roving cat sensed danger.
We have understood their position for many years.

In these sentences, the noun phrases *danger* and *their position* are not so easily construed as affected by the verbs *sensed* and *understood*. Instead, those noun phrases seem to affect the subject through the verb; it is the roving cat that is affected by sensing danger. Essentially, determining the direct object by the semantic criterion of affectedness will work best for those sentences in which the verb expresses an overt action, like *drink, elect, carry, broadcast,* etc.

There is, however, a structural means for determining direct object, and it is considerably more reliable. In short, a direct object can be made into the subject in order to construct a passive sentence. Obviously, in order to do this one has to have a reasonably good sense of what a passive sentence is. While the passive is taken up in some detail in Chapter 11, for now, consider the pairs of active and passive counterparts listed below:

Active
*John wrote **a letter**.*

Passive
***A letter** was written by John.*

Active
*The rioters have condemned **the government**.*

Passive
***The government** has been condemned by the rioters.*

Active
*The court might not accept **my witness**.*

Passive
***My witness** might not be accepted by the court.*

Even without explanation, English speakers are generally able to construct passive sentences intuitively. The important change to notice between the active and passive counterparts above is that the bolded direct objects in the active sentences become the bolded subject of the passive sentences in each case.

Syntactically, we can also note that the direct objects in the sentences all follow the verb, and this is the usual position of the direct object. However, occasionally one might **prepose** a direct object:

***Strawberries**, I like. Blackberries not so much.*

In the above example, the direct object *strawberries*, is preposed in the sentence in order to contrast it with *blackberries*.

Using the above passivization test, however, we can also see that some post-verbal nouns are not good candidates for direct object status. Consider the following active and passive pairs of sentences:

Active
*The kittens slept **the whole day**.*

Passive
*****The whole day** was slept by the kittens.*

Active
*My ticket costs **twenty dollars**.*

Passive
*****Twenty dollars** was cost (by my ticket).*

Active
*An NBA basketball weighs **22 oz**.*

Passive
*****22 oz** is weighed by an NBA basketball.*

Active
*He walked **the path** every morning.*

Passive
*?**The path** was walked by him every morning.*

In the above sentences, the noun phrases following the verb (*the whole day, twenty dollars, 22 oz.,* and *the path*) appear likely candidates for direct objects, mostly on the criterion that they follow the verb. However, they cannot be made into subjects in passive sentences (at least not well). The reason for this is that they are actually adverbial in function; these are not concepts that are affected by the verb, but instead they express extent of space (*path*), measurement of exchange (*twenty dollars*), duration of time (*the whole day*), and unit of measure (*22 oz.*)—all adverbial notions.[1] Noun phrases functioning as adverbials are treated in more detail in Chapter 7. As we will see in the next section too, other noun phrases that follow the verb are not direct objects but subject complements.

TRANSITIVITY

An important grammatical concept to learn at this point is that of transitivity. A **transitive verb** is one that has a direct object, while an **intransitive verb** is one that does not have a direct object.

> *Tamia drove her car to the meeting.* (transitive, *her car* = direct object)
> *Tamia drove to the meeting.* (intransitive)

As you can see from the examples, many verbs, like *drive*, can be either transitive or intransitive. Transitivity is a scalar concept, and as we have already seen, some verbs are more transitive than others:

> *My sister carried the wood inside.* (high transitivity since a willful agent performs an action and changes the state/location of the object)
> *He walked the path.* (low transitivity)

We have seen that in making a passive sentence, the direct object of the active sentence became the subject; in other words, passivization is a detransitivizing strategy that we may choose for any number of reasons. Again, the topic of passive sentences is taken up in Chapter 11. In addition to transitive and intransitive verbs, there is a third type, referred to as **copulative verbs**, which are important for understanding the next noun-phrase function, subject complement.

NOUN PHRASE AS SUBJECT COMPLEMENT

Subject complements are Noun Phrases (NPs), adjective phrases (Adj. Ph.) or prepositional phrases (PP) that complete the sense of a copulative verb. A copulative verb is one that expresses a specific relationship between the subject and the following NP (or Adj. Ph. or PP). The most common of these relationships, at least in terms of a following NP, is the equation in which A = B. The most common copulative verb of this sort in English is *be*.

---

[1] One of the reasons that *path* is less objectionable as the subject of the passive sentence has to do with the fact that it is about space, and space adverbials do things in the grammar that are otherwise not possible, as we will see in Chapter 7.

> *Daniel is **a good student**.*
> *Hiram was **the designated driver**.*
> *The book has been **a source of debate** for centuries.*

In each of these sentences, the noun phrase following the verb *be* (*a good student, the designated driver, a source of debate*) completes the equation set up by the subject and the verb *be*: that is, the noun phrase renames the subject in some sense, as in *Daniel = a good student*.

As was indicated above, subject complements can also take the form of adjective phrases and even PPs:

> *The children were **really happy** to see the school after such a long field trip.*
> *The cat was **on the table** when we arrived home.*

In these examples, the adjective phrase *really happy* and the PP *on the table* are complements of the copulative verb *be*, as they complete the equation *The children were...* and *The cat was...*. Consider how incomplete the sentence would be if it were only **The cat was when we arrived home*. As we will see in the next chapter, we will analyze PPs in such a subject complement role more specifically as adverbial complements.

Other common copulative verbs include *become, appear,* and *seem*. *Become* allows for both noun phrase and adjective complements:

> *Yoko will become **the president** of the club.*
> *Ferris became **despondent**.*

Appear and *seem* allow adjectives as their complements:

> *The package appeared **heavy**.*
> *They seem **angry**.*

Adjectival subject complements are sometimes called **predicate adjectives** in grammar, and noun-phrase complements are sometimes referred to **predicative nominatives** or **predicate nouns**.

Concerning noun-phrase subject complements, we note that they are not able to become subjects of passive verbs since they are not direct objects:

> *Adam was a good student.* → **A good student was been by Adam.*

However, like direct objects, noun phrase subject complements usually follow a verb. Thus the two sentences below appear to be the same structurally:

> *Adam was **a good student**.*
> *Adam found **a good student**.*

In both cases we have a noun phrase + verb + noun phrase. However, as we have learned in this chapter, *a good student* in the first sentence is a subject complement and a direct object in the second; note that, in this case, *a good student* can be made the subject of a passive sentence: *A good student was found by Adam.*

We can also note that because the subject complement renames the subject, the subject noun phrase and the subject complement noun phrase both refer to the same entity, ultimately *Adam*. However, because the direct object does not rename the subject in this way, we understand *Adam* and *a good student* to be two different people in the sentence containing a direct object.

Certain verbs involving sensory perception can also be followed by adjective subject complements. These verbs include *taste, smell, look, sound,* and *feel*.

> *The soup tasted **good**.*
> *Rotten fish smells **bad**.*
> *The future looks **bright**.*
> *His plan sounds **ridiculous**.*
> *The air feels **heavy**.*

We know that the adjectives *good, bad, bright, ridiculous,* and *heavy* are subject complements because they describe the subjects in each sentence. People sometimes debate whether a sentence like *Rotten fish smells bad* should be *Rotten fish smells badly*. Of course, since we have now identified the functions in these sentences to be subject complements, we are justified in selecting the adjective form *bad*; *badly* is an adverb.

NOUN PHRASE AS INDIRECT OBJECT

An indirect object is the noun phrase for whom or to whom something is intended or directed:

> *They have given **Cheryl** a prestigious award just this month.*
> *The volunteer has been reading **the children** stories from the Chronicles of Narnia.*
> *My husband made **me** a ring for our anniversary.*

In each of the sentences above, the first noun phrase after the verb (*Cheryl, the children,* and *me*) describes who the direct object (*a prestigious award, stories from the Chronicles of Narnia* and *a ring*) is intended for or directed to. While this sort of semantic definition is helpful, it is also necessary to take into consideration the syntax. Note that in each case there are two noun phrases following the verb. In order to have an indirect object there must be a direct object, and the direct object always follows the indirect object.

It might also be noted that indirect objects are almost always animate; inanimate indirect objects tend to be metaphorical or even idiomatic:

*The janitor gave **the house** a fresh coat of paint.*

Finally, there is a structural test for indirect object status. An indirect object can be transformed into a PP following the direct object. The preposition in such a transformed sentence will normally be *to*, but sometimes it is *for*.

Indirect object construction
*The volunteer has been reading **the children** stories from the Chronicles of Narnia.*

Prepositional phrase construction
*The volunteer has been reading stories from the Chronicles of Narnia **to the children**.*

Indirect object construction
*The group built **the family** a new barn.*

Prepositional object construction
*The group built a new barn **for the family**.*

It is important to remember that once the indirect object noun phrase has been transformed into a prepositional phrase, the noun phrase is no longer an indirect object; it is the object of the preposition *to* or *for*.

It should be noted that indirect objects may also be made into the subject of a corresponding passive sentence: *They gave Cheryl a prestigious award* → *Cheryl has been given a prestigious award*. When the indirect object becomes the subject of a passive sentence, however, we see that the direct object remains; in other words, making the indirect object into the subject of the passive sentence does not detransitivize the verb. In fact, verbs that have both indirect and direct objects are sometimes called "ditransitive" verbs. We can also note that when the direct object of a ditransitive verb is made into the subject of the corresponding passive, the indirect object must be changed to an object of *to/for*: *They gave Cheryl a prestigious award* → *A prestigious award was given to Cheryl*.

NOUN PHRASE AS OBJECT COMPLEMENT

Object complements very often occur after a select set of verbs such as *elect*, *name*, *call*, and *consider*. An object complement follows the direct object and renames it:

*The committee elected Angelina **the new president**.*
*A local news agency has named Luigi's **the best restaurant in town**.*
*His classmates called him **a bully**.*
*We have always considered her **our friend**.*

In these sentences, the object complements (*the new president, the best restaurant in town, a bully,* and *our friend*) rename, or complete, the direct objects (*Angelina, Luigi's, him,* and *her*). Sometimes a preposition like *as* is preferred instead:

The committee elected Angelina **as** *the new president.*
We have always considered her **as** *our friend.*

Of course, once *as* appears in the sentence the noun phrases are no longer to be analyzed as object complements but as objects of the preposition *as*.

Note now the contrast between indirect object (in the second sentence) and object complement (in the first sentence) constructions:

The voters elected Maria president.
The voters gave Maria an award.

In both cases, the structure of the sentences is noun phrase + verb + noun phrase + noun phrase. However, the two noun phrases in the indirect object + direct object construction refer to two different entities, but since the object complement renames the direct object, the two noun phrases in the direct object + object complement construction refer to the same entity, similar to the way in which a subject complement renamed the subject.

We can note further that object complements can also be adjectives, and in those cases the adjectival object complement will describe the noun phrase functioning as direct object:

We found the test **difficult**.
Raimundo will consider your plan **ridiculous**.
I found him **silly**.

DIAGRAMMING NOUN PHRASES

Diagramming noun phrases acting as subjects (SUBJ) and as objects of a preposition (OP) was introduced in Chapter 4, so in this section we will turn our attention to diagramming NPs in their functions as direct objects (DO), indirect objects (IO), subject complements (SC), and object complements (OC). DOs, IOs, SCs, and OCs are NPs within the inflection phrase, and the structure of those NPs is going to be the same as the NPs functioning as subjects or objects of prepositions seen in Chapter 4. However, up until now we have always diagrammed the inflection phrase as a triangle to avoid a detailed analysis. The inflection phrase is a fairly complex structure, and in this chapter and the next, as we learn to diagram the Inflection Phrase, we will learn some of its parts, but we will leave most of the detail to Chapter 8.

The inflection phrase always has three branches extending from it, one labeled Tense, another labeled Auxiliary-1 (abbreviated as Aux-1), and another Predicate Phrase (Pred. Ph.), as the tree in Figure 6.1 shows. In labeling the underlined functions, the entire Inflection Phrase has the function of INFLECTED PREDICATE.

FIGURE 6.1

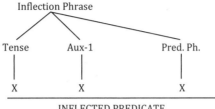

In turn, the predicate phrase has one obligatory branch, the verb phrase, or VP for short, but it may have other material coming off of it too. The V of the VP is the head of the predicate phrase, and its function is labeled Predicate. Given the principle that the head of a phrase and the entire phrase have the same function, the entire VP is also labeled as Predicate (see Figure 6.2).

FIGURE 6.2

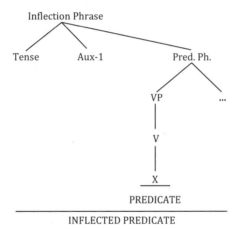

It is from the predicate phrase that various kinds of complements to the verb will appear, including NPs functioning as DO, IO, SC, and OC. (In the next chapter we will see how PPs can also be included in the predicate phrase.) For the remainder of this chapter, the Inflection Phrase will be fully diagrammed so that we can include NPs. For now, however, focus only on the structural relationship between the predicate and the NP(s). Again, Tense, Aux-1, and the VP are elaborated on in Chapter 8.

NOUN PHRASE AS DIRECT OBJECT
My sister reported the news.

FIGURE 6.3

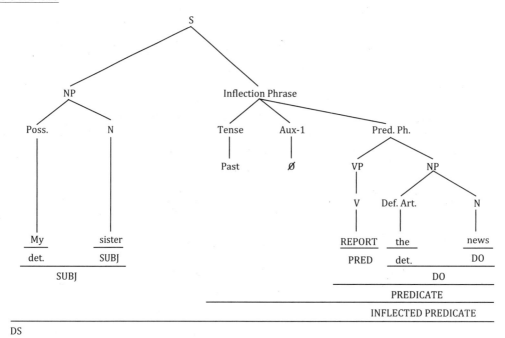

From Figure 6.3, it can be seen that the NP *the news* comes off of the predicate phrase and is labeled DO. The internal structure of the NP, however, follows the same internal NP structure as learned in Chapter 4.

The tree diagram in 6.3 also shows a few more features of diagramming within the predicate phrase. Note that the tense of the verb is indicated in the "Tense" branch of the Inflection Phrase, and for English the only two possibilities are "present" or "past." Once the tense is indicated, then the first verb, whether it be in the Aux-1 position or in the V of the VP of the predicate phrase, is presented in all caps in its base form. In the tree in 6.3, that verb is REPORT, which we understand to be "reported" because it is identified as "past" in the tense node.

NOUN PHRASE AS INDIRECT OBJECT

The man with black hair gave us our instructions.

Note that the predicate phrase now has two NPs, one with the IO function and one with the DO function. As you learned above, a sentence with an IO will also have a DO, and the IO will be the first NP. In this example, the subject NP has a PP modification, a structure we saw in the last chapter (see Figure 6.4).

FIGURE 6.4

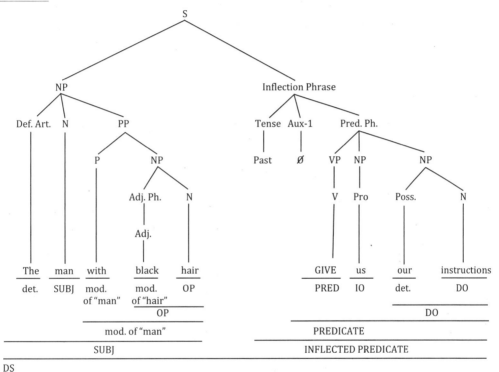

NOUN PHRASE AS SUBJECT COMPLEMENT
Allan is the director.

You may also note from the tree diagram in Figure 6.5 that when a form of *be* is the only verb, it will be analyzed as having auxiliary status (and occur in the Aux-1 node) and the predicate will be empty. The arguments for this analysis are developed more in Chapter 8.

FIGURE 6.5

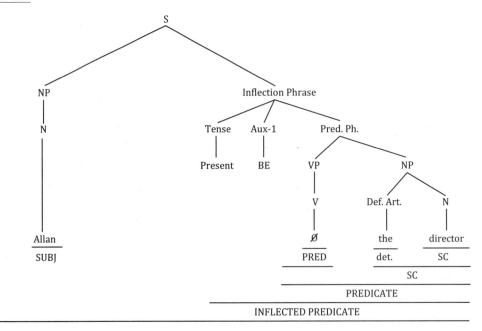

As we saw earlier in this chapter, Adjective Phrases can also fulfill the function of Subject Complement, as in Figure 6.6.

Allan is sick.

FIGURE 6.6

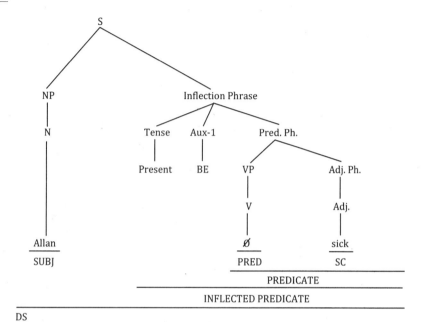

NOUN PHRASE AS OBJECT COMPLEMENT
The committee elected the new member president.

FIGURE 6.7

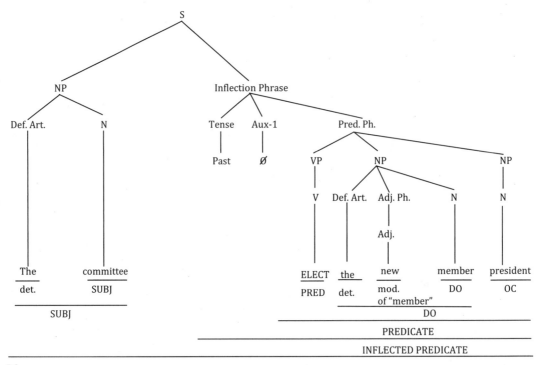

Again note that with the OC construction, there are two NPs in the predicate phrase, both of which refer to the same entity; that is, *the new member* and *president* refer to the same person (see Figure 6.7).

All of the examples of NPs in the predicate phrase so far are relatively easy. However, as we saw in Chapter 4 and above, NPs can be modified by PPs, and certainly that is true of NPs functioning as DO, IO, SC, and OC. While such PP modification may necessitate the addition of more layers into the tree diagram, they do not really add any extra complexity:

My sister reported the news about the quarantine.

About the quarantine modifies or describes *the news* and therefore it will be a PP off of the NP with the function of "Modifier of 'the news'" (see Figure 6.8).

FIGURE 6.8

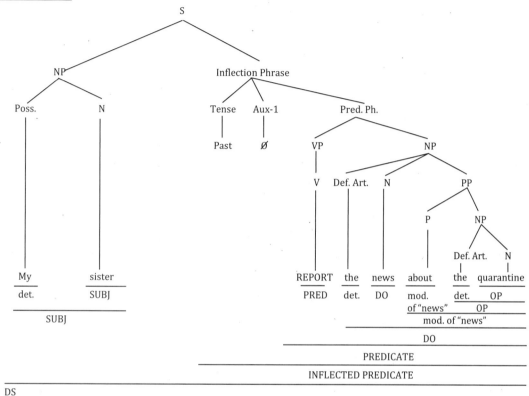

APPOSITIVES

Finally, we should note the appositive use of noun phrases, as in

Miss Ugor, ***our high school baseball coach****, won a very prestigious teaching award last year.*

Appositives give more information about a noun phrase in the sentence, and often this is information that is not, strictly speaking, necessary to the identification of the noun. Syntactically, they generally follow that noun phrase and are separated from the rest of the sentence by commas or by pauses and lower intonation in speech. For stylistic reasons, however, appositives may occur in other positions:

An unhappy boy from a young age*, Mori often appeared sulky and disinterested in groups of other children.*

In this sentence, the appositive noun phrase, *an unhappy boy from a young age*, appears at the beginning as a way of highlighting the "extra" information it expresses.

EXERCISES

A. Change the following third-person singular subjects to plural, or third-person plural subjects to singular. Make any changes necessary in the verb phrase as well.

1. **The house** was destroyed in the terrible storm that swept through on Sunday afternoon.
2. At the end of Lent, **the priests** deliver the Easter mass, which celebrates the Christian belief that Jesus ascended to heaven after his crucifixion.
3. **The treasure map** was hidden in the back of a volume from the encyclopedia set on the shelf in the library.
4. **A money order** made out to the office is considered an acceptable method of payment.
5. When we first purchased the cabin, **the carpet** was stained and **the cabinets** were grimy.

B. Make the following sentences into cleft sentences centered on the bolded noun.

1. **The paper** fell off the table.
2. **Jason** left his jacket in the library.
3. **The "f" key** on my computer keyboard was stuck.
4. **Our school** was recognized for academic excellence.
5. **This current generation of students** will spend more than $100,000 on post-secondary education.
6. You should direct all inquiries to **the writing director**.
7. We started **the fire** with dry twigs and old papers.
8. The broker had sold **the antique lamp** to my sister at a great discount.
9. We chose **oil** as the medium for the painting of the coastline.
10. Alison called **the sheriff** to investigate the noise she heard in the basement.

C. Consider each of the following sentences containing the existential *there's* construction. Does the contracted verb agree with *there* or with its subject?

1. There's too much noise in the back room and it's compromising the recording.
2. In our latest count we found that there's more than 500 books in his library.
3. Despite all the arguing, there's really only one solution to the issue.
4. Even if you can make a persuasive appeal, there's always some people who won't agree.
5. Although my silence might irritate you, there's reasons that I choose not to share that information with anybody.
6. There's much work that still needs to be done, and we are dedicated to doing it!

7. Since the sign gives a maximum capacity of only 3,000 pounds, it is my guess that there's too many people in the elevator.
8. Just as the weather forecast said, there's a lot of puffy, cumulus clouds against an intensely blue sky today.
9. There's oil spilled on the floor in the garage and I'm trying to soak it up using sand.
10. Don't worry. You won't get lost because there's signs on the walls telling you where to go.

D. Make the following active sentences passive by moving the direct object into the subject position. Decide whether it makes sense to include the by-phrase.

1. In the end, the customer bought the more expensive computer.
2. Although we didn't realize it at the time, the head chef prepared the meal especially for us.
3. After filing an intent-to-claim form, an agent will take your information.
4. One can use a stapler for putting these two panels together.
5. Starting Saturday, the gym will offer swimming classes for children 12 and under.
6. Because of the extensive weather damage caused by the extremely cold weather, the city repaved the road.
7. Because of my back injury last fall, my friends raked the leaves.
8. After some local teens vandalized the neighborhood, the township installed new mailboxes along our street.
9. As a result of several years of investigating it has been determined that Rembrandt painted the picture.
10. Ambryl sent the letter although she refused to sign her name to it.

E. Transform each of the following indirect objects into *to/for* phrases.

1. Dimitri and Arno will read the students an account of the Civil War in their history class.
2. The office gave me an extension after I explained that some of the information had not yet arrived.
3. The teacher taught her class the five rules for using the passive voice.
4. The audience handed the waiting proctors the evaluations and comments.
5. Amy transferred her mother the money via Western Union and paid a small fee.
6. The boy slid his classmate the note without the teacher suspecting a thing.
7. We will build you the strongest tree house and thus ensure the safety of your children.
8. Always tell your loved ones the truth and they will forgive you for anything.
9. When you have finished, please pass me your completed exams.

F. Determine whether the underlined NP is a DO or an SC.

1. Jason was <u>the clown</u> in the play but no one recognized him.
2. Mike hit <u>the tree</u> with his bike and luckily he wasn't hurt.

3. The ad-hoc committee is <u>the body</u> that makes all of the decisions.
4. Frank moved <u>our refrigerator</u> from the kitchen into the garage on Saturday.
5. After the party, everyone cleaned <u>the house</u> except Meg, who slept all day.
6. Honestly, I wrote <u>an email</u> about the incident although I don't think anyone will care.

Functions of Prepositional Phrases

In Chapter 4, we saw already one use of the prepositional phrase (PP) in its function as modifier of a noun phrase:

that boy **with the brown shoes**

With the brown shoes is a prepositional phrase that modifies the noun phrase *that boy*.
In this chapter, we will review some of the many other functions that prepositional phrases may have.

ADJUNCTS

Adjunct structures in grammar are in some sense "extra." They are still important to the overall message, but from a grammatical standpoint, their omission does not result in an ungrammatical sentence; in other words, they are not **obligatory**. In order to understand the concepts of optionality and obligatoriness, consider the direct object in a sentence like this:

He stacked the bricks.

Without the direct object, *the bricks*, the sentence would hardly be grammatical in the sense that speakers of the language would not generate or accept it:

*He stacked. (The only way the utterance would make sense is with considerable context.)

The non-grammaticality of *he stacked* can be understood because a direct object with the verb *stack* is obligatory; *stack* is a strongly transitive verb and therefore requires a direct object. Now consider the following sentence:

In my opinion, cats are better than dogs.

The prepositional phrase, *in my opinion*, here is not obligatory in the way that the direct object was in the previous sentence. In fact, if I omit the prepositional phrase, the sentence is still grammatical:

Cats are better than dogs.

While it's true that I might lose some potentially important information (especially for dog lovers and potential cat haters), the sentence is still complete. *In my opinion* is not a grammatically obligatory structure; it is an adjunct.

THE CORE OF THE CLAUSE

The idea of the core of a clause has to do with those items that are obligatory within the clause. Every clause must have a subject and a predicate, and depending on the type of predicate, the clause may also obligatorily contain a subject complement, a direct object, an indirect object, and/or an object complement. Also contained within the core of a clause are the modifying structures of the core elements. Each of the clauses below contains only core elements and their modifiers:

Mary had a little lamb.
The tourists have become dissatisfied.
Jan gave Billy a book on Spanish fairy tales.

It should be noted that the core of the sentence is completely contained within the subject and predicate phrase branches of the S in a tree diagram, as shown in Figure 7.1.

FIGURE 7.1

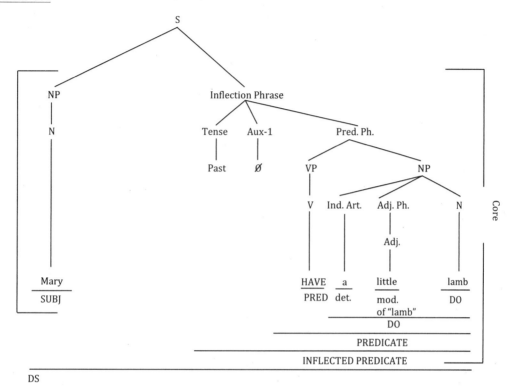

Material that occurs outside of the core of the sentence will be considered **adjunct** in nature. This notion of the core of a clause and adjunct material is important as we look at the first two functions that we will identify for prepositional phrases: **attitudinal adjuncts** and **adverbial adjuncts**.

ATTITUDINAL ADJUNCTS

The first function of prepositional phrases that we will consider under the concept of adjunct is what we will call **attitudinal adjuncts**. Attitudinal adjuncts are those that situate the entire sentence within the attitude or subjective stance of the speaker:

In my opinion, the price of gas is outrageous.
In all honesty, her taste in clothes is questionable.
With all my heart, I will endeavor to answer every question.
Without a doubt, this restaurant is the worst.
For God's sake, don't mollycoddle the child.

In each of the sentences above, the prepositional phrase at the beginning of the sentence has the function of expressing the speaker's attitude or subjective involvement in what they are saying. The price of gas may or may not really be outrageous, but it is *my* opinion that it is. In each case, we would identify the prepositional phrases as appearing in the pre-core area of the clause, that is, the area outside of the core before the subject in a declarative sentence, as in Figure 7.2.

FIGURE 7.2

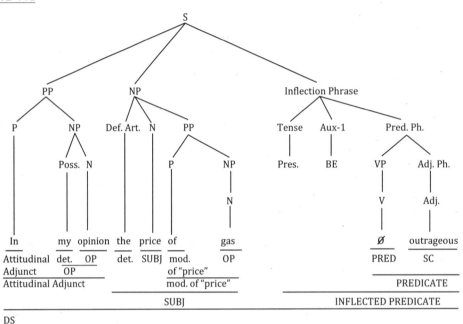

In this case then, the PP *in my opinion* comes off of S before the NP subject. The function of the P is "attitudinal adjunct," and the NP inside the PP is the object of the preposition (of course, the whole PP has the same function as the P, namely, "attitudinal adjunct").

One syntactic property of attitudinal adjuncts is that they may be moved easily to the post-core position. The post-core position is after the inflection phrase:

The price of gas is outrageous, **in my opinion**.
Her taste in clothes is questionable, **in all honesty**.
I will endeavor to answer every question, **with all my heart**.
This restaurant is the worst, **without a doubt**.
Don't mollycoddle the child, **for God's sake**.

In writing, attitudinal adjuncts are generally set apart from the core by commas.

Attitudinal adjunct is a function, and prepositional phrases are only one structure that can fulfill the attitudinal adjunct function. Structures that we refer to as ADVERB may also fulfill that function, as in the following sentence:

Seriously, we are very late.

The adverb *seriously* in the above sentence serves the function of giving the speaker's/writer's attitude or subjective evaluation of the rest of the sentence. In diagramming such a sentence, the adverb is indicated as the structure and attitudinal adjunct is the function (see Figure 7.3). As with all word classes, even if the sentence involves a single word of that category, the tree will include a layer of phrase. Thus, the tree has an Adverb Phrase (Adv. Ph.) branch before Adverb (Adv.).

FIGURE 7.3

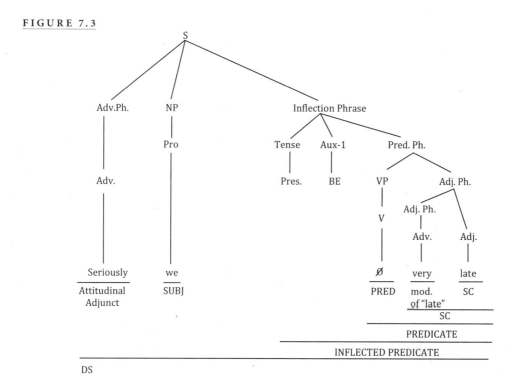

ADVERBIAL ADJUNCTS

Prepositional phrases can also serve in the function of **adverbial adjuncts**. An adverbial adjunct is one that expresses where, when (including duration), or how the predication takes place:

***In the kitchen**, Molly and her brother sat playing UNO **for hours**.*

After my birthday, *the weather turns cold.*
With great stealth, *the burglar crept into the exhibit room of the museum.*

In the above sentences, *in the kitchen* expresses where Molly and her brother sat playing UNO, and *for hours* gives the duration. *After my birthday* says when the weather usually turns cold, and *with great stealth* explains how the burglar crept into the exhibit room.

Like attitudinal adjuncts, adverbial adjuncts can move between the pre-core and post-core positions with relative ease:

For hours, *Molly and her brother sat playing UNO **in the kitchen**.*
*The weather turns cold **after my birthday**.*
*The burglar crept into the exhibit room of the museum **with great stealth**.*

The structure of a PP functioning as an adverbial adjunct is like that of an attitudinal adjunct; the PP will descend from S, either in the pre- or post-core areas. It will be labeled, however, as an adverbial adjunct, in the function lines (see Figure 7.4).

FIGURE 7.4

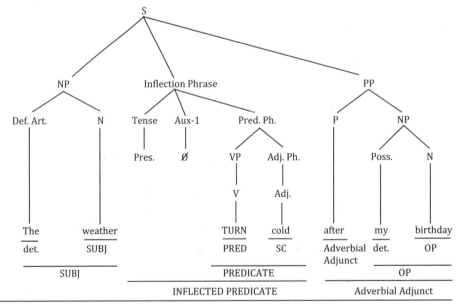

Although usage may vary on this point, a common practice is to separate the adverbial adjunct from the core with a comma when it appears in pre-core position but not when it is in post-core position.

Note, too, that as with most grammatical functions, the adverbial adjunct function can also be fulfilled by other structures. For example, certain kinds of noun phrases can also function as adverbial adjuncts. Nouns like *week*, *month*, and *year*, together with sequencing adjectives like *last* and *next* or demonstratives like *this* and *that*, frequently fulfill an adverbial adjunct function:

Last week, we bought a new puppy.
I will get the report to you **this month**.

Last week and *this month*, both noun phrases, express when the predicate happened or will happen. They are adverbial adjuncts in function and as such they are identified as NPs in terms of their structure but labeled as adverbial adjuncts (see Figure 7.5).

FIGURE 7.5

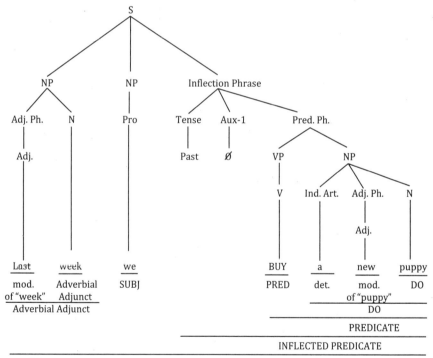

The function of adverbial adjunct may also be fulfilled by an adverb:

***Yesterday**, the speaker gave us the resources.*

Yesterday gives information about when the predicate happened. As such, it fulfills an adverbial adjunct function (see Figure 7.6).

FIGURE 7.6

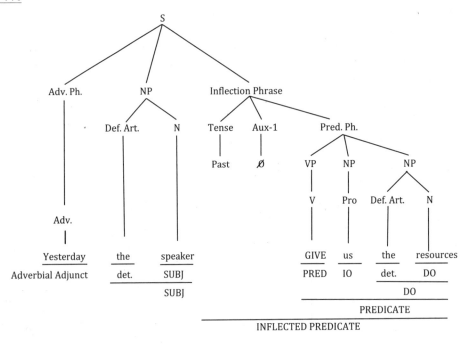

DS

In some cases, and without any other context, there may be some ambiguity between attitudinal adjuncts and adverbial adjuncts. Consider the following sentence:

Sadly, the couple walked out of the hearing knowing they would never see each other again.

Who exactly is sad? If it is the writer's opinion that what happened is sad, *sadly* is an attitudinal adjunct. If, however, *sadly* is meant to describe the manner in which the couple walked out of the hearing, it is an adverbial adjunct. In diagramming, the structure of the two sentences would be identical; however, the function of the two readings would necessitate two different labels for *sadly*.

The different senses of the attitudinal adjunct and adverbial adjunct meanings can be captured through paraphrasing. Attitudinal adjuncts can be paraphrased as "It is _____ that....," where the adjective form of the adverb is placed in the blank. Thus, if *sadly* is the opinion of the writer, *sadly* means *It was sad that the couple walked out of the hearing knowing they would never see each other again*. However, adverbial adjuncts of manner can be paraphrased by placing "in a _____ way" at the end of the sentence, where again the adjective form is placed in the blank: *The couple walked out of the hearing in a sad way knowing that they would never see each other again*. *In a sad way* describes how the couple walked out of the hearing.

ADVERBIAL COMPLEMENTS

It is important to remember that the concept of adjunct is not to be found in the prepositional phrase itself but in its relationship to the entire utterance. While the prepositional phrase *in the kitchen* in a sentence like *Molly and her brother sat playing UNO for hours in the kitchen* is, grammatically speaking, optional in the sense discussed above, it is not in a sentence like *Mike was in the kitchen*, as proved by the grammaticality and non-grammaticality of the following sentences in which the prepositional phrase has been removed:

Molly and her brother sat playing UNO for hours.
*Mike was.

Therefore, merely because the prepositional phrase *in the kitchen* expresses the concept of *where*, that fact alone does not make it an adjunct; and since it is necessary for the grammaticality, or completion, of the predicate *was* in the sentence *Mike was in the kitchen*, its function in that sentence is **adverbial complement**.

The major way, then, in which adverbial complements differ from adverbial adjuncts is that they are more necessary to the predicate from a grammatical standpoint. Another way of thinking of adverbial complements is that they are necessary because they complete the sense of the predicate. This sense of completion is of four types:

1. Occurrence with a copulative verb, usually the verb *be* (as introduced above)[1]
2. Completion of the trajectory of a verb
3. Prepositional verbs
4. Phrasal verb constructions

Each of these is treated in the next sections of this chapter.

---

1 Strictly speaking, too, adverbial complements may occur with stative verbs other than copulative verbs. For example, *The commanders kept their troops out of danger* has *out of danger* as an adverbial complement.

Adverbial Complements Following Copulative Verbs

Further to what was introduced above, note the incompleteness of the following:

*Jack is.

Such an utterance would not constitute a complete sentence except as a truncated response to a more complete question such as *Is anyone available for a late shift on Friday?* In that case, the sentence is made complete by ample context. On its own, the sentence is incomplete. The utterance is made complete, however, by the addition of a prepositional phrase:

Jack is in the hospital.

Thus it is apparent that the prepositional phrase *in the hospital*, which in this case indicates where Jack is, is grammatically obligatory and therefore is an adverbial complement. Other examples include the following:

*The mariachi band was **on break**.*
*A pharmacist is **behind the counter**.*
*The lecture will be **after lunch**.*

On break, *behind the counter*, and *after lunch* all express the adverbial notions of either place or time, but in each case the prepositional phrase expressing that time or place is obligatory; that is, it functions as a complement.

Structurally speaking, adverbial complements differ in an important way from adverbial adjuncts. Recall that adverbial adjuncts, whatever their structure as PP, NP, or Adv. Ph., attached to S in the pre- and/or post-core areas. Adverbial complements, since they have a more intimate relationship with the predicate, attach to material within the inflection phrase, something that is similar to the placement of NPs with DO, IO, SC, and OC functions that we saw in the last chapter.

Diagramming Adverbial Complements

As indicated in the last section, adverbial complements extend from the predicate phrase. If we return to the sentence *Jack is in the hospital*, we note that the adverbial complement function is being fulfilled by the PP *in the hospital*. Thus, the PP extends from the predicate phrase and is labeled as an adverbial complement (AC). (See Figure 7.7, and again, as in the last chapter, do not focus for now on the Tense, Aux-1, or VP branches.)

FIGURE 7.7

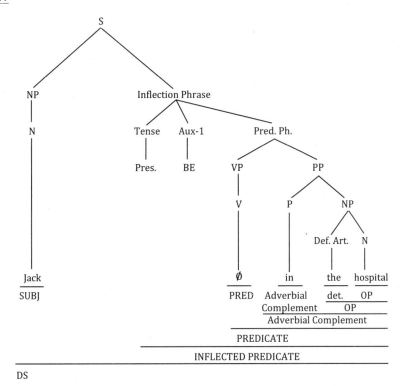

Note that the more intimate the structural and semantic relationship an adverbial complement has with the predicate, the more difficult it is to move it around in the sentence; in fact, it is sometimes impossible:

*After lunch the lecture will be.

This kind of restricted mobility is quite different from that of adverbial adjuncts, which moved easily around the sentence:

The children rode their bikes after lunch.
After lunch, the children rode their bikes.

Like so many of the other functions we have seen throughout this book, the function of an adverbial complement need not always be fulfilled by a prepositional phrase. For example, it is quite possible for that function to be expressed by an adverb itself (see Figure 7.8):

*Jack will be **here**.*

FIGURE 7.8

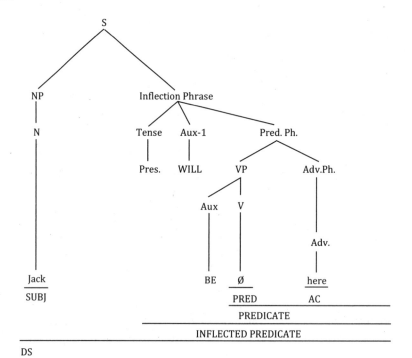

Note that in the tree, the structure of *here* is Adverb; its function is Adverbial Complement. An adverbial complement may also be fulfilled by a noun phrase (see Figure 7.9):

*The party is **next week**.*

FIGURE 7.9

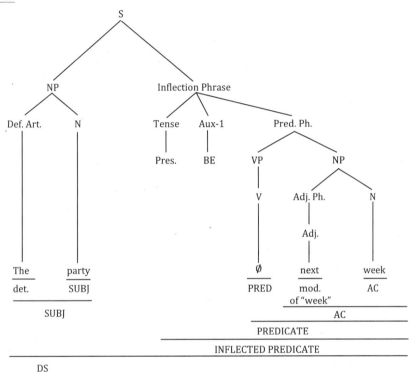

In addition to the verb *be*, there are some other verbs that may be followed by adverbial complements:

*The show will take place **in Vegas**.*
*The accident occurred **after several safety courses**.*

With these examples, it might be noted that the omission of the prepositional phrase is less objectionable:

The show will take place.
?The accident occurred.

The ability of these predicates to appear without the adverbial complement is an indication that the line between adjunct and complement status is not discrete but instead, like most grammatical concepts, continuous. It is not a reasonable grammatical task to decide whether sentences such as these should fall in the complement or adjunct categories, but instead it is the grammarian's task to understand their position on a scale from greater to lesser adjunct status:

*Jan rented a room **on Monday**.*

On Monday rates high as an adjunct since its omission is quite possible while maintaining grammaticality:

Jan rented a room.

However, in a different sentence like

*Mike is **on the roof**.*

on the roof rates high as a complement since its omission is impossible while maintaining grammaticality:

*Mike is.

Again, the prepositional phrase *in Vegas* in *The show will take place in Vegas* falls between these two extremes, although I would suggest it leans toward complement status; however, such a grammaticality judgment depends on other contextual factors such as the importance of the prepositional phrase to the predicate.

Adverbial complementation may take place after other kinds of copulative-like verbs, such as *weigh* and *cost*.

*The book costs **$200**.*
*My cat weighed **15lbs**.*

$200 and *15lbs* are adverbial complements; note the ungrammaticality of **The book costs* or **My cat weighed*.

Completion of the Trajectory of a Verb

Contrast these two sentences:

*The partiers danced **in the streets**.*
*The rioters ran **into the streets**.*

In the first sentence, the prepositional phrase *in the streets* tells us where the partiers danced; the general location is static and non-changing. However, in the second sentence, the prepositional phrase tells us where the rioters ran *into*; the location is the endpoint of the action of the verb *ran*. Therefore, the sense of the predicate in the second sentence would not be complete without the prepositional phrase; it is an adverbial complement.

For those adverbial complements that complete the movement or trajectory of the verb, one can try to envision the verb as it is happening (or was or will be happening) in order to "see" if the prepositional phrase completes the movement or not.

>Maria pulled the string **from her sweater**.
>The boy stuck his arm **through the window**.
>A library worker will put the book **on the shelf**.
>The picture fell **off the wall** with a loud crash.

In each of these sentences, the prepositional phrases delimit the movement of each of the verbs: The origin of the movement of pulling the string begins *from her sweater*; *through the window* indicates the trajectory of the boy's sticking his arm; *on the shelf* gives the destination of where the book will be put; and *off the wall* sets up the path of motion for the falling picture.

The difference between adverbial adjuncts and adverbial complements can be contrasted in the following set of sentences:

>The dog bit the child **on the playground**.
>The dog bit the child **on the arm**.

In the first sentence, *on the playground* tells us where the subject was when it did the verb. In other words, it modifies the entire core of the sentence; it is an adverbial adjunct. But in the second sentence, *on the arm* tells us only the location of the bite; it is part of the predicate, that is, an adverbial complement.

Furthermore, we might note the relative freedom of the adverbial adjunct to move to the beginning of the sentence:

>**On the playground**, *the dog bit the child*.

Placing the adverbial complement at the beginning of the second sentence, however, sounds odd or overly poetic:

>**?On the arm**, *the dog bit the child*.

Analyzing Sentences with Multiple Prepositional Phrases

As can be seen from the example sentences in the last section, grammatical analysis is now becoming increasingly complex. If we take, for example, the sentence *The picture fell off the wall with a loud crash*, we note there are two prepositional phrases, *off the wall* and *with a loud crash*. What is the status of each? To carry out that analysis, it is important to remember that omission as a test for adverbial complement status is not a test that works in both directions. It is true that a prepositional phrase that cannot be omitted is very likely an adverbial complement, as in *Jack is in the kitchen*, in which *in the kitchen* is not omissible and therefore an adverbial complement. However, just because a prepositional phrase can be omitted does not preclude its status as adverbial complement. As we saw above, some adverbial complements can be omitted, although certainly a lot of information is lost by doing so. Let's consider for a moment the criterion of omissibility for the two prepositional phrases in *The picture fell off the wall with a loud crash*. Grammatically speaking, both *off the wall* and *with a loud crash* are omissible because there is nothing ungrammatical about the sentence *The picture fell*.

However, if we consider the relationship of the two prepositional phrases to the verb *fell*, we find that *off the wall* has a more intimate connection to that verb, while *with a loud crash* has a lesser relationship. To be specific, *off the wall* describes the path of motion for falling, while *with a loud crash* describes how the picture fell. Based on the information learned so far in this chapter, a prepositional phrase that delimits the motion of the verb is in some way an adverbial complement, and a prepositional phrase that gives the manner in which the verb happens is an adverbial adjunct. Applying that to the sentence in question, *off the wall* is an adverbial complement and *with a loud crash* is an adverbial adjunct.

In diagramming the two prepositional phrases, we simply follow what we have learned so far concerning the two functions for prepositional phrases; adverbial adjuncts come off of the pre- or post-core part of the sentence, that is, off the S, and adverbial complements come off of the predicate phrase, as in Figure 7.10.

FIGURE 7.10

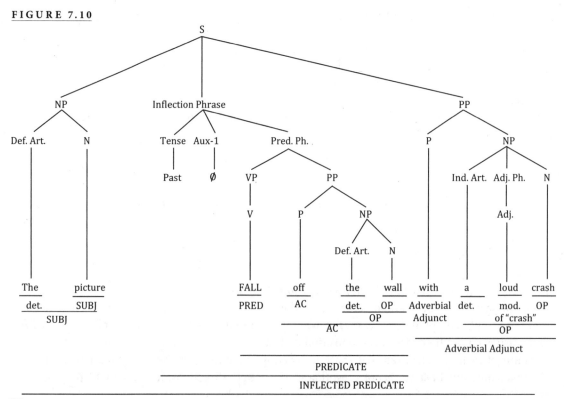

Now let's consider another sentence in which there is more than one prepositional phrase:

They marched from the Capitol Building to the White House.

In our analysis of these two prepositional phrases, we might begin by noticing that both are omissible; there is nothing ungrammatical about *They marched*. Of course, just because the prepositional phrases can be omitted does not conclude our analysis. Next we must ask what their relationship to the verb is, and we note that *from the Capitol Building* and *to the White House* both serve to delimit the trajectory of the verb *march*. In other words, they both serve adverbial complement functions. Sometimes when learning grammar, students do not expect it to be possible to have two prepositional phrases (or more) fulfilling the adverbial complement role. However, there is nothing at all that prohibits multiple structures fulfilling adverbial complement roles, even two or more prepositional phrases. When we are diagramming such structures, both prepositional phrases are simply placed into the tree in the predicate phrase, as shown in Figure 7.11.

FIGURE 7.11

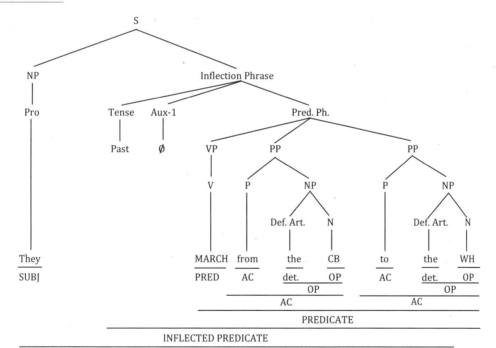

Prepositional Verbs

Prepositional verbs are those that regularly select a specific preposition to follow. Examples include the following:

depend on (someone or something)
sneer at (someone or something)
rebel against (someone or something)
repent for (something)
coincide with (something)
shrink from (someone or something)

Pets **depend on** their owners for their basic survival needs.
We **sneered at** her explanation of the events.
The combatants have been **rebelling against** the illegally imposed government since the summer.
The accused have not **repented for** the crimes they committed.
The children's concert **coincided with** the first day of Spring.
Devorah always **shrinks from** large crowds.

In each of the verb + preposition combinations, it is the verb that governs the selection of the preposition. Consider, in contrast, the sentence

Alan **sat in** the chair.

In this case, the preposition *in* is selected by the relationship among Alan, his posture, and the chair. Indeed, if he were in a different place, we would use a different preposition:

Alan **sat under** the boardwalk.

In other words, *sit* does not "select" the preposition *in* in the same sense that *depend* "selects" *on* in a sentence like *Pets depend on their owners*. How many other prepositions could occur with *depend*? **Depend for, *depend with, *depend in* are all ungrammatical in the sense that they would not be accepted or generated by native speakers. So we say that *depend* and *on* have an intimate relationship, and consequently the PP beginning with *on*—*on their owners*—is an adverbial complement (see Figure 7.12).

FIGURE 7.12

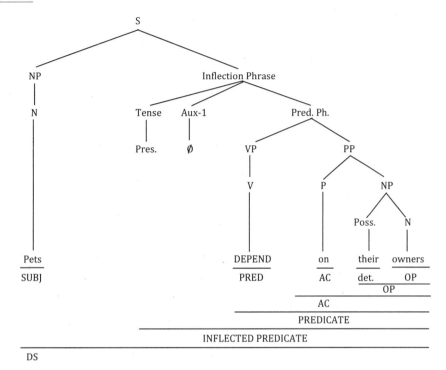

Phrasal Verbs

Phrasal verbs are verb + preposition combinations which together derive a unique and usually unpredictable meaning. Phrasal verbs are usually paraphrasable by a single-word near-synonym:

*The runner **gave up**.* (= quit)
*The flight **took off** from Dallas at 3:12 p.m.* (= depart)
*They decided to **throw out** the old couch together.* (= discard)
*Unfortunately, we will have to **put off** the reading.* (= postpone)

Phrasal verbs may be intransitive or transitive.

Intransitive Phrasal Verbs

Some phrasal verbs are intransitive, meaning that they do not have a direct object and therefore will occur only with a preposition:

*The runner **gave up**.*
*We were afraid of how the project would **turn out**.*

*Because of the extreme weather, the plane was not able to **take off**.*

In such cases, the predicate phrase will contain a PP, but the PP will simply be made up of a P, the function of which is adverbial complement (see Figure 7.13). This is remarkable because so far in this book, PPs have always had NP objects.

FIGURE 7.13

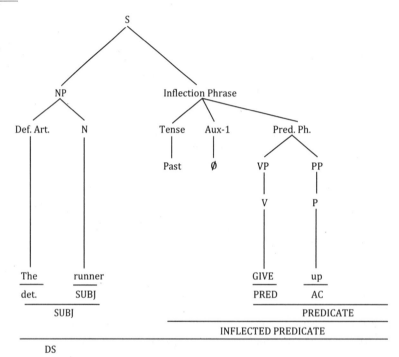

Also note how a short sentence with an intransitive phrasal verb will often have the preposition as the last element in the sentence, as in each of the examples above. As mentioned in the introduction to this book, quite often even if a person does not have extensive training in grammar, they will have heard the "rule" not to end a sentence with a preposition. Phrasal verbs are very common in English, and their use will frequently leave or "strand" a preposition at the end of a sentence. The rule forbidding sentence-final prepositions is neither in line with the linguistic facts about English nor even a grammar rule, because it is really much more about stylistics.

During certain periods of English, writing styles have varied between those that attempt to achieve a stilted and complex voice and those that prefer simplicity and homeliness. Phrasal verbs belong very much to the natural stuff of English, descending from the Germanic origins of the language. The semantic equivalents of the phrasal verbs are most often words borrowed during the history of English, often from Latin or French. Therefore, the avoidance of phrasal verbs as a means of avoiding sentence-final prepositions (although phrasal verbs are not the only source for sentence final prepositions) will involve the use of one of these borrowed verbs and will lend a different tone to the sentence, probably one that sounds more erudite, but maybe even "highfalutin'." Still, the decision about whether to use phrasal verbs like *take off* versus borrowed terms like *depart* is not really grammatical but stylistic, so it depends on speaker/writer choice and on context.

In certain cases, an intransitive phrasal verb might look very much like a sentence with an adverb. Contrast the following set of sentences:

He looked up.
He messed up.

In the first sentence, *up* is an adverb, telling us the direction *he* looked. *Up* in the second sentence, however, is the prepositional part of a phrasal verb; we can note, for example, that *messed up* is idiomatic and that *up* may be placed at the front of the first sentence but not the second, suggesting that *up* in the second sentence is more intimately tied to the predicate:

Up he looked.
*Up he messed.

Transitive Phrasal Verbs
Other uses of phrasal verbs reveal them to be transitive; that is, they have a direct object:

*Hideki **turned off the light** as he exited the room.*
*The bandits **held up the bank**, but luckily no one was hurt in the heist.*
*That charitable foundation **has been calling up past donors** in its search to meet its $200,000 goal.*

In each of the cases above, the noun phrase following the prepositional element is not the object of the preposition but instead is a direct object within the predicate phrase. The preposition is a PP consisting only of a P with an adverbial function (see Figure 7.14).

FIGURE 7.14

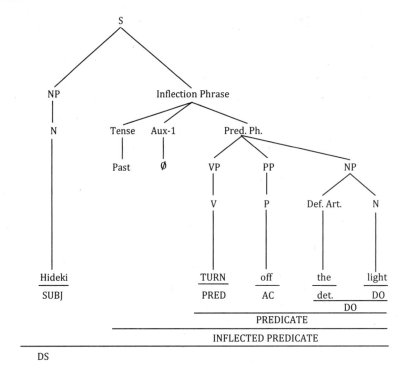

On the surface of things, prepositional verbs and transitive phrasal verbs would appear to be structurally identical:

We depended on their kindness.
We turned down their kindness.

In both cases, there is a preposition following the verb and a noun phrase following that preposition. However, while the noun phrase in the first sentence is the object of that preposition, it is not so in the second sentence. Instead, in the second sentence, the noun phrase comes off the predicate phrase directly and functions as a direct object and the PP contains only a preposition, the function of which is adverbial. Contrast the two trees in Figures 7.15 and 7.16 carefully.

FIGURE 7.15

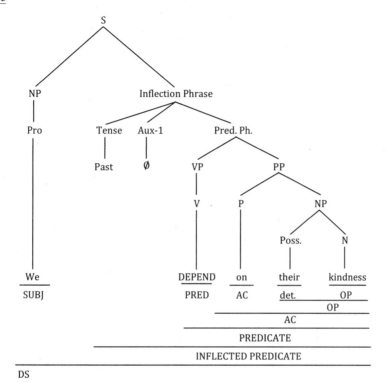

FIGURE 7.16

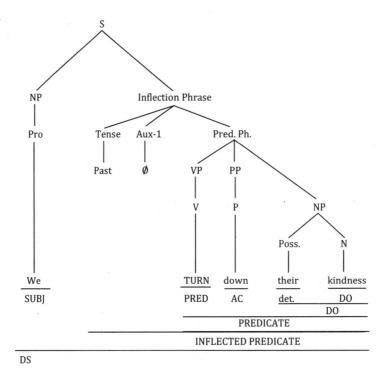

There is a simple test to determine whether a verb + preposition combination is a phrasal verb or a prepositional verb. In a phrasal verb construction, the prepositional element may be moved to the position following the noun phrase direct object (but see below on inseparable phrasal verbs).

*We turned **down** their kindness.*
*We turned their kindness **down**.*

Such movement is not possible in prepositional verb constructions:

*We depended **on** their kindness.*
We depended their kindness **on.*

Whether the preposition in a phrasal verb is before or after the noun phrase direct object, its basic structure is the same, as can be seen in Figure 7.17.

FIGURE 7.17

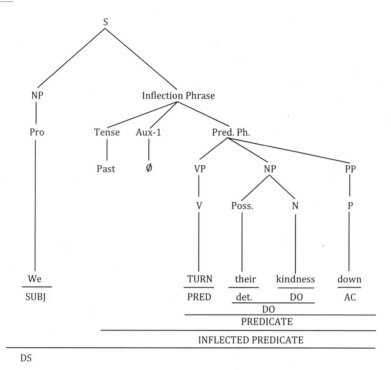

Note that when the direct object is a pronoun, the prepositional element of the phrasal verb *must* follow that pronoun:

*The belligerent customer **took** them **on**.*
The belligerent customer **took on them.*

However, sometimes, in speech, a pronominal direct object of a phrasal verb may follow the prepositional element for contrast or emphasis.

The belligerent customer took on THEM and not those other people.

Separable and Inseparable Phrasal Verbs
Traditionally, phrasal verbs are divided into those that are separable, like the example with *turn down* above, and inseparable ones, like the example below. A **separable phrasal verb** allows the prepositional element to be moved to the position after the noun phrase direct object, as we saw in the section above. However, some other situations, which seem very similar, do not allow that kind of movement:

My sister ran across her old boyfriend.

Run across is often treated as an **inseparable phrasal verb**. Its designation as a phrasal verb is along semantic lines in that it is a verb + preposition combination that derives a unique or unpredictable meaning—in the case of *run across* it means "meet by chance." Structurally, however, *run across* does not act like *turn down* since it cannot be separated from the verb and placed after the noun phrase:

*My sister ran her old boyfriend across.

Thus, inseparable phrasal verbs behave structurally more like prepositional verbs. We could then debate their exact analysis: should we consider *her old boyfriend* a direct object and leave *across* as a PP with only a P, or should we consider *her old boyfriend* the object of the P *across*? While there are good arguments for both sides of the debate, in this book we will defer to the structural criterion of mobility. Since the preposition cannot be moved, we will consider the NP to be the object of the preposition, as diagrammed in Figure 7.18.

FIGURE 7.18

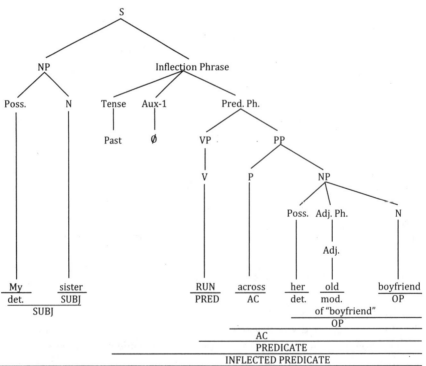

Note, then, that it is not necessary to distinguish, at least for now, the difference between a prepositional verb and an inseparable phrasal verb. The important criterion for deciding the status of the noun phrase after the prepositional element is whether it can move. If it can, the noun phrase is a direct object; if it cannot, it is the object of the preposition.

Prepositional-Phrasal Verbs

Finally, we should also recognize that there are some phrasal verbs that also "select" a preposition. These are fairly easy to recognize since they will generally involve two prepositions after the verb. These too may be intransitive:

*The teachers **put up with** the noise in the classroom.*
*We **gave up on** the problem.*

With intransitive prepositional-phrasal verbs, the first preposition is a single P within a PP, and the second PP will contain the regular P and NP, with both PPs functioning as adverbial complements (see Figure 7.19).

FIGURE 7.19

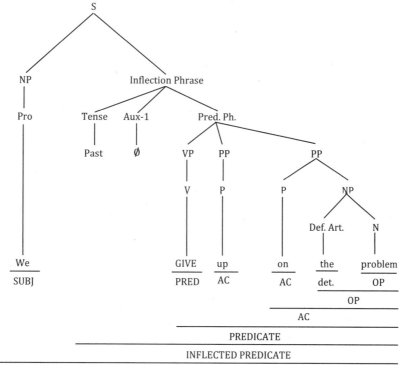

Prepositional-phrasal verbs may also be transitive:

*The boy **took out** his frustration **on** his brother.*

Note that like other transitive phrasal verbs, the preposition can move before or after the NP (see Figure 7.20):

*The boy **took** his frustration **out on** his brother.*

FIGURE 7.20

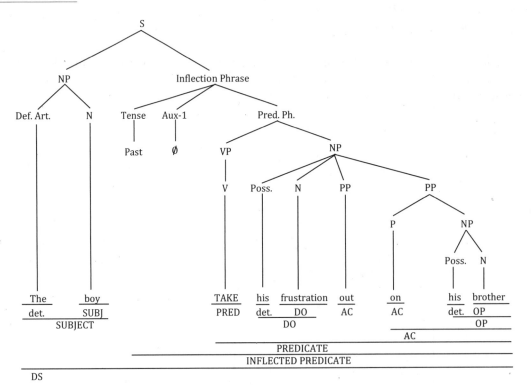

Some transitive prepositional-phrasal verbs require the first preposition to be placed after the direct object NP (see Figure 7.21):

The factory locked the workers out of the building.

FIGURE 7.21

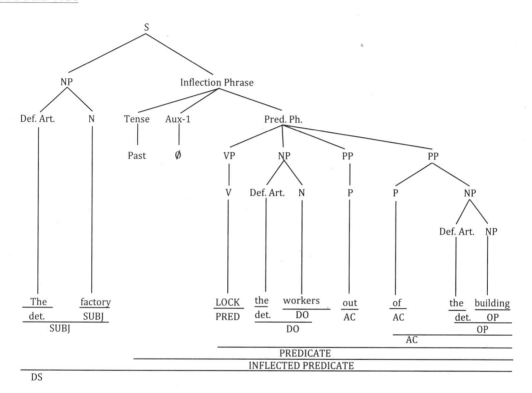

Adverbial Complements Following Adjectives

There are certain adjectives that require a following prepositional phrase in order to complete their sense:

*Edcel is fond **of his nieces**.*

In this sentence, the adjective *fond* cannot be used without the complement PP *of his nieces*:

*Edcel is fond.

In analyzing such complement PPs using form-function trees, the PP extends from the Adj. Ph. and is labeled as "adverbial complement" (see Figure 7.22).

FIGURE 7.22

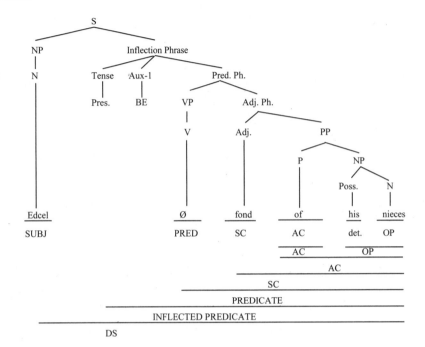

Other adjectives commonly followed by adverbial complements include *angry at, mad at, good at, afraid of, ashamed of, full of, proud of, scared of, dependent on, keen on, close to, similar to, angry with, content with, familiar with, furious with, uncomfortable with, happy with/about, glad about*, etc.

EXERCISES

A. Determine whether the italicized portions in the following sentences are obligatory or optional.

1. Nick placed *the glove* into the drawer.
2. The ceremony will be *in the garden*.
3. Those books were found *on the third floor*.
4. Although we made up *the beginning*, the ending was completely true.
5. Tom and Brett ran *a marathon* last year, but neither chose to this year.
6. The townsfolk elected *Roberto* mayor in the last election.

7. Novelists are often *surprised* to find their original idea and the critics' reading of their work to be completely different.
8. The *scented* candle gave off a putrid aroma after it had sat on the window sill all summer.

B. Determine whether the italicized PPs in the following sentences are adjuncts or complements.

1. Our painting will be hung *on the wall*.
2. Their house is *on the market* now.
3. The guest arrived *at eight*, a full hour later than the invitation indicated.
4. The actor walked *off the stage* and swore never to return.
5. The couple will have their long-awaited wedding *in the Square*.
6. Once the birds learned that the cats could not reach them, they sat *on the perch* very close to the side of the cage.
7. The man put the hat *on his head* only to realize it wasn't his.
8. Our neighbors' car has stood *in the street* unmoved for several days.
9. Alfonso placed the marker *in the book* to remind him to reread the passage later.
10. Generally I am very good at math but that problem was *over my head*.

C. Make full form–function trees for the following sentences. In the next chapter, you will learn the details of the Tense and Aux-1 nodes. For now, do not focus on those but on the position of the PP as an adjunct (coming off S) or complement (coming off the predicate phrase).

1. Mary placed the cup onto the counter.
2. The gloomy children are in school.
3. The curious cat hid behind the books.
4. Bill is a handyman here in this city.
5. Obviously, we will be there at noon.
6. After the sermon, the parishioners had a potluck on the lawn of the church.
7. At the park, my dog runs from person to person repeatedly.
8. In summary, I deem our profits miserable in this quarter.
9. Luckily, my students could find the materials in the library.
10. I will be at the courthouse next week before the trial.

D. In this chapter, you have learned to apply a structural test to determine whether the preposition can be moved from the position immediately following the verb to the position following the noun phrase. Based on the application of that test, determine whether each of the following bolded verb + preposition combinations is a prepositional verb or a phrasal verb. (Hint: don't forget that if the preposition can move it would move best to the position after the noun *and anything else that might modify that noun*.)

1. We have **moved over** the column and placed a new set of figures next to it.
2. The strikers **decided on** a strategy to stay off the job until management met their demands.
3. The dieters **craved for** sweets but found willpower in the inspirational talks given to them by their trainer.
4. All students were required to **hand in** their assignments on the Tuesday before class.
5. Do not **deviate from** the specific directions given to you by the engineers.
6. The radio hosts **called up** the winner and announced her prize on the air.
7. Although we didn't really want to, we inadvertently **brought up** their marital problems during dinner.
8. In order to find the correct solution, you will need to **dispense with** unnecessary data.
9. The vacationers were excited to **embark upon** their cruise, completely unaware of the dangers that lay beneath the waves.
10. The gunmen **held up** the convenience store on Jefferson and Main shortly after midnight.

E. In this chapter, you have learned that a prepositional phrase may be an adverbial complement because of one of the following:

   a. Occurrence with a copulative verb, usually the verb *be* (in which case its removal results in an incomplete/ungrammatical sentence)
   b. Completion of the trajectory of a verb
   c. The verb + preposition is a prepositional verb
   d. The verb + preposition is a phrasal verb

Consider the following sentences and determine why the bolded preposition is the head of a prepositional phrase functioning as an adverbial complement, selecting from the four criteria listed.

1. Duncan tossed his hat **into** the ring.
2. The dog dug **up** his bone.
3. The judge decided **on** the case.
4. The boy pulled the crayon **from** the box.
5. The cat gazed **at** the mouse.
6. Rezalda took **down** the picture.
7. Alan called **up** his friend.
8. The students depend **on** their teacher.
9. My sister jumped **off** the porch.

F. Make full form–function trees for the following sentences. In the next chapter, you will learn the details of the Tense and Aux-1 nodes. For now, do not focus on those but on the position of the PP as an adjunct (coming off S) or complement (coming off the predicate phrase).

1. My blind dog has been digging up our flowers in the garden. (Note that *in the garden* is intended to describe where the dog is digging.)
2. That neighbor will look at yours after Sunday.
3. I looked at a new car with black stripes on Sunday.
4. Unfortunately, these customers bought a bag of marbles with their money.
5. We put up with their nonsense in school.
6. Frank placed the envelope with the money on the desk last night.
7. My father set me up with a new job.

The Inflection Phrase

It is in the area of verbs that grammatical terminology has perhaps been most misused, leading to much confusion on the part of learners. One of the most important things to do when learning about verbs is to acquire the vocabulary concerning verbs and to use that vocabulary consistently. While some of the terms may be new, many will be familiar, although it may be that misuse of them has made their understanding "fuzzy.")

One of the most important sets of terms to learn in discussing verbs is the difference between a synthetic verb form and a periphrastic verb form. Note carefully, too, the use of the term "form" here to discuss these structures. One of the unfortunate misuses of grammatical verbal terminology is the use of "tense" to talk about all verb forms. "Tense" has a very specific meaning in grammar; the term and its exact meaning are presented in the next section.

To return to the concepts of synthetic and periphrastic verb forms, note these two sentences:

*The lawn service workers **pruned** the trees in the front yard.*
*The lawn service workers **are pruning** the trees in the front yard.*

In the first sentence, the verb is the single word *pruned*; it signals past time through the suffix *-ed*. In the second sentence, the verb is made up of the two words, *are* and *pruning*; it signals that the activity of pruning is ongoing at the moment of speech. That sense of ongoingness is made by the connection of the auxiliary verb *are* with the verb ending in *-ing*. We say of the first verb form that it is **synthetic** because the grammatical information (pastness) is contained within a single word form. We say of the second verb form that it is **periphrastic** because the grammatical information (present time, ongoingness) is contained in a multi-word phrase.

TENSE VERSUS ASPECT

Tense is a concept that refers to the encoding of time through specific verbal morphemes, like the *-ed* in the example in the last section. *-ed* is the past tense morpheme. English has, *in a linguistics sense*, only two tenses: the simple present and the simple past, exemplified respectively in the two sentences below.

> *Tom **eats** lunch at 12:00 every day.*
> *Tom **traveled** to Europe last summer.*

Note that in both cases, the verbs *eats* and *traveled* are synthetic.[1]

Aspect refers to the finer-grained temporal or situational meanings that a verb might have. Consider for instance the difference between the following:

> *Tom **eats** lunch at 12:00 every day.*
> *Tom **is eating** lunch right now.*

In the first sentence, the present-tense verb form *eats* signals what we call **habitual** aspect, that is, an activity, situation, or event repeated at regular intervals. In the second sentence, the periphrastic verb form *is eating* refers to an activity that is ongoing at the moment of speech, an aspect most often called **progressive**. While it is true that the aspectual sense of habituality is supported by the adverbial expression *every day* in the first sentence and that the sense of ongoingness is supported by the adverbial expression *right now* in the second sentence, the verb forms alone would still signal those same meanings:

> *Tom eats lunch at 12:00.*
> *Tom is eating lunch.*

Thus, we might think of tense as referring to macro-time divisions, like present, past, and future, and in English we have specific synthetic forms that correspond to present and past times, namely, the present and past tenses. Aspect, however, refers to a set of finer semantic designations that we use to describe verbal meaning. There is no one-to-one correspondence for aspectual meaning and verbal form in the way there often is with the present and past tenses. So while the *is eating* form of the verb can signal progressive aspect, that form can also signal habitual meaning, albeit with an added sense of irony, frustration, etc., often with the addition of the adverb *always*.

> *Sanjev is always riding his bike past our house in the afternoon.*

---

1 Strictly speaking, tense may be periphrastically expressed, as in English when we use a form of the auxiliary *do* in sentences such as *We did not wash the dishes*. In that sentence, the past time of the verb phrase is expressed in the auxiliary verb *did*. Auxiliary *do* is treated in Chapters 10 and 12.

(Actually, the meaning is more like this: on any given occasion in the afternoon, Sanjev is in the ongoing activity of riding his bike past our house.) Thus progressivity and the form of the auxiliary verb *be* + the *-ing* form of the verb are not exclusively linked; that linkage can derive other meanings as well.

In some other instances, however, certain verb forms have arisen in English that have only habitual as their aspectual meaning. For example, *used to* is exclusively used for past habitual activities or events:

Sanjev used to ride his bike past our house every afternoon.

We return to various aspectual meanings after presentation of the verb forms in the next section.

VERB FORMS

In order to learn English verb forms, the use of the following terms/concepts is necessary. Finite forms are those that have an inflection for tense as well as person and number governed by a grammatical subject; non-finite forms do not (see Table 8.1).

TABLE 8.1: VERB FORMS

Finite Forms

General present:	*take*
Third singular present:	*takes*
Simple past:	*took*

Non-Finite Forms

Base form:	*take*
Simple active participle:	*taking*
Simple perfect participle:	*taken*

NOTES ON THE FORMS

Base form. The base form is sometimes referred to as the "bare infinitive" or the "infinitive without *to*." During the Middle English period (1100–1500) (the infinitive, which formerly had been signaled by a suffix) as it is in the majority of European languages today, came to be exclusively periphrastic, with the form *to* + the base form of the verb: *to take, to love, to have*, etc. Compare the infinitive in Spanish, *tomar* 'to take,' or German, *nehmen* 'to take,' in which the infinitive is still signaled by a suffix; that is, the infinitive is synthetic in those languages but periphrastic in English.

The form referred to as the **simple active participle** above is often called the "present participle," and sometimes the "*-ing* participle" in some grammatical traditions. The **simple perfect participle** is traditionally called the past participle, and sometimes the *-en* participle in some grammatical works. People have objected to the terms "present" and "past" for participles because participles themselves do not signal time; that is, they are not tensed forms. Consider the following example:

> **Carrying** *their distinct speech features from their East Anglian home, the Puritan settlers replanted their Norfolk whine as the Yankee drawl.*

The so-called "present" participle in this sentence, *carrying*, has no present time association but instead gets its time (past in this case) from the main verb *replanted* in the second part of the sentence. Similarly, in a sentence like

> **Taken** *in small doses, aspirin may be effective in preventing heart disease.*

the so-called "past" participle *taken* refers to a habitual or perhaps even future time (if the sentence were part of a doctor's recommendation for a future course of preventative actions).[1]

However, the alternative terms, *-ing participle* and *-en participle*, respectively, for the present and past participles, are not wholly satisfying either. While the term *-ing participle* is rather well justified, since every single verb in English will admit the *-ing* suffix, the *-en* suffix is quite restricted to a small set of irregular verbs. In fact, the majority of verbs in English have a simple perfect participle identical in form to the simple past, most frequently *-ed*. Thus the simple perfect participle form of *look* is *looked*, which is the same as the simple past form.

In this book, we will use the terms simple active participle and simple perfect participle for reasons that will be made even clearer in Chapters 11 and 17.

As stated above, finite forms have traditionally been identified as carrying an inflection for tense and an inflection for person and number that is governed by a grammatical subject, at least for English and structurally related languages. This property of finite verb forms is most easily seen in the **third-person singular present**, because in that category an *–s* will always appear.

> *Jane drive**s** an SUV.*
> *The President come**s** from Hawaii.*
> *It rain**s** too often in that city.*

Readers familiar with a language like Spanish (or Italian, Russian, Latin, German, etc.) will know that this kind of agreement suffix is more widespread in those languages. As we have seen in earlier chapters, languages like Spanish, for instance, show many different forms in agreement with a subject:

tom**o**	tom**amos**
tom**as**	tom**áis**
tom**a**	tom**an**

---

1 The simple perfect participle is also regularly passive in meaning for transitive verbs, in contradistinction to the active meaning of the simple active participle.

English used to have more of these kinds of inflections throughout the verbal system (consider *-est* with *thou* in Shakespeare, as in *thou speakest*). However, during its history, English lost most of its inflections such that most of the time no overt agreement marker appears. Perhaps not really justifiably, we often say that the inflection for tense/person/number is simply "zero" for most persons. Therefore, a paradigm for the verb *take* in the present tense in English is:

I	takeØ	we	takeØ
you	takeØ	you	takeØ
he she it	takes	they	takeØ

Every form other than the one that agrees with *he*, *she*, *it* (or indeed any singular noun) has a zero-inflection. This zero-inflected form is the **general present**. Because the general present has a zero inflection, it will be identical to the base form for every verb in English except for the verb *be*, for which the base form is *be* and the present is either *am*, *is*, or *are*. The *-s* form of the third-person singular present and the general present make up the present-tense category in English.

The **simple past** form signals past time; along with the present tense, it is one of the true tenses in English. While past-tense forms show past-tense inflections, they do not show person/number inflections. Additionally, in the simple past, verbs in English are either regular or irregular. A regular verb is one that signals the past tense with the addition of a past-tense suffix, what we usually think of as *-ed*:

talked
mowed
assembled
opened
needed

In fact, the majority of verbs in English are regular, and essentially all new verbs admitted into the language are regular as well, for example, *texted*. An irregular verb is any verb that does not form its past in this way. Such irregular verbs may indicate past through a vowel change, a vowel change and a suffix, or no change at all:

sing~sang
keep~kept
cut~cut

Since the simple past form and the simple perfect participle form of irregular verbs cannot be predicted, they are learned as three-part synopses, the so-called **principal parts** of the verb. Thus an irregular verb is most often presented and learned as something like this:

take-took-taken

In that set of three forms, the first is the base form (which again is almost always identical to the general present), followed by the simple past form, and finally the simple perfect participle.

In the next section, we will consider the compound, or periphrastic, verb forms in English.

SYNOPSIS OF THE ENGLISH VERB

Table 8.2 presents the forms of the English verb using the sample verb *take*.

TABLE 8.2: ENGLISH VERB FORMS

	simple	progressive	perfect	perfect-progressive
present time	take/takes	am/is/are taking	has/have taken	has/have been taking
past time	took	was/were taking	had taken	had been taking

Again, remember that the only two forms that are "tenses" are the simple present (the general present and the -*s* present), *take/takes*, and the simple past, *took*. All others should be referred to as "forms," and it can be noted that each of them involves an auxiliary verb and some form of the main verb. Such combinations are sometimes called **compound verb forms** or, as discussed earlier, periphrastic verb forms. Thus, *take*, *takes*, and *took* are synthetic, but *am taking*, *had taken*, *was taking*, and so on are periphrastic. The following chart lists the names of the various verb forms along with the example form using *take*;

    simple present: *take* (general present)/*takes* (-s present)
    present progressive: *am/is/are taking*
    present perfect: *has/have taken*
    present-perfect progressive: *has/have been taking*

    simple past: *took*
    past progressive: *was/were taking*
    past perfect: *had taken*
    past-perfect progressive: *had been taking*

Present Progressive

The present progressive is made up of the present form of auxiliary *be* + the simple active participle. It is used chiefly to signal **progressive aspect** in the present time. Progressive aspect means that an action is ongoing at the time of reference; the time of reference with the present progressive is the present moment.

    Bill **is taking** his cat to the vet.
    Our mayor **is running** for his second term.

In both cases, the action signaled by the verb is being done by the subject at the moment of the present time. The progressive typically signals a subject that is an agent, someone or something that intentionally performs the verb. The verb in the progressive is normally an action verb, like *take* or *run (for a term)*, things an agent intends to do and has some control over. Also, the progressive is not bound temporally, meaning we do not really know its beginning or end; the point of the progressive is an action in progress, and we understand that action to be temporary. At some point, Bill will arrive at the vet and the taking will be complete. At some point, the mayor will win or lose his bid for re-election and his running will be over.

For these reasons, the progressive does not appear normally with certain verbs, particularly those in which the subject cannot be agentive, the action is not overt, or the time of the verb is not understood as temporally restricted. This is true of some verbs of emotion or mental processing, as well as those that express stative situations, that is, those that don't change for a long time:[1]

love
like
hate
think
feel
contain
hold
matter
depend
resemble
belong

Note the oddity of sentences like:

?Oh Val, I am loving you with all my heart.
?My dog is feeling cold when he spends too much time in the snow.
?You're resembling your father.

In the first sentence, the subject *I* is not an agent; I don't make love happen. Nor is the verb *love* an action verb. Instead the emotion of love is something that the subject experiences. Also, the emotion of loving someone, while it may truly be only temporal, is not supposed to be. Similarly, the subject in the second sentence is not an agent and the verb is not an action verb. Again the subject, *my dog*, is the experiencer of *feel*. And, in the third sentence, if *you* resemble your father, it's a stative situation and not likely to change, at least any time soon.

---

1 In non-stative senses, some of these verbs can occur in the progressive. Contrast the following:

I think that the red one suits you better.
I am thinking about our meeting next week.

However, as discussed in the next paragraph, even among these verbs the progressive is extending into stative territory.

Given the restricted use of the progressive in the above contexts, one may ask why, then, sentences such as the following happen at all:

I'm loving your new shoes.

This usage is common enough and may in fact be increasing. Of course, its use is somewhat marked; by saying "I am loving your new shoes," I seemingly put myself more into the moment and take a more active role in my assertion about my adoration of the shoes. Its use is wrapped up in the social moment of my convincing the listener that I *really do* love the shoes, rather than about my stating an experience. This is a common theme in language change; as grammatical forms move into new contexts/uses, the meaning is at first often emphatic or reinforcing.

Present Perfect

The present perfect is made up of the present form of the auxiliary verb *have* + the simple perfect participle:

*The agents **have taken** the file and will deliver it to the spies.*
*The judges **have chosen** our project for the award.*
*This issue **has caused** a lot of pain for a lot of people.*

The present perfect is used in order to do one of the following:

1. Express **resultative aspect**. Resultative aspect reports an action, state, or event as having happened in the past yet setting up a resultant state:

*We won't be able to buy posters since Mike **has stolen** all of the funds.*
*The president **has resigned**!*

In the first example, Mike's stealing of the funds results in the present state of the funds being absent and having no money to buy posters. In the second, the president's resignation, probably quite recent, ushers in a new state of affairs.

2. Express **present anterior aspect**. Present anterior aspect reports an action, state, or event as having happened in the past and being relevant to the present:

*I **have** already **seen** that movie. Let's see a different one.*
*Angie **has finished** her part of the work and now it's time for you to kick in.*

In both sentences, that action or event of the past is relevant for some current situation. In the first sentence, the fact that I saw the movie in the past causes me to encourage us to see a different one now. In the second sentence, the fact that Angie finished her part of the task means that it is now time for you to do your part.

3. Express **anterior-continuing aspect**. In anterior-continuing aspect, an action, state, or event that began in the past continues into the present time:

> I **have lived** here for nearly 10 years.
> Amy **has worked** in our department since 2003.

In the first sentence, I began living here in the past and continue to do so. In the second sentence, Amy began working in our department in 2003 and continues working in our department now. This particular use of the present perfect is somewhat unique to English. Many other languages express these kinds of sentiments with the simple present form, which explains why learning the present perfect is often so difficult for speakers of English as a second language.

Present-Perfect Progressive

The chief sense of the present-perfect progressive is an anterior-continuing use, which we just examined in the present progressive:

> We **have been taking** French since high school.
> I **have been living** in this dump for too long!

Past Progressive

The past progressive is similar to the present progressive in that it refers to an ongoing action that takes place at a specific reference point. However, whereas the specific reference point in the present progressive is the present moment, it is a past moment for the past progressive:

> Fatimah **was talking** to Jahanara when the van drove up.
> Evan and Brian **were editing** their paper yesterday in the library.

In the first sentence, the subject was engaged agentively in the action of talking at a specific point in the past, established by the simple past verb in the clause *when the van drove up*. Similarly, in the second sentence, the subjects *Evan and Brian* were engaged in editing at the point in the past established by the adverb *yesterday*.

Past Perfect

The past perfect, sometimes called the pluperfect in grammar, is also a relational verb form, which, like the present perfect, expresses anterior aspect, but in the past. That is, it sets up a situation, action, or event prior to another point of reference but which is relevant to that point of reference. However, whereas that point of reference for the present perfect is the present moment, for the past perfect it is some past point.

> After they **had called** for help, they waited by the hissing and smoking car.
> Many families **had lived** there before the Great Depression.

In the sentences above, the actions of calling and living happen before the other point in the past set up in the same sentence, the past action *waited* in the first sentence and the past event *the Great Depression* in the second.

Past-Perfect Progressive

The past-perfect progressive is used to express the past anterior-continuing aspect and underscores that an action or situation began in the past before another action, event, or situation and continues up to that second past point.

> The bird **had been singing** in its cage all day before the cat finally noticed its existence.
> Although Apollo finally called the doctor about his sore throat, his friends **had been advising** him to do so for more than a week.

In the first sentence, the bird's activity of singing had been going on continuously until the second past action, the cat's noticing the bird. In the second sentence, Apollo's calling the doctor happens in the past, but before that past action another past action, his friends' advising him to do so, took place continuously until Apollo finally called the doctor.

DIAGRAMMING VERBS

A point that has been made many times in this book is the fact that English has only two tenses, a present and past. Note, too, that in Table 8.2 above, it is only the simple present and the simple past forms that do not include an auxiliary. However, even for those verb forms that do have an auxiliary, the only two choices for the form of that auxiliary is a simple present or a simple past form: *have/has* versus *had*; *am/is/are* versus *was/were*. (We will discuss modal auxiliaries in the next chapter.)

Therefore, in diagramming verbs in English, tense is an important and top priority in analyzing what is going on in the predicate part of the sentence. However, not all predicates need to have tense. We noted earlier the inappropriateness of the terms "present" and "past" to describe the participles, which are non-finite and therefore by definition do not signal tense or agree with a grammatical subject. We saw that in a sentence like

> **Carrying** their distinct speech features from their East Anglian home, the Puritan settlers converted their Norfolk whine into the Yankee drawl.

we could not say that *carrying* had tense; it is non-finite, that is, uninflected for tense or subject-verb agreement. However, it does make a predication; it says something, specifically something about the Puritans carrying their accent from East Anglia to New England. For this reason, we want to make a distinction between finite and non-finite predicates, and as we have seen, that distinction rides on tense and person/number inflection. Therefore the basic split that we learned earlier as the subject–

predicate division can now be formulated as the more specific split between the subject, which is almost always an NP, and the inflection phrase (see Figure 8.1).

FIGURE 8.1

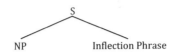

Inflection on the predicate involves tense and person/number agreement, and in diagramming we foreground the importance of these inflectional parts of the predicate. We do so by giving each of the two inflectional categories, tense on the one hand and person/number on the other, their own branches immediately off of the Inflection Phrase node. Thus Tense appears as its own branch and is always labeled either "Present" (Pres.) or "Past," as seen in Figure 8.2.

FIGURE 8.2

Person/number inflection, which we have seen above to be quite abstract for English since it can very frequently be Ø, is much more frequently expressed when it occurs on an auxiliary verb, a point also made above. It is in this sense that the auxiliary verb in English is quite important because it acts as an **operator**, carrying agreement and tense information. The operator is also important for English because it is a linguistic piece that "moves around" in the syntax to achieve certain kinds of meanings.

Consider this plain, unmarked declarative sentence:

*Philippe **has** sent his application to the school.*

In this basic sentence type, notice that the subject precedes the auxiliary verb and that the main verb comes immediately after it. However, if we change this sentence into a yes/no question, we "move" the auxiliary verb in front of the subject:

***Has** Philippe sent his application to the school?*

Because we want the auxiliary to maintain syntactic looseness and because it carries agreement inflections, we will give it its own branch off of the Inflection Phrase and label it as Aux-1 (see Figure 8.3). It is referred to as Aux-1 because, as can be seen from the verb synopsis above, there are several verb forms in English that employ multiple auxiliaries, for example, *has been taking*. And, as we will see in subsequent chapters, it is the first auxiliary that acts as an operator in the sense given above, so it occupies an independent branch in an inflection phrase.

FIGURE 8.3

The third branch to extend from the Inflection Phrase is the Predicate Phrase (Pred. Ph.) (see Figure 8.4).

FIGURE 8.4

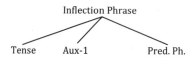

The Predicate Phrase in this example is understood to be finite because it occurs under the Inflection Phrase that also carries branches for Tense and Aux-1. Aux-1 is the site where, among other things, person and number inflections appear. As we have already seen, some predicates may be non-finite, like **Carrying** *their distinct speech features from their East Anglian home*. We will address analysis and diagramming of such non-finite structures in Chapter 17.

The head element of the Predicate Phrase is the Verb Phrase, commonly abbreviated as VP (see Figure 8.5). The VP will obviously accommodate the lexical verb (i.e., the verb that is not an auxiliary).

FIGURE 8.5

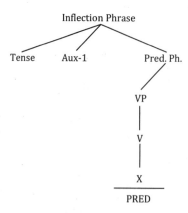

Note that since the tense is indicated in its own branch off of the Inflection Phrase node, the lexical verb is represented as the base form, all in caps. The specific form of that verb is determined by applying the tense signaled in the Tense branch to the form. Since the VP is the head of the predicate phrase, its function is PREDICATE; again, the function of a head and its phrase always have the same function.

The VP node may also accommodate auxiliaries other than the first auxiliary or operator auxiliary (see Figure 8.6).

FIGURE 8.6

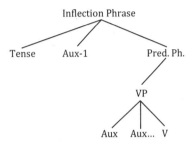

In labeling auxiliary uses, for now we can note that auxiliary BE is used to build progressive forms, and auxiliary HAVE is used to build perfect forms. So those auxiliaries, whether they appear in the Aux-1 position or in the VP, are labeled progressive and perfect, respectively. Note, too, that if there is a verb in Aux-1, it is written in all capital letters and the lexical verb appears as it would in the sentence. The exact form of Aux-1 is derived by applying the tense signaled in the Tense branch to the base form of Aux-1 (see Figures 8.7–8.9).

FIGURE 8.7

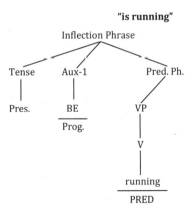

FIGURE 8.8

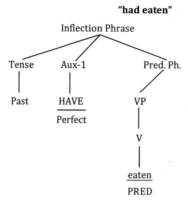

FIGURE 8.9

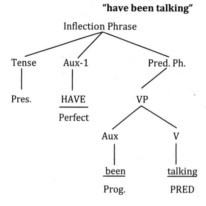

As we saw in the last chapters, the predicate phrase can also accommodate an NP functioning as the DO, IO, or OC, as shown in Figure 8.10.

FIGURE 8.10

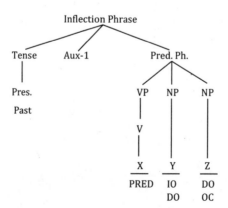

Remember that the object complement (OC) and subject complement (SC) functions can also be filled by adjective phrases (see Figure 8.11; on the labeling of BE as "copulative" and the V of VP as Ø, see below).

FIGURE 8.11

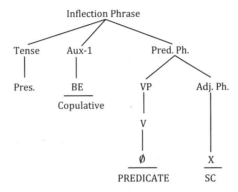

The predicate phrase also accommodates a prepositional phrase (PP) when it functions as an adverbial complement (AC), as in Figure 8.12.

FIGURE 8.12

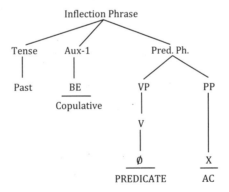

BE AS THE ONLY VERB IN A SENTENCE

The verb *be* may be the only verb in a sentence, in which case it is referred to as a copulative verb, because its function is to link a subject with a complement, usually an NP or adjective phrase with the function of subject complement:

*Janie **is** our new representative.*
*Alfred **was** weak during the battle.*

In some grammatical treatments, this use of *be* is even considered to be a "lexical *be*," as opposed to "auxiliary *be*," and to occupy the V position within VP. However, it is not clear that *be* can ever actually be a lexical verb, either semantically or syntactically. Semantically we should note that the use of *be* in its copulative function is quite abstract in meaning and not easily definable in the way that a lexical verb like *buy* or *walk* would be. Syntactically, too, copulative *be* acts like an auxiliary verb in that it obeys the so-called NICE properties of auxiliary verbs. NICE is an acronym that refers to Negation, Inversion, Coding, and Emphasis. These properties of auxiliary verbs will be presented here briefly and then treated in much more detail in subsequent chapters.

Negation refers to the fact that in English the negator *not* is placed after Aux-1:

*Amy has **not** seen our new home yet.*

Notice, too, that when there is no auxiliary in the verb phrase, one is inserted in the negative (in the form of *do, does,* or *did*) and *not* appears after that auxiliary:

Sarah writes in her journal everyday.
*Sarah **does not** write in her journal everyday.*

When *be* is the only verb, it does not require the insertion of an auxiliary, and *not* appears directly after it, as it would after any auxiliary.[1]

Amy is the bandleader.
*Amy is **not** the bandleader.*

Inversion refers to the movement of Aux-1 before the subject in questions:

*Ralph **has** finished the race.*
***Has** Ralph finished the race?*

Similar to the situation with negatives, when the verb form contains no auxiliary, a form of *do/does/did* is inserted and appears before the subject in questions:

Ralph goes to the same bar every Friday.
***Does** Ralph go to the same bar every Friday?*

---

[1] Imperative sentences involving *be* act a little differently in this regard in that they require auxiliary *do*, especially in the negative: *Don't be such a baby!* In some varieties of English, auxiliary *do* even appears in positive commands: "Do be quiet, Henry!" This may be some indication of the more general spread of auxiliary *do* in English, and we can even see its use in declarative sentences in some varieties of English, such as Irish English and Newfoundland English: *She does always be complaining*.

When *be* is the only verb, it does not require the insertion of an auxiliary but instead inverts with the subject like any other Aux-1:

*Ralph **is** a full member of the group.*
***Is** Ralph a full member of the group?*

Coding has to do with special kinds of constructions, usually at the end of the sentence, that reidentify a subject with the predication. A common type of construction that involves coding is a **tag question**.[1] Tag questions were introduced in Chapter 3 and are taken up more fully in Chapter 12, but for the present purposes it is enough to know that they are resumptive questions that appear after a declarative statement. If the verb form in the declarative statement contains an auxiliary, then it is that auxiliary that is used in the tag question:

*Bruce **was** working in Joliet for a while, **wasn't** he?*
*Bruce **has** called our office several time, **hasn't** he?*

As might be expected now, when the verb form in the declarative does not contain an auxiliary, a form of *do/does/did* appears in the tag question:

*Bruce knows a lot about cars, **doesn't** he?*

However, when it is the only verb in the declarative sentence, *be* can appear in the tag-question, as auxiliaries do:

*Bruce **is** a lineman, **isn't** he?*

Finally in terms of emphasis, when we want to emphasize certain aspects of the predication like the tense, we emphasize the auxiliary:

Corey WAS writing a novel but decided to turn it into a book of poems.

If no auxiliary is available, *do/does/did* is inserted for such emphasis:

Corey DID finish his book.

But *be* as the only verb in a sentence, again like the auxiliary, can carry such emphasis:

Corey WAS at the party, but he left before you got there.

---

1 Another kind of construction that shows coding information involves *nor*-clauses, as in *I didn't say he wasn't welcome, **nor did Tony**.*

For these reasons, it is reasonable to treat *be*, even when it is the only verb, as an auxiliary. Therefore, when it is the only verb in the sentence, the form BE will occupy the Aux-1 position and the V of the VP will be Ø. BE is labeled in such instances as "copulative," and the Ø VP is still labeled as "predicate" (see Figure 8.13).

FIGURE 8.13

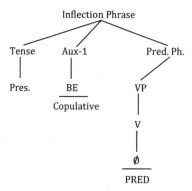

When *be* occurs with another auxiliary, or auxiliaries, it occupies the additional auxiliary position(s) off of the VP. The V of VP will still be Ø. *Be* is still labeled "copulative" and Ø is labeled as "predicate," as shown in Figure 8.14. A simple way of looking at the situation with *be* is that it never occupies the V of VP.

FIGURE 8.14

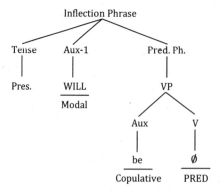

EXERCISES

A. Fill in the chart to present the forms for the verbs given in the infinitive:

Infinitive: **to forget**

Non-finite forms
base form: _____
simple active participle: _____
simple perfect participle: _____

Finite forms
general present: _____
-s present: _____
past tense form: _____

Infinitive: **to type**

Non-finite forms
base form: _____
simple active participle: _____
simple perfect participle: _____

Finite forms
general present: _____
-s present: _____
past tense form: _____

Infinitive: **to please**

Non-finite forms
base form: _____
simple active participle: _____
simple perfect participle: _____

Finite forms
general present: _____
-s present: _____
past tense form: _____

Infinitive: **to fight**

Non-finite forms
base form: _____
simple active participle: _____
simple perfect participle: _____

Finite forms
general present: _____
-s present: _____
past tense form: _____

B. Define "non-finite" and "finite" as the terms pertain to verbs in grammatical theory.

Non-finite   _____

Finite   _____

C. Use the following chart to fill out the verb forms in the past and present times in English for the verbs given in A above:

to forget	simple	progressive	perfect	perfect-progressive
present time				
past time				

to type	simple	progressive	perfect	perfect-progressive
present time				
past time				

to please	simple	progressive	perfect	perfect-progressive
present time				
past time				

to fight	simple	progressive	perfect	perfect-progressive
present time				
past time				

4. Define "synthetic verb form" and "periphrastic verb form."

   Synthetic _____

   Periphrastic_____

5. Give the formula for the following verb forms, e.g., "The present progressive is made up of the present tense form of the auxiliary BE + the simple active participle":

simple present
present progressive
present perfect
present-perfect progressive

simple past
past progressive
past perfect
past-perfect progressive

6. Make diagrams for the following sentences. Take care to note the functions of the NPs and Adj. Ph.s.

   1. The office gave my boss a promotion.
   2. We saw a good movie.
   3. Troy is a total jerk.
   4. The really happy students confirmed it.
   5. We made Arnold the captain of the ship.
   6. The students with concerns read the Provost their statements.
   7. These former employees will be litigants against the company.
   8. The school in Springfield was the best choice.
   9. A shopper bought the entire collection of miniatures.
   10. We will nominate you chair of the committee.

Other Verb Forms

THE SUBJUNCTIVE MOOD

Students who have studied Spanish, French, Latin, German, or any number of other European languages have likely encountered the subjunctive mood. **Mood** is a category of language that some define as marking the speaker's subjectivity toward the information being given as uncertain, contrary to fact, non-assertive, etc. In other words, subjectivity has to do with how much the speaker/writer believes in the information or to what degree they are supposing it to be true, etc. Although we do consider the subjunctive in languages like Spanish to be a mood, it is mostly because of the form, because the truth is that quite often the subjunctive is required by the syntax and not really a result of speaker/writer choice.

Some argue about whether the subjunctive still exists in English; it certainly used to. And, in truth, if we consider the subjunctive to be about meaning, then we would have to say that it still very much exists today, although in a much-reduced capacity and with very few special forms. Approached in this way, in English we have to distinguish two subjunctives, which we will call here the first and second subjunctive.[1]

THE FIRST SUBJUNCTIVE
The first subjunctive form for every verb is identical to the base form. It is used in certain established expressions that often sound formal or even archaic:

---

[1] I am using the terms "first" and "second" subjunctive in accordance with the traditional treatment of similar subjunctives in other Germanic languages.

Be that as it may…
Be it ever so humble, there's no place like home.
*Whether it **be** true or not.*

The first subjunctive is also used in clauses with a sense of urging, requesting, commanding, demanding, advising, and the like:

*The law required that all drivers **wear** a seat belt.*
*I demand that he **stop** this business at once.*
*We advise that you **drop** the course and **take** a different one.*

That sense of urging, requesting, commanding, etc. may be established with a verb, as in the above examples (so-called **suasive** verbs), or it may be set up by a noun phrase:

*It was **a requirement** that all employees **wash** their hands several times throughout the day.*

an adjective:

*It is nothing less than **imperative** that Sharona **leave** that job immediately!*

or some other part of language, for example a prepositional phrase:

*It is **without question** that Faviola **be** the leader of this project team.*

Note that the form of the first subjunctive is exactly the same, regardless of time or the number of its subject. In the first sentence, *The law required that all drivers **wear** a seat belt*, the verb *required* in the main clause sets up a past time reference. However, the subjunctive verb form *wear* remains uninflected for tense. Similarly, in the second sentence, *I demand that he **stop** this business at once*, the subject of the verb *stop* is *he*, which in the present tense, indicative mood would take the inflection *-s*. However, no such inflection appears because of the subjunctive force set up by the verb *demand* in the first part of the sentence.

The use of the first subjunctive may sound rather archaic and overly formal to many Modern English speakers/writers and it is not uncommon to find that it is avoided, particularly in UK English. Therefore, if the following sentence sounds overly formal with the subjunctive:

*James's new boss requires that he **be** five minutes early every day.*

one is likely to express it with a **modal verb** instead:

*James's new boss requires that he **must** be five minutes early every day.*

or to express it with a **quasi-modal verb**:

*James's new boss requires that he **has to be** five minutes early every day.*

Modal verbs and quasi-modal verbs are topics taken up later in this chapter.

THE SECOND SUBJUNCTIVE

The second subjunctive is more complicated. It involves a shift in the tense marking of a verb form and occurs in clauses that set up contrary-to-fact meanings, often with an *if*-**clause** (and the negative *unless*-**clause**).

*If I **had known** you were coming, I would have baked a cake.*
*The neighborhood watch committee would be angry if they **knew** you were keeping a known criminal in your basement.*
*Unless she **had wanted** to destroy the plans intentionally, I do not think she can be blamed.*

Notice that the bolded verb in each sentence refers to a situation that is contrary-to-fact, that is, something that did not happen or is not happening in reality. In the first sentence, the fact is that I didn't know you were coming. In the second example, the neighborhood watch committee doesn't know you are keeping a criminal in your basement. And in the third sentence, she did not want to destroy the plans intentionally, or at least the speaker/writer of this sentence does not believe so. This second subjunctive does not occur only in *if*-clauses but may occur in other expressions as well, in which the meaning is contrary to fact or only very tentatively true.

*Say I **were** to agree, what then?*

Since *if*- and *unless*-clauses set up a specific type of subordination, the second subjunctive is readdressed in detail in Chapter 14 when we discuss adverbial clauses.

MODAL VERBS

It is presumed that modal verbs developed in English as a means of carrying some of the weight of the dying subjunctive, although replacement is hardly the only motivation. It is true that by the time the modal verbs began to emerge in Old English (ca. 950 CE) and definitely by the time of their establishment as a class of verbs in Middle English (ca. 1400), the subjunctive was already quite attenuated, but it is not quite right to say that the modal verbs directly replaced older uses of the subjunctive in all cases, since modal verbs exist in other Germanic languages as well. Modal verbs include these:

can~could
may~might

shall~should
will~would
must

Modal verbs make up a special class of verbs in terms of both meaning and syntactic behavior. In terms of meaning, they have the ability to adjust the speaker's/writer's subjective stance or attitude toward the information expressed by the verb. Syntactically, they are auxiliary verbs, and each of them is followed by the base form of the main verb. They are morphologically remarkable because they do not take the third-person singular *-s* inflection in the present.[1]

*Simon **could** never **understand** Sarah's unwillingness to have a pet.*
*Congress **must pass** a bill within the next few days to avoid government shutdown.*
*The band **might get** together for one final tour—one more time.*

Modal verbs like *can/could, may/might, shall/should,* and *must* have both **deontic** and **epistemic** uses. Deontic meaning has to do with obligations and permissions, while epistemicity is about the speaker's/writer's judgment or commitment to the truth of the verb. The modal *can/could* also expresses ability. *Will/would* expresses future and conditional meanings, often with a tint of desire or wanting.

DEONTIC MEANING

As stated above, deontic meaning is about permission or obligation. Modals are used to express permission in the following sentences:

*Jan **may** go whenever she chooses.*
*You **can** check out anytime you like, but you **can** never leave.*
*You **could** simply leave your hat on the credenza, but it would be better to hang it in the hallway.*

The use of *can* for permission is often cited by language purists as incorrect, but of course such usage is well attested, and insistence on the use of *may* for *can* in sentences such as *Can I have a piece of cake?* is merely pedantic (and, frankly, teachers of young people could be spending their energies on more important matters of language!).

Modals are used to express obligation in the following sentences:

*Mariam **should** shovel the snow before she leaves.* (weak obligation, maybe even suggestion)
*You **must** file your tax return on or before April 15th.* (strong obligation)
*I **shall** not give in to their whims and caprices.* (self-imposed obligation/determination)

---

[1] Some consider *dare* and *need* as partially modal since in some varieties of English they can be followed by the base form of the verb and lack *-s* in the third person in the present tense: *Dare he speak the truth? She need not bother to answer the question.*

Shall is archaic and formal sounding in American English. It is more normally heard in certain kinds of requests, but still with a degree of formality:

Shall *we dance?*

Shall is usually now replaced with *will* or *should*.

ABILITY

Can and *could* are used to express ability. When *can/could* expresses ability, the difference in their use is one of tense; *can* is present tense in form and signals present-tense meanings, and *could* is past tense in form and signals past-tense meanings.

*Alan **can** sing very well.* (present time)
*The students **could** cause a lot of problems when they wanted to.* (past time)

EPISTEMICITY

Modal verbs express a range of nuances about how true the speaker/writer assumes the information expressed in the predicate to be. Consider the following scenario: there is a knock on the door. The speaker guesses at the identity of the knocker with the following statements:

*That **will** be the pizza-delivery guy.*
*That **would** be the pizza-delivery guy.*
*That **must** be the pizza-delivery guy.*
*That **should** be the pizza-delivery guy.*
*That **may** be the pizza-delivery guy.*
*That **might** be the pizza-delivery guy.*
*That **could** be the pizza-delivery guy.*

In each of the statements, the speaker/writer becomes less sure of who the knocker is, such that *will be* is a very certain statement, while *could be* is rather weak in terms of the speaker's certainty about whether it is the pizza-delivery guy. Note that *shall* does not really participate in this set of uses, and while *can*, as in *That can be the pizza-delivery guy*, is heard in UK English, it is less frequent in American English.

FUTURE TIME

In Modern English, we have at least two ways of signaling future time. One is with the modal verb *will*, and the other is with the periphrastic auxiliary *be going to*.

Will developed from the Old English verb *willan*, which meant 'to desire.' That meaning of desire is still apparent in the noun form of that word: *where there is a will, there is a way*, or in the expression *if you will*. The desire meaning in the (auxiliary) verb form of the word is quite "bleached out," and its meaning is almost always about future prediction:

*My computer **will** last another couple of years.*
*I **will** see you at the library at 3:00.*

In some cases, the desire meaning seems still to be present:

I will not stand here and listen to such nonsense.

Will is an interesting kind of word in grammar; it has an alternate form, *'ll*, known as an enclitic. An enclitic has a status somewhere between word and affix. However, whereas a word can stand alone and an affix is always bound to the same kind of word (e.g., *-ed* always appears on the end of regular verbs), an enclitic like *'ll* can "float" around and attach to many different kinds of structures.

It can attach to a pronoun:

I'll be seeing you in all the old familiar places.

It can attach to a noun:

Kevin'll be here soon.

It can attach to a PP modifying the subject:

The box in the corner'll have to do.

It can even attach to a whole clause modifying the subject:

The man who helped you earlier'll be glad to check up on your application.

In more formal types of writing, the enclitic spelling is acceptable only, if at all, with the pronoun, but in speech, the other structures are very often heard.

To express future time, we also use the periphrastic auxiliary *be going to*, as in

*This pipe **is going to** blow at any time.*

In speech, *going to* is most often expressed as *gonna*, and indeed we have even conventionalized the spelling as *gonna*, although it isn't acceptable in formal writing. But it is easy to find in less formal writing contexts, like internet writing. One interesting thing to note about *gonna* (and proof of its auxiliary verb status) is the fact that *going + to* can reduce to *gonna* when it means the future time for a verb, but not when it has the more literal meaning of 'move toward.' Thus *I am going to send him a message* can become *I'm gonna send him a message*. But *I'm going to Istanbul* cannot be **I'm gonna Istanbul*.

There is a difference in meaning between the two futures in English. *Will* tends to be vaguer in many uses, referring to a more general future time. *Be going to*, however, is more often used for actions, situations, or events that are imminent (about to happen) or in situations where the speaker is quite determined about carrying on the action. That difference can be seen in this contrastive pair:

I will call you later.
I'm going to call you later.

In the first sentence, the event is vague in terms of time and perhaps speaker commitment. It's the kind of thing one might say to a somewhat distant friend upon running into them on the street—and we all know how often we say *I'll call you* or *I'll give you a call* with no intention of doing so. The second sentence sounds more like a plan has been made and the speaker is more committed to carrying out the verb.

QUASI-MODALS

As stated above, modals are considered to be a separate class of verbs, not only because they form a semantic class but also because of their unique syntax, appearing before the base form of the word. Quasi-modals are similar to modal verbs in terms of the kinds of meaning they convey, but they appear with *to*-infinitives rather than the base form of the main verb. The quasi-modals in English include

Have (got) to (obligation): **Mark has (got) to** *put the boxes on the shelf before he can leave.*
Be able to (ability): *Sarah* **is able to** *help if needed.*
Ought to (obligation): *Aaron* **ought to** *pay off his bills before incurring more debt.*
Be supposed to (obligation): *You* **are supposed to** *remove your shoes before entering.*
Want to (desire): *I* **want to** *visit Kyoto while we are there.*

Some of the quasi-modals can also express epistemic meaning:

That **has to** *hurt!* (strong certainty)
Well, she **ought to** *be regretting her words now.* (weaker certainty)

Many of the quasi-modals also have reduced forms in regular speech:

gotta (< *have got to*)
oughta (< *ought to*)
wanna (< *want to*; cf. the compound *wannabe* = a person who wants to be someone or something else)

MODAL VERBS IN COMBINATION WITH THE PROGRESSIVE AND PERFECT VERB FORMS

All of the modals and quasi-modals are combinable with the progressive and perfect verb forms:

It **can be raining** *one minute and then the sun* **can be shining** *brightly the next.*

*He **must have said** something.*
*We **should have been helping** the cause all along.*

With the quasi-modals, however, it is the infinitive that will take the progressive and perfect forms:

*He **has to have said** something.*
*We **need to be talking** to them directly and not merely sitting around guessing what is going on.*

Progressive and perfect forms of the participle and infinitive are discussed in detail in Chapter 17.

DIAGRAMMING MODALS

Modals are auxiliary verbs. When there is a single modal verb + main verb, the modal fills the Aux-1 position and the main verb (in the base form) fills the V of the VP. The tense of the modal is indicated as Present or Past in the Tense node; *can, must, will, shall,* and *may* are present-tense forms, while *could, would, should,* and *might* are past-tense forms. Modals, like all elements in Aux-1, are expressed in their base form in all caps (CAN, MAY, WILL, SHALL, MUST), as shown in Figures 9.1–9.2.

FIGURE 9.1

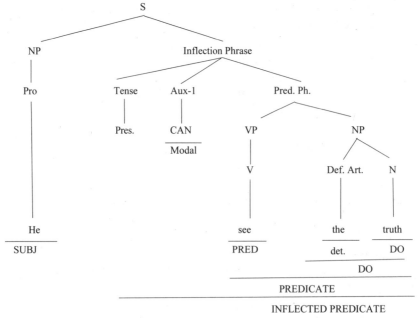

FIGURE 9.2

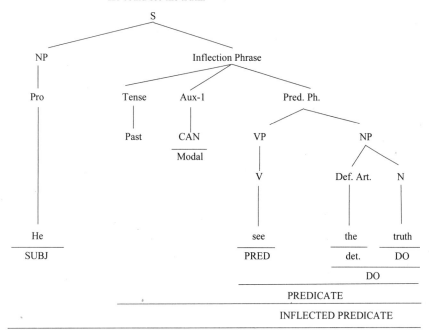

In sentences with a modal verb combined with progressive or perfect verb forms, the modal verb is always Aux-1. Other auxiliary verbs appear as additional auxiliary (Aux) branches off of the VP. Tense is expressed as Present or Past in the Tense node. Aux-1, as always, appears in its base form in all caps (see Figures 9.3–9.5).

FIGURE 9.3

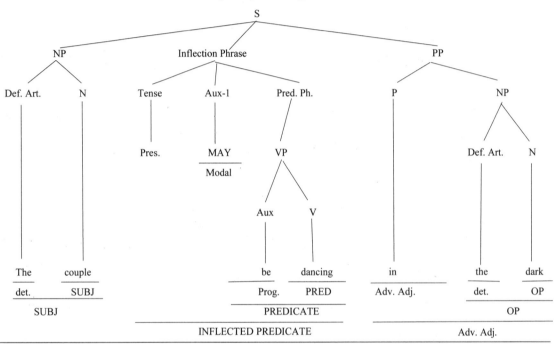

OTHER VERB FORMS 185

FIGURE 9.4

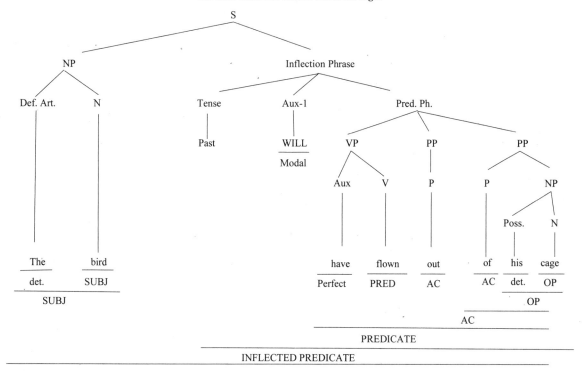

FIGURE 9.5

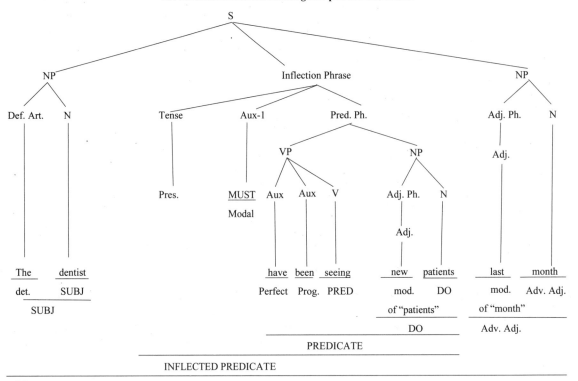

OTHER VERB FORMS 187

Quasi-modal verb constructions are of two different types: those that occur with the verb *be* as the first element and those that do not use *be*. Those that use *be* are diagrammed with BE as Aux-1 and the next word with *to* as an Aux off of VP. Tense is expressed as Present or Past in the Tense node. Aux-1, as always, appears in its base form in all caps.

FIGURE 9.6

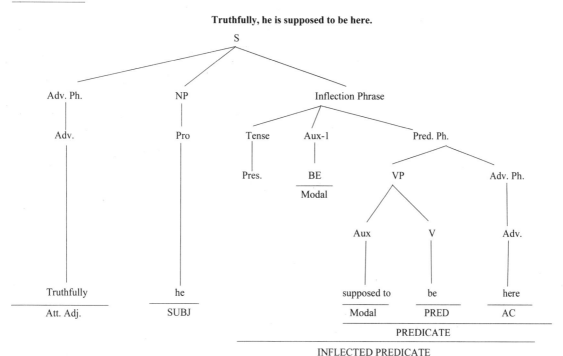

FIGURE 9.7

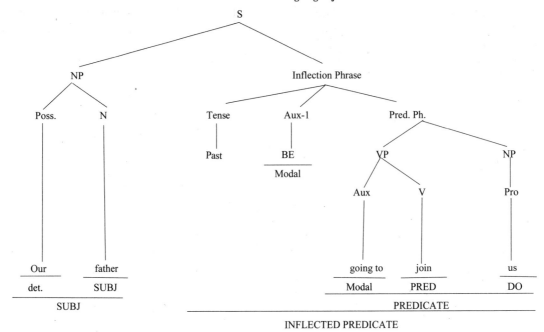

OTHER VERB FORMS 189

In quasi-modal constructions without *be*, such as *have to*, the first verb along with *to* is Aux-1, and the main verb appears in the VP. Tense is expressed as Present or Past in the Tense node. Aux-1, as always, appears in its base form in all caps.[1]

FIGURE 9.8

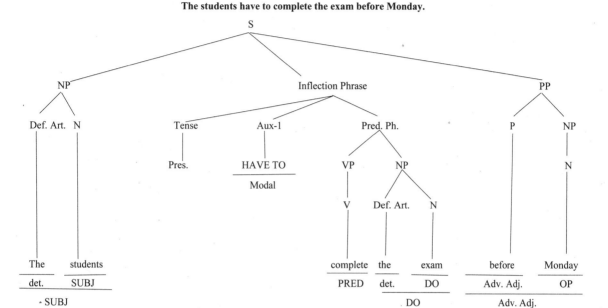

---

[1] Note that quasi-modals without *be* are a different kind of auxiliary from the others in that they do not undergo the characteristic inversion for making a question and they are not followed by *not*. Instead, they act like lexical verbs and require *do*-support.

FIGURE 9.9

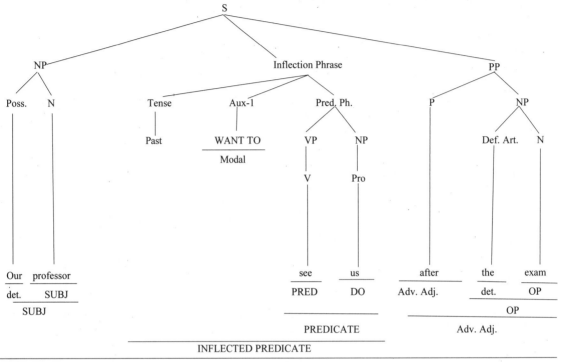

EXERCISES

A. List all of the modal verbs in English. Indicate in your list which forms are present and which are past in form.

B. Construct sentences using the first subjunctive for the following prompts. Remember that the second part of the sentence should begin with *that* and contain a subject and a finite subjunctive verb.

    Example: The university demanded _____

                                The university demands *that all full-time students **take** at least 12 hours each semester.*

1. My parents urged _____
2. The report suggests _____
3. My boss required _____
4. His wife demanded _____
5. The law expects _____
6. It is imperative _____
7. It is a requirement of the city_____
8. It was obligatory _____
9. The statute _____ was upheld in the last council meeting.
10. We made sure _____

C. Make full form–function trees for the following sentences.

1. Tomorrow we will take the bus to Miami.
2. Unfortunately, I might be wrong.
3. Those students might have been taking French.
4. We have to buy groceries this weekend.
5. Our neighbors were supposed to move to a new town.

10

Negation

NEGATION IN THE PREDICATE PHRASE

Negation in English is syntactically tricky and often involves one of the most unique of English syntactic operations: ***do*-support**. In this chapter we will look at some of the major ways of expressing negation, starting with negation in the inflection phrase and then turning our attention to negation within noun phrases.

NOT

The most common strategy for negation is negating the predicate by including the adverb *not* in the predicate phrase before the VP:

> *The applicants have **not** completed the correct forms.*
> *We are **not** destroying his credibility.*
> *Alice might **not** have been driving after all when the accident happened.*

In each of the sentences above, you will notice that negation is achieved by placing *not* after the first auxiliary verb (Aux-1). It is syntactically placed between the Aux-1 and the VP by extending it from the Predicate Phrase (see Figure 10.1). It is labeled Adverb[1] (Adv.), the function of which is Negator (Neg.).

---

1 For consistency, we will first include a layer of adverb phrase before adverb.

FIGURE 10.1

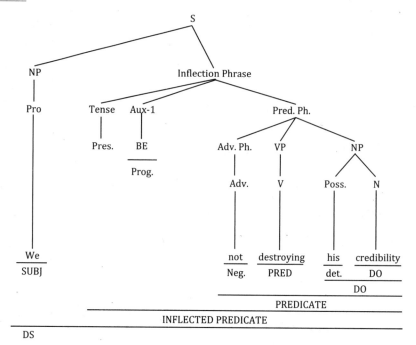

However, if the rule for this strategy of negation is to place *not* after the first auxiliary, what about synthetic verb forms that do not have an auxiliary verb? From the chart of English verb forms presented in Chapter 8, it will be recalled that of the English verb forms, only the simple present and the simple past have no auxiliary. In previous stages of English, it was possible to negate synthetic verb forms by simply placing *not* after the verb:

*They know **not** what they do.*

But in present-day English it has become syntactically obligatory to include some form of the auxiliary *do* in sentences negated with *not* when the simple present or simple past tense is used. Observe the following correspondences:

Elroy speaks Dutch. → *Elroy **does** not speak Dutch.*
Fatima and her brother have a good relationship. → *Fatima and her brother **do** not have a good relationship.*
Simon sang for his club. → *Simon **did** not sing for his club.*

From the above examples, it can be seen that the possible forms of the auxiliary *do* are *do*, *does*, and *did*. Each is chosen based on agreement with the subject and the desired tense. *Does* is used in the present with a third-person singular subject, and *do* is used in the present with all other persons. *Did* is used for all past-tense contexts (note all past-*tense* contexts, not all past-*time* contexts). Once the tense and person inflection is expressed through auxiliary *do*, it will not appear again on the main verb. Thus, in the change from *Elroy speaks Dutch* to *Elroy does not speak Dutch*, the inflection -s, which shows third-person present agreement, switches from being suffixed on the lexical verb to appearing on the auxiliary, that is, *does*; the main verb is always in the base form following auxiliary *do*.[1]

Do itself in this use is essentially meaningless; it is an **operator**. Its function is to carry person/number marking (if relevant), but perhaps more importantly it achieves the syntactic operation of placing *not* after the first auxiliary by providing an auxiliary to carry out the syntactic rule. Other auxiliaries, like modals, *have*, and *be*, are also operators, strictly speaking, but they contribute some meaning to the verb form as well. That contribution of meaning is why we label them "modal," "perf.," and "prog.," but again, those labels are more about form than about meaning, since verbal meaning is derived more holistically and a given verb form like the PERFECT, for example, can actually appear with several aspectual profiles—resultative, anterior, etc. In diagramming, *do* simply appears in the Aux-1 position in the inflection phrase, as shown in Figure 10.2.

FIGURE 10.2

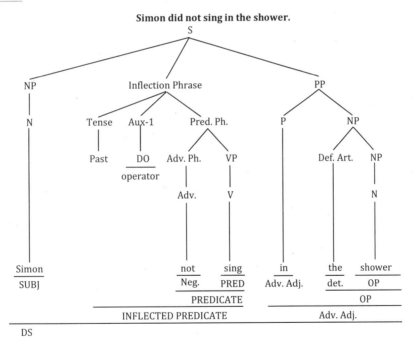

---

1 It may be noted that the first subjunctive uses discussed in Chapter 9 do not require auxiliary *do* in the negative: *The company urges all employees strongly that they not go on vacation the second week in August when business is at its height for the year.* The non-use of *do* with that construction is an indication of its archaic origin in English, before auxiliary *do* became obligatory.

The verb *be*, however, when used as the only verb in a clause, does not require the operator *do* in the negative. It will be recalled from Chapter 8 that even in the simple present and the simple past, *not* is placed directly after the verb *be* since we are taking the view that *be* is always an auxiliary.

*John was **not** the source of the leaked information.*
*December is **not** the coldest month of the year in Illinois.*
*I am **not** happy with these results.*

NEAR-NEGATIVES

A number of other negative adverbs can appear in the inflection phrase; some of these are actually better thought of as **near-negatives**. These include *never, hardly, scarcely,* and *barely*. When these appear in the Inflection Phase, they do not require auxiliary *do*, although if the Inflection Phase has an auxiliary, the near-negative adverb is regularly placed after the first auxiliary.

*They have **barely** made enough money this month.*

However, sometimes these near negative adverbs are placed at the beginning of a sentence. When appearing there, they sometimes cause changes from the normal syntactic order of a declarative sentence:

***Scarcely** had Ethel arrived before the paparazzi descended upon her entourage.*

In this case, we find that the placement of *scarcely* as the first element in the sentence has forced a syntactic change involving juxtaposition of the subject and the first auxiliary, a process called subject-auxiliary inversion, which we will return to in Chapter 12 when we discuss question formation.

Note that since the simple present and the simple past do not have an auxiliary to undergo the syntactic operation of subject-auxiliary inversion, auxiliary *do* must be inserted for those verbal categories in order to provide an auxiliary for inversion:

We never followed his orders. → *Never **did** we follow his orders.*

Again, the verb *be*, when used as the only verb, does not require *do* and may invert with the subject directly in the simple present and the simple past, just like an auxiliary:

*He **was** never so happy in his life.* → *Never **was** he so happy in his life.*

NEGATION IN THE NOUN PHRASE

Negation in English can also be achieved in the NP. This can be done in two ways: with the negative determiner *no* or with a negative indefinite pronoun.

THE NEGATIVE DETERMINER *NO*

No may be used as a determiner to negate a noun:

No *child will go without food or shelter during my administration.*
I have accepted **no** *money from their company.*

In these kinds of sentences, *no* is treated formally as negation (Neg.), and it is treated functionally as a determiner, as in the sentence *We have no time* (see Figure 10.3).

FIGURE 10.3

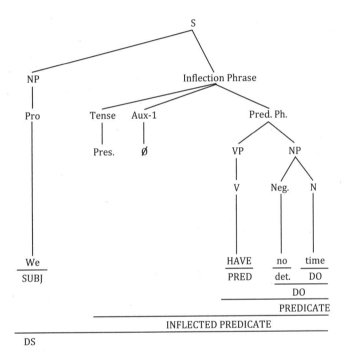

Negating the NP as opposed to the predicate often carries a different meaning. Contrast these two sentences:

He is not a teacher.
He is no teacher.

The meaning of the first sentence is unmarked negation, meaning just what it seems to say: "He is not a teacher." The second sentence, however, implies that at least nominally he is a teacher, but not a normal one somehow.

Sometimes, for stylistic effect, a negated NP of this type will be moved to the front of the sentence. For instance, a direct object has its regular position after the verb in English, as in

*She has received **no criticism** during her many years as director.*

In this sentence, *no criticism* is an NP with the function of DO. However, one may place the negated NP as the first element in the sentence. If so, the fronted negative will trigger subject-verb inversion:

*No criticism **has she** received during her many years as director.*

As would be expected by now, if the verb is in the simple present or simple past, that is, if it does not have an auxiliary already, the operator *do* would be supplied in such sentences:

The man committed no crime, yet he spent more than 50 years in prison.
*No crime **did** the man commit, yet he spent more than 50 years in prison.*

NEGATIVE INDEFINITE PRONOUNS

Negative indefinite pronouns in English include *no one, nothing, nobody,* and *nowhere*, although *nowhere* sometimes functions as an adverbial. It is rather easy to see that some of these expressions originated in English as the nouns *thing* and *body*, with a negative determiner, as in *no + body*. As pronouns, they will function as NPs in a sentence.

As a subject:	***Nobody*** *told me about his plan.*
As a direct object:	*I have received **nothing** from them.*
As an indirect object:	*They will tell **no one** the news until May.*
As a subject complement:	*That is **nothing** to worry about.*
As an object of a preposition:	*The office has been talking **to no one*** (see Figure 10.4).

FIGURE 10.4

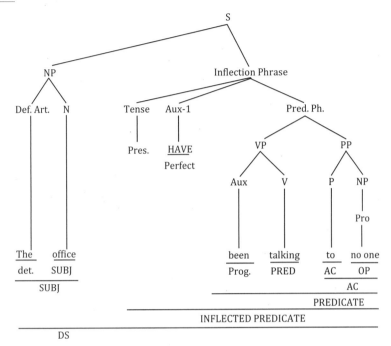

For stylistic effect, these negative indefinite pronouns may be fronted to the beginning of the sentence, and when they are they invoke subject-auxiliary inversion and *do*-support when necessary:

Nothing would he like more.
No one did she see who interested her in the least.

ANY
In English, at least in the prescribed standard, there is an injunction against the use of multiple negatives in a clause. Multiple negation, however, appears in many dialects of English, where it is a continuation of the older acceptable pattern of negation in older English. The English classics of *Beowulf* and *The Canterbury Tales*, composed many centuries apart, contain multiple negation throughout, for example:

*He **nevere** yet **no** vileynye **ne** sayde.* (*Canterbury Tales*, General Prologue, line 70)

In present-day English, multiple negation of the following type is avoided by using the negative determiner *any* instead of *no*.

*He did not have **no** reason to doubt her.* → *He did not have **any** reason to doubt her.*

Similarly, the plural indefinite determiner *some* is changed into *any* when negation appears in the verb phrase:

*The children want **some** ice-cream.* → *The children do not want **any** ice-cream.*

In diagramming, *any* may function as a determiner (for our purposes we will say it is a negator in form) when it occurs with a noun (see Figure 10.5):

*We did not receive **any** assistance.*

FIGURE 10.5

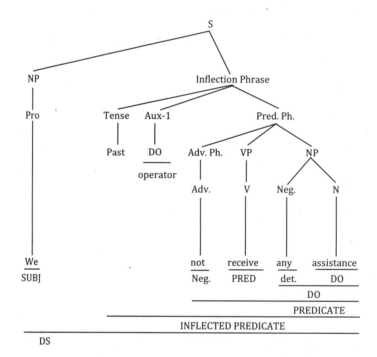

Or *any* may be a pronoun, when it refers to a noun phrase (see Figure 10.6):

*Sadly, I did not have **any**.*

FIGURE 10.6

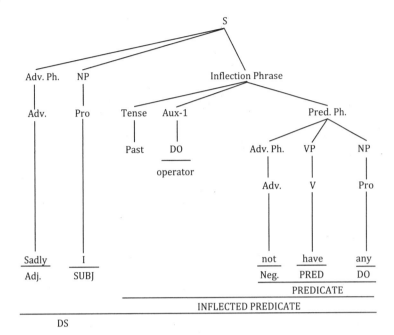

TWO NEGATIVES MAKE A POSITIVE?

While true of numbers in math, the rule that one should not use two negatives because it makes a positive is familiar to everyone and has become part and parcel of a list of well-known grammatical axioms that, in fact, few completely understand (and see Chapter 18 on language myths).

First, it should be noted on empirical grounds (observable facts) that when speakers or writers use two negatives, they most often do not in any sense intend a positive meaning:

The team hasn't lost no games this season.

This sentence does not mean the team has lost *some* games this season. No one intends that meaning, and no one understands that meaning either (unless they are perversely misconstruing the message).

There are, however, some ways of using double negatives that do create a non-negative meaning:

He's not unhappy.
We did not NOT tell him the truth.

In these cases, the negatives do work to partially reverse each other, but they do not make a positive meaning exactly. Saying "he's not unhappy" does not mean "he is happy." Such constructions allow for a middle space between negative and positive meanings, which can be rhetorically useful.

EXERCISES

A. Change the following sentences to place the near-negative adverb to the front of the sentence. Make any other syntactic changes necessary.

    Example: *He never claimed to know everything.* → *Never did he claim to know everything.*

1. The builders seldom used pine to make their beams.
2. We had hardly arrived before they began asking us questions.
3. During the play, the actors never look one another directly in the eye.
4. Although I enjoy swimming, I have seldom swum in oceans or lakes.
5. I have never worked with such a difficult set of colleagues in my entire career.

B. Move the following negated direct object to the beginning of the sentence and make any other syntactic changes necessary.

    Example: *He had no vacation during his entire four years with the company.*
                        No vacation did he have during his entire four years with the company.

1. The packages contained no directions.
2. The prisoners had received no warnings prior to the lockdown.
3. Retired teachers in the district will receive no benefits after the first of the month.
4. The children made no complaints and set out on the work with alacrity.
5. The new retail outlet is offering no incentive for shoppers during the Christmas season.

C. Make full form–function trees for the following sentences:

1. The makers of this product do not endorse its use on bare skin.
2. We will never see that money again.
3. I offer no apology for my actions.
4. The jury had seen nothing from the earlier trial.
5. We do not require any proof of purchase.

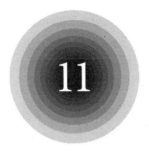

Active and Passive Voice

SEMANTIC ROLES

A theme that emerged earlier in this book was the unfortunate confusion of meaning (including semantics and function) with form (including word, morpheme, and syntactic form), leading to such unhelpful definitions as that for subject, which some have defined as "the noun that does the verb." This is not to say that meaning is not relevant or important to grammatical description; it certainly can be. But we need to be clearer on the relationship between form and meaning. This chapter on **active** and **passive voice** especially requires attention to that relationship.

It is possible to provide an analysis of the meaning that noun phrases play in a sentence by examining their **semantic roles**. Semantic role theory can be understood by thinking of the metaphor of a stage. If the sentence is a stage, then the noun phrases are the actors or props and play certain roles or functions on that stage. Some nouns do things; other nouns take things; and still other nouns stand there witnessing or experiencing things. In this brief introduction to semantic roles, we will focus on two semantic roles as they relate most directly to active and passive voice.

The **agent** role describes a noun phrase that consciously and intentionally performs an overt action:

***Felicity** tore down the photo from the bulletin board.*

The **patient** role describes a noun phrase that changes in some way as a result of an action performed on it:

*Munira kicked **the ball**.*

Note that the ball changes its state after having been kicked, presumably to some new position.

The two examples above present prototypical sentences in English (and many other languages) in which the subject is an agent and the direct object is a patient, illustrated below by noting the syntactic function under and the semantic role above the noun phrase:

Agent   Patient
Munira kicked the ball
SUBJ   DO

However, there is no necessary relationship between syntactic functions and semantic roles. In other words, not all agents are subjects and not all subjects are agents. Likewise, not all direct objects are patients and not all patients are direct objects.

Patient   Agent
The ball was kicked by Munira.
SUBJ   OP

In this version of the sentence, the meaning has remained the same overall; we still understand *Munira* as the agent and *the ball* as the patient. However, *the ball* is now the subject and *Munira* is now the object of the preposition *by*. Grammatically, we call the first sentence an active sentence and the second one a passive sentence. Thus, active and passive structures serve to realign syntactic and semantic roles for specific discourse functions. To continue the stage metaphor, the passive is a means of refocusing the spotlight away from the agent and onto the patient by making the direct object into the subject. In other words, the general purpose of the passive voice is to promote the identity of the patient or theme and to demote the agent.

PASSIVIZATION

Most grammar treatments present the passive as a derivation from the active. If approached in this way, we would note the following steps in that derivation:

Active: *Munira kicked the ball.*

1. Make the direct object into the subject.
2. Change the verb to the passive form.
3. Make the subject into the object of the preposition *by*.

Passive: *The ball was kicked by Munira.*

Since one of the functions of the passive is to demote the agent, the agent may be omitted altogether, and in fact most often the agent is not expressed in a passive sentence by leaving off the entire *by*-phrase:

> The ball was kicked.

WHEN TO USE THE PASSIVE

It is not at all difficult to find much disparagement about the passive in traditional grammars—even some that say simply not to use the passive at all (see Chapter 18 on grammar myths). The truth is that the passive is used in all types of writing, although it appears in certain genres, like science writing, more frequently than in others. And there are times when the active voice is perhaps a better choice *stylistically*. For example, consider the use of the passive in the following short paragraph:

> Bill and Susan finally decided to buy a new car and went to the dealership. They fell in love with a blue, slightly used Honda Civic. At first, Bill was unsure whether buying a used car was a good idea, but since the dealer was willing to offer a one-year warranty, he agreed. **The car was bought on a five-year, low-interest loan**, and Bill and Susan drove the car home that same day.

While the bolded passive might not sound totally wrong, consider the version with an active verb in that sentence:

> Bill and Susan finally decided to buy a new car and went to the dealership. They fell in love with a blue, slightly used, Honda Civic. At first, Bill was unsure whether buying a used car was a good idea, but since the dealer was willing to offer a one-year warranty, he agreed. **Bill and Susan bought the car on a five-year, low-interest loan** and drove it home that same day.

Since the paragraph deals with the thinking, actions, and decisions by the agents Bill and Susan, the paragraph flows best, other things being equal, when those agents are the subject of the sentences that express their thinking and actions.

In other contexts, however, there are several very good reasons that the passive may be chosen. For example, the focus may be on the event or the patient.

> Ahmed: "I haven't received my check from the office yet."
> Amy: "Payments were sent out last week. I got mine."

In this exchange, Amy wishes to focus on the event of the checks having been sent or on the payments themselves. If that speaker had said "The office sent out payments last week," she might sound slightly off topic and perhaps even a little defensive of the office. Therefore, another reason to consider when using the passive is that it can serve specific politeness functions. Say, for instance, that a person knows who did something but for politeness reasons does not want to name that agent:

> The rice was a little overdone and the sauce was too salty.

While the person saying or writing this sentence is probably asking for trouble, especially if the cook hears/reads the sentence, avoiding the agent may be a way to avoid such trouble.

In some cases, however, the agent may simply be unknown or completely out of the picture, so to speak:

The explosive device was found under a seat in the stadium. No suspects have been identified.

Obviously, this type of passive is useful in news reporting of events as they roll out before all of the participants are known.

PASSIVE VERB FORMS

In Chapter 8, we saw the forms of the active verb. Each of those active forms has a passive counterpart, presented in Table 11.1, again using the example verb *take*.

TABLE 11.1: PASSIVE VERB FORMS

Simple Present
Active
take (general present)/takes (-s present)

Passive
am/is/are taken

Present Progressive
Active
am/is/are taking

Passive
am/is/are being taken

Present Perfect
Active
has/have taken

Passive
has/have been taken

Present-Perfect Progressive
Active
has/have been taking

Passive
has/have been being taken

Simple Past
Active
took

Passive
was/were taken

Past Progressive
Active
was/were taking

Passive
was/were being taken

Past Perfect

Active	Passive
had taken	had been taken

Past-Perfect Progressive

Active	Passive
had been taking	had been being taken

The progressive and perfect-progressive forms are possible since they are generated by English speakers and writers. However, they are often rejected as stylistically awkward. Instead, the simple and perfect forms, respectively, are more often used.

STATIVE VERSUS INCHOATIVE PASSIVE

There is another type of passive construction used frequently in English, sometimes called the ***got-passive***, but whose linguistic name is the **inchoative passive**. Both names are telling. As the name *got-passive* implies, these are passive forms made with the auxiliary verb *got*:

Hannah **got** married last week.

The verb *got* is sometimes avoided in writing, so the verb *become* may be used instead:

Hannah **became** married last week.

However, in speech the *got*-passive is very frequent. The name *inchoative passive* contrasts that form with the regular passive that we were discussing above, which is a stative passive. *Inchoative* means 'to begin or enter into a new state' while *stative* means to already be in a state. Thus, if we contrast *Hannah got married* to *Hannah is married*, the difference is that the first expresses her entrance into the state of being married and the second presents her status as already married. There are some verbs in English that we do not consider to set up states, usually those verbs that are viewed as happening at a single point, a kind of either-or meaning, like *win*. For such verbs, the *got*-passive will often sound odd because we do not view such verbs as having significant beginning, middle, and end stages—just an end.

?*The race got won by Zeze.*

DIAGRAMMING PASSIVE SENTENCES

Diagramming passive sentences creates no new difficulties. The auxiliary verb, either *get* (for the inchoative passive) or *be*, occupies an auxiliary position and is labeled passive in function. If the *by*-phrase stating the agent of the verb is included, it is a PP extending from the S, and its function will be adverbial adjunct (see Figure 11.1). We consider it an adjunct because it is not obligatory, as discussed earlier (and see Chapter 7 on the non-obligatory status of adjuncts).

FIGURE 11.1

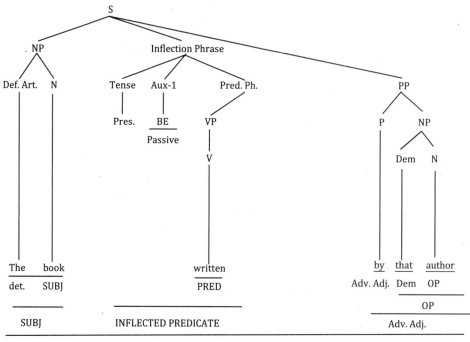

In the sentence in Figure 11.1, *is* is the only auxiliary, so it occupies Aux-1 of the Inflection Phrase and is labeled "Passive." Of course, if the verb form were more complex, as in *The book might have been written by that author* (see Figure 11.2), *been* would still occupy an auxiliary position, but that position would be from the VP, since the Aux-1 position is now occupied by *may*; the function would still be passive.

FIGURE 11.2

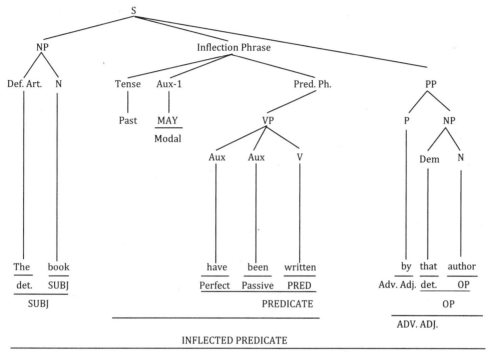

Note, however, that there are three different functions that *be* can have in the Aux-1 position: copulative, progressive, and passive. While the function of each should be obvious from a close analysis, there is a structural trick to check your analysis. If the verb form immediately after auxiliary *be* is the simple active participle, the function of *be* is progressive, as in Figure 11.3.

FIGURE 11.3

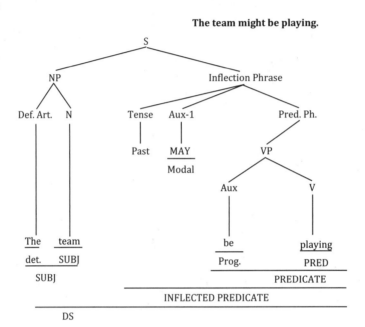

ACTIVE AND PASSIVE VOICE   211

If the verb form immediately after auxiliary *be* is the simple passive participle, the function of *be* is passive, as in Figure 11.4.

FIGURE 11.4

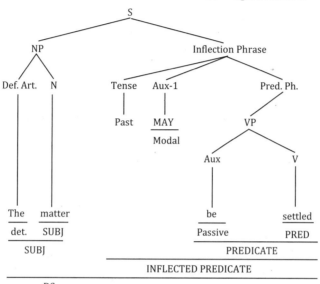

If there is no verb immediately after auxiliary *be*, the function of *be* is copulative, as in Figure 11.5.

FIGURE 11.5

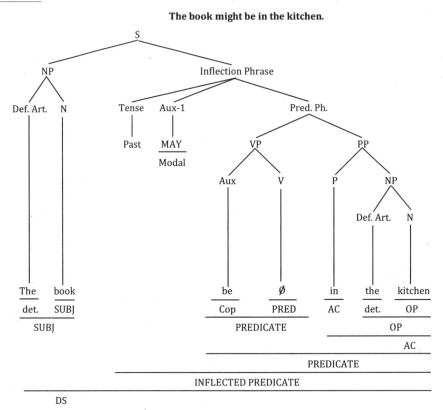

EXERCISES

A. Give the complete formula for the following verb forms. The first is done for you as an example:

1. Simple present (passive): "The simple present passive is made up of a present form of the auxiliary verb BE + the simple passive participle."
2. Present progressive (passive)
3. Present perfect (passive)
4. Present-perfect progressive (passive)
5. Simple past (passive)
6. Past progressive (passive)
7. Past perfect (passive)
8. Past-perfect progressive (passive)

B. Make the bolded parts of the following sentences into the passive. (In some cases it's the entire sentence.) Only include the agent if it seems necessary. Be very sure to maintain the same verb category, e.g., present perfect → present perfect.

1. **Martin had cleaned the dog pen before the show.**
2. **Someone has sent a warning to the network.**
3. **Landscapers pruned the trees last spring.**
4. The demilitarized zone was placed on high security risk **when the President and his entourage were visiting the area.**
5. **The design department has been designing all of the book covers for the publisher since 1973.**
6. **When the laboratory assistant added a glucose derivative to the cooling epoxide,** the viscosity rose.
7. Billy always said "please" and "thank you" **when someone asked him to do so.**
8. **The DJ has been putting together a playlist for Maureen's wedding reception.**
9. **The teacher has explained the instructions to the students in the class so that they can begin their assignment.**
10. **His family buried Mr. Jackson in the cemetery on the edge of town.**

C. Determine what the function of *be* would be in each of the following sentences (progressive auxiliary, passive auxiliary, or copulative verb). State how you came to that judgment in the space provided.

1. Maria could be our first choice.

2. The director was reneging on his commitment within a month of his appointment.

3. Right is right.

4. We have been told to change our route because of weather.

5. The lecture will be in the auditorium and we may go if we have enough time.

6. Jack is complaining about everything these days!

7. The service vehicles were decommissioned last year after the flood.

8. We may be taking donations in the hall outside the main office but we haven't decided yet.

9. Melissa has been getting a lot of attention for her work in the past few months.

10. The computer must have been running the entire time.

D. Diagram the following sentences with full form–function trees.

1. The photos will be released next month after the show.
2. The new arrangements were made on Saturday by Alice.
3. Sadly those fresh vegetables have been thrown out.
4. Jackson was being praised for her hard work on the project.
5. Our statue was taken down from the pedestal by an angry mob.

Question Formation

TYPES OF QUESTIONS

So far in this book we have been dealing exclusively with declarative sentences, although some other sentence types were briefly described in Chapter 3. In many senses, declarative sentences can be thought of as "unmarked," in the sense that they are basic, most frequent in most contexts, and likely to be the first type of sentence that children acquire in language. Other types of sentences, like questions, are often analyzed by contrasting their structure to declarative sentences.

The basic order of elements in a declarative sentence is subject + predicate:

The tree fell.
The cat chased a mouse.
Angela read the children a story.
We threw pennies into the fountain.

While the above list is not exhaustive of all the various types of possible declarative sentences, they all have one important feature in common: in each, the subject comes before the entire predicate. That canonical subject-predicate order is key to understanding what happens when a question is formed.

YES/NO QUESTIONS

The first type of question we will consider is the **yes/no question** type.[1] A yes/no question is one for which the appropriate answer is "yes," "no," or "maybe" (or any one of a number of expressions indicating assent, denial, or ambivalence: "Youbetcha!" "No way, Jose!" "Whatever"):

Are you leaving tomorrow?
Had Kai met her in person before they agreed to take a trip together?
Has your sister returned with the ice cream?
Have Amos and Mary been waiting a long time?

If we consider the declarative counterpart to each of these sentences, we have:

You are leaving tomorrow.
Kai had met her in person before they agreed to take a trip together.
Your sister has returned with the ice cream.
Amos and Mary have been waiting a long time.

By comparing the declarative and yes/no question forms, it becomes obvious that what has happened is that the subject and the first auxiliary have been juxtaposed (or have undergone **subject-auxiliary inversion**, as we say in linguistics):

You are → *Are you* (*are* is the auxiliary verb for the verb form *are leaving*)
Kai had → *Had Kai* (*had* is the auxiliary verb for the verb form *had met*)
Your sister has → *Has your sister* (*has* in the auxiliary verb for the verb form *has returned*)
Amos and Mary have → *Have Amos and Mary* (*have* is the first auxiliary verb for the verb form *have been waiting*)

Syntactic operations involving the first auxiliary were important in Chapter 10 as well. In that chapter on negation, we learned that the negating element *not* was placed after the first auxiliary. However, when there was no auxiliary, some form of the auxiliary *do* was inserted after the first auxiliary:

Jane goes to yoga on Thursdays. → *Jane does not go to yoga on Thursdays.*

The auxiliary *do* allowed for the syntactic rule of placing *not* after the first auxiliary to be carried out.
   Similarly, in making yes/no questions, if the verb form does not contain an auxiliary, a situation again that will obtain only in the case that the verb is in the simple present or the simple past (review the chart of verb forms in Chapter 8), then a form of the auxiliary *do* is included so that the syntactic rule of inverting the subject and the (first) auxiliary can be carried out:

---

[1] Yes/no questions are also called "polar questions" or "closed interrogatives."

Jane goes to yoga on Thursdays. → *Does Jane go to yoga on Thursdays?*
They drive their kids to school. → *Do they drive their kids to school?*
You sent the package yesterday. → *Did you send the package yesterday?*

Again, note that the forms of the auxiliary are *do*, *does*, or *did* according to subject agreement and the tense of the verb form.

WH-QUESTIONS

Wh-questions seek information through a *wh*-word. The *wh*-words are as follows:

who (whom)
what
where
why
when
how

They may also include any number of *wh*- compound expressions:

what time
how often
how much
how many
what kind of person
etc.

A key concept in understanding *wh*-words is that they have a function in their sentences. This concept is abstract in some ways because the *wh*-word is "incomplete" in a semantic sense; it doesn't seem to have substance. Still, from a grammatical point of view it has a form and function, just like every word in every sentence must. No word, no matter how general or underspecified, is ever "free" in the grammar.

The *wh*-words *where*, *when*, *why*, and *how* are always adverbial adjuncts or adverbial complements. The *wh*-words *who* (*whom*), *what*, and *which* are interrogative pronouns (so they are NPs), although *what* and *which* sometimes serve an interrogative determiner function too.

The best way to figure out the function of a *wh*-word is simply to make up an answer to the *wh*-question:

Where is Hamid?
Hamid is **in school**.

In the above exchange, *in school* answers the question *where*. The function of the structure that answers the question will most often also be the function of the original *wh*-word. In this case, *in school* is an adverbial complement since it follows a copulative verb (see Chapter 7), so the question word *where* was originally an adverbial complement in the first sentence. Now consider

***Who** called?*
***Sherry** called.*

In this exchange, *Sherry*, the answer to *who*, is the subject of the verb; therefore, *who* was the subject in the original question as well.

Things can become more complicated in cases like the following:

***What** did you buy?*
*I bought **shoes**.*

In this exchange, *shoes* answers the question *what*. *Shoes* is the direct object in the answer, so we can then apply the same method for analysis that we did above and say that since *shoes* is the direct object in the response question, then *what* in the original question also has the function of direct object. What makes this situation more difficult is the fact that the *wh*-word *what* does not appear in the normal position for direct objects, which usually follow the verb. That's because *wh*-words "float" to the front of the sentence.

***Who** does John love?* → *John loves **his mother**.*
***Why** have you complained?* → *I complained **because of the service**.*
***How** are you getting there?* → *I'm getting there **by car**.*
***What** were you carrying?* → *I was carrying **a toolbox**.*

In each case, the question begins with the *wh*-word, while in the declarative sentence (i.e., the answers to those *wh*-words) the order of words is in their syntactically expected positions. When a *wh*-word "moves" to the front of the sentence, the by-now familiar set of changes take place:

1. The subject and the (first) auxiliary are inverted
2. A form of auxiliary *do* is inserted when there is no auxiliary

Now consider the following questions and answers:

***Who** has left the book on the table?* → ***Jordan** has left the book on the table.*
***What** caused so much destruction?* → ***A tornado** caused so much destruction.*

In these two sentences, the noun phrases that answered the questions *who* and *what* are subjects, which again means that we can work backwards to know that *who* and *what* are the subjects in the questions as well. As subjects, they appear at the beginning of the sentence already, so in these cases where the *wh*-word is the subject, there is no *wh*-word "movement" to the front of the sentence. This then means that there are no syntactic changes involving inversion or *do*-insertion. Now consider these questions:

Who *lives in that house?*
Who *saw you?*
What *makes the ocean so blue?*

In each of these sentences, there are no syntactic changes. Since the *wh*-question words *when*, *where*, *why*, and *how* (and their compounds) are always adverbial adjuncts or adverbial complements, they always involve "movement" to the front of the sentence and always trigger the by-now familiar syntactic changes of inverting the subject and first auxiliary and/or inserting *do*.

Why do you treat me this way?
Where have you taken my couch?
When did he leave?

WHO/WHOM

The debate as to whether one should use *who* or *whom* in certain kinds of sentences continues on, and it is a good example of the kinds of omnipresent ideologies in grammar in which people believe a construction to be "correct" or "desirable" but do not themselves use or even know how to use it. For example, if you asked some people whether maintaining the *who/whom* distinction was necessary, you would likely find some who would agree wholeheartedly, although some of them may not really understand the distinction themselves. Of course, as a matter of practice, very few speakers/writers of English distinguish *who* and *whom*, in most instances.

Who is a subject form of the interrogative pronoun, while *whom* is the object form. Therefore, according to the most conservative rules of grammar, *who* is used for the subject and subject complement functions, and *whom* is used in all object functions (direct object, indirect object, and object of a preposition). However, the use of *whom*, even as an object form, is likely to sound overly stilted, and probably very often out of place:

Whom *did you blame for the incident?*

In the above sentence, *whom* is the direct object of the verb *blame*. Most English users do not use *whom* in this context, and there is very little grammatical censure for using *who* instead. In fact, in present-day English, *who* is usually preferable since its use is more reflective of actual usage:

Who did you blame for the incident?

Insistence on *whom* in contexts like the one above is pedantic, and given the stilted, archaic ring that *whom* lends to a sentence, its use is probably rhetorically misguided since it distances the audience.

Nevertheless, there remains in present-day English at least one syntactic domain in which *whom* is obligatory—when it appears after a preposition. The function of *who/whom* as object of the preposition is treated in the next section.

WH-WORDS AS OBJECTS OF A PREPOSITION: PIED-PIPING VERSUS PREPOSITION STRANDING

When *who/whom* or *what* acts as the object of a preposition, a number of choices arise concerning the structure and placement of the prepositional phrase. Consider the following sentence:

What did you talk about?

Using the method introduced above in which an answer is provided for the question in order to determine the function of the *wh*-word, we can see that *what* is the object of the preposition *about*.

What did you argue **about**? → We argued **about school**.

Since the word that answers *what* is *school* and since *school* is clearly the object of the preposition *about*, *what* is the object of the preposition in the original question. Since *wh*-words must appear as the first element in the clause, it might seem strange to see it as the object of a preposition so far away, yet it is definitely the object of *about*. But again, we might imagine *what* as having begun its life in the normal position after the preposition and then having migrated to the front of the sentence. When the *wh*-word migrates to the front of the clause and the preposition is "left behind," we say that the preposition is "stranded."

The other possibility is to bring the preposition to the front of the clause along with the *wh*-word:

About what did you argue?

Those instances in which the preposition "follows" the *wh*-word to the front of the sentence are called pied-piped prepositions, after the story of the Pied Piper who led the children out of the village when he was refused payment for having rid the town of mice.

Who/whom can also be the object of a preposition:

Who did you argue **about**? → We argued **about Felicité**.

Again, since the answer to *who*, Felicité, is the object of the preposition *about*, then we know that *who* was the object in the original sentence as well. As an object, *who* could be expressed as *whom* in such sentences:

Whom did you argue about?

While perhaps still overly stilted in such uses, *whom* is required by most English speakers/writers if the preposition is pied-piped:

About whom *did you argue?*
?About who did you argue?

Additionally, the prepositions *during* and *since* generally require pied-piping:

During what time did you attend ISU?
*What time did you attend ISU during?

Since when have you been in your new Job?
*When have you been in your new job since?

ECHO QUESTIONS

Echo questions are those in which the *wh*-word does not "move" from its normal syntactic position. Echo questions are used to set up emphatic questions, often ones that express surprise, so they do not really seek the same kind of information as do regular *wh*-questions. They may also be used as a clarification-seeking strategy when the listener did not hear the statement or is unsure whether they heard it correctly:

You ate what?!
They got there how?!
Li-Yu goes to bed when?!

Some people find echo questions useful for thinking about the grammatical function of the *wh*-word in a question. If a regular *wh*-question gets converted into an echo question, it will place the *wh*-word into a more regular syntactic position, a placement that may make analyzing its grammatical function easier:

What have you decided? → *You have decided what?!*
Where has he gone? → *He has gone where?!*

In the above sentences, *what* is the direct object and *where* is an adverbial complement. Note that in the echo questions, *what* and *where* now appear after the verb, the more regular position for direct objects and adjuncts.

TAG QUESTIONS

Tag questions are usually found in speech. They are rejoinders to a statement that do not so much ask for information but instead seek agreement from the listener:

> It's a little kitten, **isn't it?**
> The buses have left, **haven't they?**

Tag questions are made by repeating the (first) auxiliary and repeating the subject as a pronoun after it. Additionally, the **polarity** of the tag is reversed. Polarity refers to whether the sentence is negative or positive. Therefore, if the sentence is positive, as it is in the sentences above, the tag question is negative. If the sentence is negative, the tag question is positive:

> Rachel didn't stop by, **did she?**
> You aren't wearing that, **are you?**

Polarity reversal applies also to near-negative adverbials, such as *hardly*, *seldom*, and *scarcely*:

> We hardly had a chance, did we?

Obviously, if syntactic inversion of first auxiliary and subject is invoked, then *do*-insertion is necessary in the case that the main clause verb has no auxiliary:

> Alan loves chocolate, **doesn't he?**
> Charlotte went back to Peoria, **didn't she?**

How to answer a negative tag question can cause confusion for some non-native speakers. However, the answer to a negative tag is the same as it would be for a positive tag:

> You aren't wearing the black sweater, are you? → Yes, I am.
> You are wearing the black sweater, aren't you? → Yes, I am.

There are some tag questions that maintain the same polarity, as in

> So you dropped the class, did you?

Such tag questions generally express feelings such as irritation, disbelief, and mockery.

AREN'T I OR AM I NOT?

The tag for *I am* may cause some confusion. While most speakers prefer *aren't I*, some grammarians might point out that such a usage is illogical because we don't say *I are*.

I am here, **aren't I**?

Those purist-minded grammarians might suggest instead *am I not*?

I am here, **am I not**?

Am I not, however, sounds very formal to most English speakers. In this instance, there really doesn't seem to be an agreed-upon solution. Probably since most speakers use "aren't I," that is the preferable and least problematic tag. However, if someone ever points out the alleged illogicality of "aren't I," a speaker knowledgeable of grammar can explain their choice. What is probably going on here is the attraction toward the use of contractions in tag questions and the fact that the only contracted form available for *am not* is *ain't* (although *ain't* may not originally have been *am + not*), a heavily stigmatized form and thus one avoided by many speakers.

However, it should always be remembered that claims of illogicality for language are weak because language structure is full of seeming contradictions, illogicalities, and redundancy. The application of logic, regularity, and/or uniformity can often fail. Another example of what might seem "illogical" is treated in the next section of this chapter, involving tag questions with *there is* or *there are*.

TAG QUESTIONS WITH *THERE IS* AND *THERE ARE*

Sentences like the following are called existentials because their purpose is to say that something exists (see again Chapter 6):

There is a car parked in the driveway.
There are a lot of tomatoes in the garden.

While in many languages the existential expression is invariable—that is, always the same form, as in Spanish *hay*—in English we have to decide between the singular or the plural form of the verb, as with *is* and *are* in the examples above. Although in speech, English speakers have long opted for *there is (there's)* in all grammatical contexts, as in *There's a lot of tomatoes in the garden*, the prescriptive rule is that the noun after the verb agrees with it. Thus, *a car* is singular so the singular *is* appears in the first example; *a lot of tomatoes* is plural, so *are* is chosen in the second sentence. Since it is the noun after the verb in such existential sentences that decides the form of the verb, it is clearly the subject of the verb. (See again Chapter 6, where we saw that agreement with the verb was the best test for subjecthood.)

However, as we saw above in the formation of tag questions, the subject is repeated (often as a pronoun). But notice that with existentials it is not the subject that is repeated, but the word *there*:

There is a car parked in the driveway, isn't there?
There are a lot of tomatoes in the garden, aren't there?

Again, we can offer some motivation for this apparent illogicality; the preverbal slot is strongly identified with the subject of the clause, so even though *there* is not the grammatical subject of the sentence, it does occupy the regular subject slot and therefore is chosen for tag question formation.

EXERCISES

A. Make the following sentences into yes/no questions, being sure to maintain exactly the same verb tense/form.

1. The bottle has been sitting on the table for two days.
2. Raymond and Jasmine have been studying in the library.
3. The road was repaved last summer.
4. In April, the trees begin to bloom.
5. Ahmed wrote the poem during lunch.
6. Our finances are in terrible condition.
7. They have taken down the old calendar.

B. Determine the grammatical function of *who* or *what* by (1) answering the question posed, and (2) creating an echo question. Is it possible for *who* in any of the sentences to be *whom*? (Be sure to use a single NP in your answer.)

Example: *Who did you see at the park?*

   a. I saw *Ramon* at the park.
   b. You saw *who* at the park?
   c. *Who* in the original sentence is the direct object and it could be expressed as *whom*.

1. Who is it?
2. What did the boys say about the program?
3. Who have we selected for the scholarship?
4. Who made this mess?
5. What are you going to take to the party?
6. Who did they give the prize to?
7. What did you suggest to the students?
8. What did the committee talk about yesterday?
9. Who has Brian been referring to all this time?
10. What dwells in the hearts of evil men?

C. Make tag questions for the following sentences.

1. The bottle has been sitting on the table for two days.
2. Raymond and Jasmine have been studying in the library.
3. The road was repaved last summer.
4. In April, the trees begin to bloom.
5. Ahmed wrote the poem during lunch.
6. Our finances are in terrible condition.
7. They have taken down the old calendar.

Coordination and Compound Sentences

COORDINATING CONJUNCTIONS

The coordinating conjunctions in English are *and, but, or, nor, for, yet* and *so*.[1]

Coordinating conjunctions are used to link together structures in language in a range of senses:

an additive sense	*and*
a concessive sense	*but, yet*
a resultative sense	*so*
a conditional/elective sense	*or*

These may link single words:

Nouns   ***Jack*** and ***Jill*** went up the hill.

---

1 *Yet* and *so* behave differently from the other coordinating conjunctions in some ways. We might note here, for example, that they can occur with other conjunctions: *The thieves were caught red-handed, but yet they refused to confess*. Or, *We didn't have money for the tolls, and so we took the back roads*. And, technically, *or* and *nor* function as disjunction, rather than conjunction, but since grammatically they behave like coordinating conjunctions and since it is not common to speak of coordinate disjunction, we will treat *or* and *nor* along with the coordinating conjunctions.

Verbs	We **danced** and **sang** all night long.
Adjectives	the **big** and **terrifying** rollercoaster
Prepositions	The teens drove **up** and **down** the street.
Adverbs	The team worked **quickly** and **carefully** to get the product on the market in time.

They also link phrases:

NP	**An angry alligator** and **a friendly antelope** walk into a bar...
VP	The students **have written** and **will perform** their play next year.
PP	We hid the eggs **under the sofa** and **next to the television**.
Adj. Ph.	The builders added **very elaborate** but **poorly designed** columns to the front porch.

Coordinating conjunctions can also link together entire clauses.

I ran out of paper, but **Esme bought some for me**.

In certain cases even parts of words, like prefixes, can be conjoined:

pro- and anti-government protesters
pre- and post-graduation parties

But with other prefixes, such coordination is not possible, in the case below because the word *verged doesn't exist:

**During the meeting their opinions con- and diverged.

LISTS AND THE OXFORD COMMA
In the examples above, all of the coordinated items have been just two things, but of course coordinating conjunctions can also be used in a list:

The children spent the day swimming, hiking, picnicking and playing baseball.
We need eggs, butter, milk and sugar for this recipe.

Style manuals differ as to whether a comma is necessary after the final item in the series before the conjunction. The last example could have been written

We need eggs, butter, milk, and sugar for this recipe.

A comma placed before the conjunction is known as the **Oxford comma**, and while often debated, its use is a matter of style or preference and not really about grammatical correctness. Sometimes, however, a comma before the conjunction is necessary in case there might otherwise be some confusion, as for instance when there is a list of already coordinated items:

You can snack on bread and jam, cheese and crackers, or grapes before dinner.

PARALLEL STRUCTURE

An important concept within the topic of coordination is that of parallel structure, a prescriptive grammar concern stipulating that only like grammatical structures can be conjoined, for example, a noun with a noun, a verb phrase with a verb phrase, a prepositional phrase with a prepositional phrase, and so on. Observe the following cases of faulty parallelism, some of which may sound perfectly acceptable to the ear:

*The runners glided **swiftly** and **in highly coordinated movements** across the finish line.*
*We are learning **about the decline of the Roman Empire** and **how the later emperors became increasingly corrupt**.*

In the first sentence, what is being coordinated is *swiftly* and *in highly coordinated movements*. The structures are not parallel because the first element is an adverb and the second is a prepositional phrase. The coordination of these two items might sound acceptable to the ear because both have an adverbial function. However, parallelism, as it is practiced in grammar, is predicated chiefly upon structure or form. Therefore, the above sentence might be corrected to

The runners glided across the finish line in swift and highly coordinated movements.

Now *swift* and *highly coordinated* are both adjective phrases modifying the noun *movements*.

In the second sentence, the non-parallel structure comes about because what is being coordinated is *the decline of the Roman Empire*, a noun phrase, and *how the later emperors became increasingly corrupt*, a noun clause (noun clauses are treated in Chapter 16). A phrase and clause cannot be coordinated according to the prescriptive rule concerning parallel structure. This faulty parallelism might be corrected to

We are learning about the decline of the Roman Empire and the increasing corruption of the later emperors.

Now the former noun clause *how the later emperors became increasingly corrupt* has been changed into a noun phrase headed by the noun *corruption*.

CORRELATIVE CONJUNCTIONS

Within the class of conjunctions, there is a group known as **correlative conjunctions**. Correlative conjunctions may be thought of as discontinuous conjunctions made up of sets of coordinating words. The correlative conjunctions in English are the following:

both...and
neither...nor
either...or
not only...but also

Both *regular sleep* **and** *a good diet are necessary for long-term health.*
In order to get there, you can take **either** *Rt. 127 to Murphysboro* **or** *Interstate 57 to Marion.*
Not only *did he buy the treadmill* **but also** *he signed up for the extended warranty along with it.*

As in the earlier examples, the rules of parallel structure apply; whatever structure is placed after the first element of the correlative pair must also follow the second element. For example, in the first sentence, the noun phrase *regular sleep* follows *both* and the noun phrase *a good diet* follows *and*.

FALSE COORDINATION

Sometimes there may appear an additive sense to a noun of the following type:

That reporter, *along with several other members of the press*, **has been hounding** *the couple for weeks.*

In this sentence, *that reporter* is the subject and therefore requires the singular form of the auxiliary *has*. The prepositional phrase *along with several other members of the press* may seem to make the subject plural, and semantically it does. Still, grammatical agreement is based on the grammatical number of the subject, and nouns inside prepositional phrases already function as objects of prepositions; the noun phrase cannot be both the object of a preposition and a subject. The verb should agree with the subject only.

Some quantifying expressions in English have developed out of earlier noun + preposition combinations. The following list shows some of the more common ones:

a lot of
lots of
a large (small) quantity of
a large (small) amount of
a number of
a bunch of

These expressions are no longer analyzed as a noun + preposition but as a single quantifier (see Chapter 3 on the analysis of multiple word phrases as a single word). For this reason, the noun following such quantifying expressions does not function as the object of the preposition *of* but instead may act as the subject of a verb (or DO, IO, etc.). Consider these contrasting sets:

*A lot of books **were** lying on the table.*
*A lot of dough **was** lying on the table.*

*A great amount of money **was** spent on the project.*
*A great amount of trees **were** cut down to provide material for the project.*

In each case, it is the nouns *books, dough, money,* and *trees* that are controlling agreement with the verb, so they are the actual subjects of the sentences. While a prescriptive grammar tradition will object to the use of a count noun like *trees* with the quantifying expression *amount*, it is increasingly found in more spoken and written contexts. Some would prefer the quantifying expression *a number of* for plural count nouns:

*A number of students **have** chosen to major in foreign languages.*

In this sentence, *a number* is a quantifying expression and *students* is the true subject, again as evidenced by the plural number of the verb with which it agrees, *have*. We can contrast the quantifying expression *a number* with the legitimate noun phrase *the number*:

*The number of students **has** increased over the years.*

In this sentence, *the number* is the subject as shown by the singular number of the verb, *has*.
Along these same lines, it should be remembered that the expression *none of* in the prescriptive tradition of standard English always takes a singular verb:

*None of the students **has** arrived on campus yet.*

Of course, in less formal English, the plural verb in such uses is common:

None of the students **have** *arrived on campus yet.*

CONJUNCTIVE ADVERBS

There are also a number of adverbs whose sense is very similar and overlapping with that of coordinating conjunctions, so-called **conjunctive adverbs**. There are many conjunctive adverbs, but the ones that cause problems, prescriptively speaking, are *however, otherwise, therefore,* and *nevertheless*. Since these adverbs are single words and have meanings very similar to conjunctions, many writers will treat them the same, making sentences like this:

The door was locked, therefore we couldn't enter the room.
Mary had a little lamb, however the lamb contracted rabies and ran away.

In these sentences, the writer has created a comma splice by attempting to coordinate two sentences by simply placing a comma and a conjunctive adverb between them. However, they are not coordinating conjunctions and in writing cannot be conjoined in this way. To avoid this problem, one may do one of the following:

1. Use a coordinating conjunction instead:

   The door was locked, **and** *we couldn't enter the room.*

2. Use a coordinating conjunction and the conjunctive adverb:

   The door was locked, **and therefore** *we couldn't enter the room.*

3. Use a period:

   The door was locked. **Therefore,** *we couldn't enter the room.*

4. Use a semi-colon:

   The door was locked; **therefore,** *we couldn't enter the room.*

For stylistic purposes, the period may also occur with the coordinating conjunction:

The door was locked. **And** *we couldn't enter the room.*

SUBORDINATION VERSUS COORDINATION

Sentences may be coordinated, as in:

The house burnt down, **and** *the neighbors responded by helping the unfortunate victims with clothing and new home supplies.*
We tried to warn him, **but** *he just wouldn't listen.*

Two clauses can also have a different relationship to one another in that one may be subordinate to the other. Subordination is the topic of the next several chapters, but one thing to note for now is that when a clause is subordinate it depends on another grammatical structure in the sentence. By definition, a subordinate clause does not stand alone as a sentence, except for stylistic effect or in dialogue.

The man left the money by the tree **because** *the kidnappers insisted he do so.*

In this case, the part of the whole sentence *The man left the money by the tree* is what we refer to as the main or independent clause and *because the kidnappers insisted he do so* is the subordinate or dependent clause. Again, whereas the main or independent clause can be a sentence by itself—

The man left the money by the tree.

—the subordinate or dependent clause cannot normally be a sentence by itself:

Because the kidnappers insisted he do so.

Of course, subordinate clauses may appear as standalone sentences in the representation of dialogue:

A: Why did you kill that spider?
B: Because I love you.

Or for rhetorical effect:

And why, you ask, should we believe their story? Because it's true!

The last example underscores an important fact about grammar. If you know the rules, you can break them for certain kinds of effect. Just as with any socially conventionalized behavior, breaking the rules calls attention to the rule itself and forces people to figure out why the rule is being broken.

SIMPLE, COMPOUND, AND COMPLEX SENTENCES

We are now ready to consider four levels of sentence complexity. Sentences may be **simple**, **compound**, **complex**, or **compound-complex**.

A simple sentence is one that has a single subject and predicate:

The cat sat on the mat.
Lulu has released a new album.

The subject or the predicate, or both, may be compounded (i.e., conjoined), but the result will still be a simple sentence:

The cat and the dog sat on the mat.
Lulu has released a new album and has begun a tour of the UK.

Note that in the tree representation of such sentences, there is still just one NP subject and one inflection/predicate phrase immediately under S.

A compound sentence is one in which multiple (at least two) subject–predicate pairings are conjoined:

I will go this way, and you go that way.
I love you, but I must leave you.
Jan left her bag in the room, or it is really missing!

A complex sentence is one in which there is a main or independent clause and one or more subordinate or dependent clauses:

Although he is right, I still don't want to listen to him.
The band stopped playing because a storm blew in over the field.

And, finally, sentences may be both complex and compound:

Although he is right, I still don't want to listen to him, but since we have to work together, I will do my best.

Again, complex sentences are the topic of the next several chapters, in which we will divide subordinate or dependent clauses into adverbial, relative, and noun clauses.

DIAGRAMMING COORDINATING CONJUNCTIONS

The essential matter to consider when diagramming conjunctions is that they cause a **regeneration** of structure at the phrase or clause level, meaning that a given node "generates" two (or more) nodes of its same kind. Those regenerated nodes are conjoined by a coordinating conjunction, as in Figure 13.1.

FIGURE 13.1

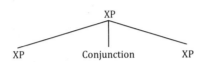

The conjoined structures can be at the highest level of clause; that is, the S may regenerate two S's that are then conjoined. This would be the case of a compound sentence, as in Figure 13.2.

FIGURE 13.2

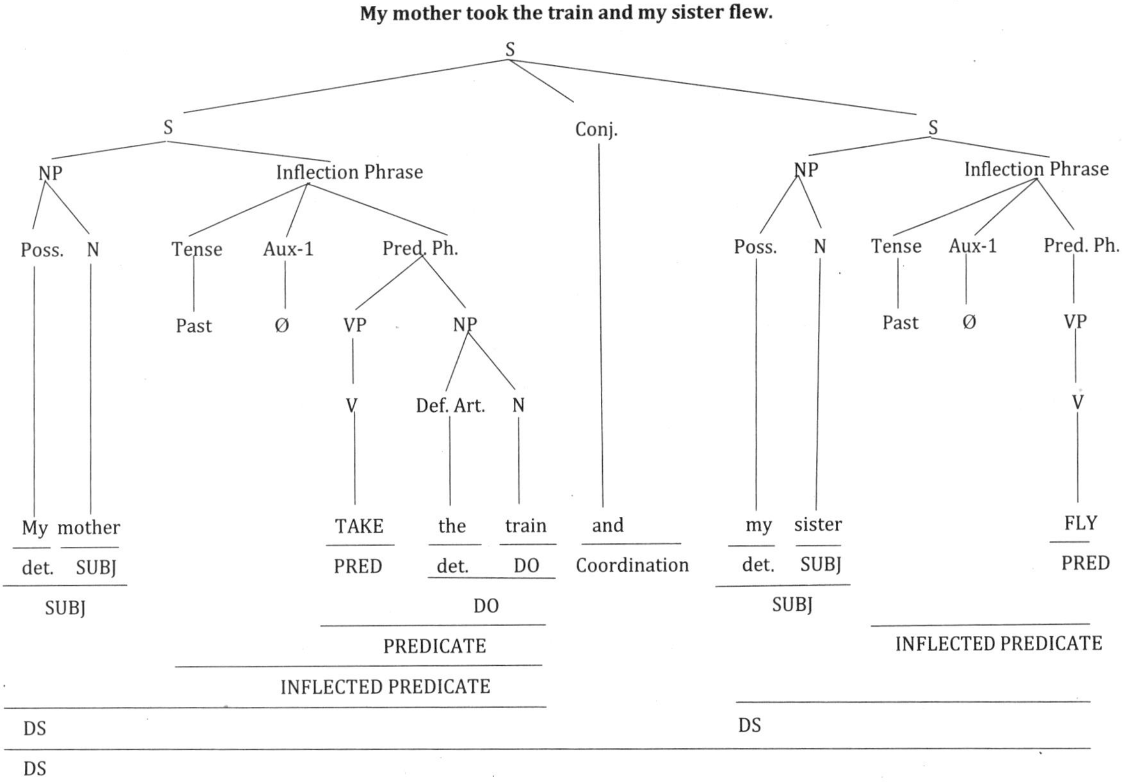

Virtually, then, any structure in the sentence can be regenerated in this way: for example, two noun phrases (Figure 13.3) or two inflection phrases (Figure 13.4).

FIGURE 13.3

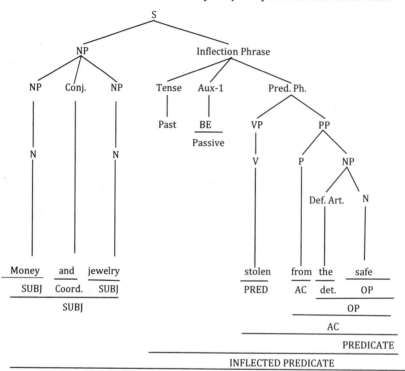

Money and jewelry were stolen from the safe.

FIGURE 13.4

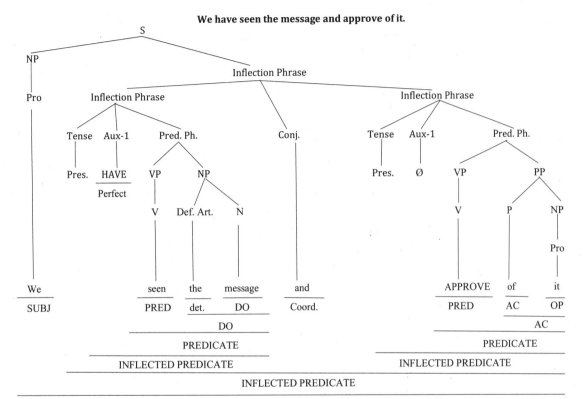

Modifiers must be considered carefully in conjoined structures. If a given modifier applies to both conjoined items, it appears off of the highest node of that particular structure. For example, in the compound NP *the long chapter and exercise*, *long* is meant to modify both nouns, *chapter* and *exercise*. Therefore, that adjective (Adj. Ph.) should come off of the highest NP designation (see Figure 13.5).

FIGURE 13.5

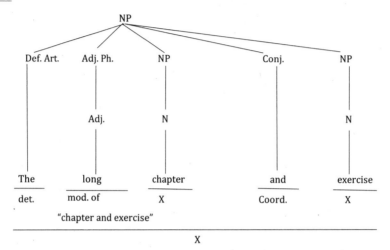

However, in the compound NP *the long table and low chair*, the adjective *long* is meant to modify only *table*. Therefore, that adjective (Adj. Ph.) comes off of the NP for *table* only. The definite article, however, determines both *table* and *chair*, and consequently it should extend from the highest NP, as in Figure 13.6.

FIGURE 13.6

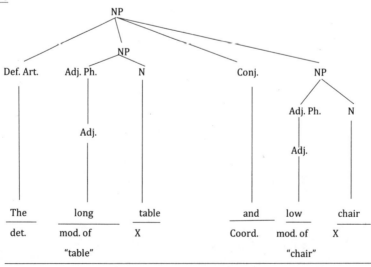

For the coordination of verbal structures, it is the entire inflection phrase that is regenerated if there are two finite verbs. That includes finite auxiliary verbs, as in Figure 13.7.

FIGURE 13.7

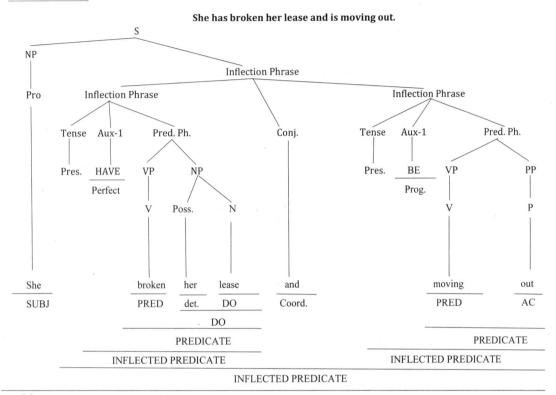

However, if there is only one finite verb form and it is only the non-finite verb forms that are being coordinated, then it may be that two predicate phrases are coordinated, as in Figure 13.8.

FIGURE 13.8

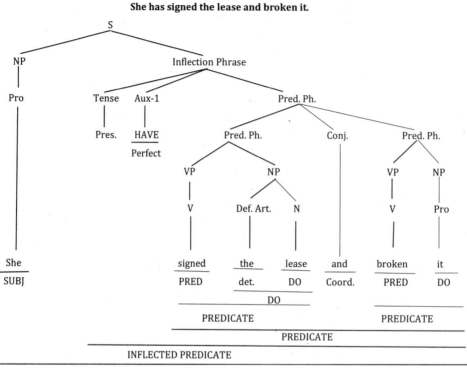

However, if two non-finite verbs have the same object(s) or complement(s), it is two verb phrases that are coordinated, as shown in Figure 13.9.

FIGURE 13.9

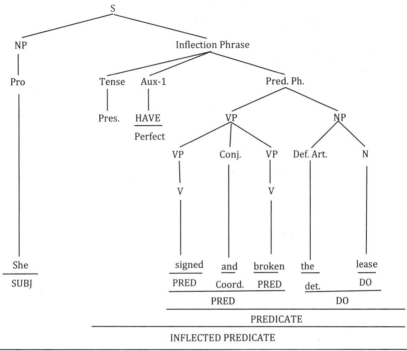

EXERCISES

A. The following sentences all contain some items being coordinated with conjunctions (some are correlative conjunctions). State what is being coordinated, e.g., two verb phrases, two nouns, etc. Be explicit about how you made your determination.

1. We couldn't decide whether to see the new blockbuster or that old movie about the college sweethearts.
2. Abedi twisted his ankle while he was running and jumping into the pool.
3. We tried to call last night around 8:00 p.m., but no one answered the telephone.
4. You will need to use either blue or black ink to fill out this form.
5. Micah was so impressed by all of the support he received that he was eternally and deeply thankful to all of his friends.

6. Your application is currently under review but will be processed no later than the end of next month.
7. The bridesmaids complained that their shoes and dresses did not match.
8. Over the mountain and through the woods to grandmother's house we go.
9. I think that Bashkim must have heard and repeated the news about the downsizing.
10. We were ultimately successful in getting the Chair to step down, yet he continued to voice his unpopular decision.

B. The sentence below may contain false coordination with the effect that there are subject-verb agreement errors. Indicate what is wrong and propose an edited sentence correcting the agreement problem that arose from the false coordination. If there is no fault in the structure, state so.

1. Austin, together with his fellow-business owners in the area, have decided to hold a street fair in the later spring.
2. Unfortunately, I found out that Anne, along with Gabriel and Sharon, are not eligible for the award this year.
3. It has been repeatedly shown that exercise alongside a good diet are still most effective in preventing disease.
4. Maroc told us that Tasha's contribution in combination with a matching grant from City Council are more than enough money to fund the project for over a year.
5. You can rest assured that I, in addition to my entire staff, are totally committed to customer satisfaction.

C. Each of the sentences below contains examples of faulty parallelism. Identify why the conjoined structures are not parallel (using grammatical terminology to refer to the structures) and suggest a possible rewriting of the sentence that would not result in such faulty parallelism.

1. The new dining hall was completed swiftly and within budget even though the project manager left her position midway through the construction.
2. Rochelle wrote an editorial in which she praised both the editing of the new film and how the director used camera angle to build suspense.
3. Difficult to afford but still within budget, the vacation package looks like a rather good bargain.
4. Recipients will be notified of available funds before April 30th or after the new fiscal year begins on June 1st.
5. If you look hard enough you can find a good used car that is cheap and in the paper.

D. Each of the following sentences contains an error in the use of conjunctive adverbs. Suggest a possible rewriting of the sentence to correct the error.

1. The directions for assembling the furniture appeared easy to follow, however, I couldn't figure out what I was supposed to do from pages 2–12.

2. The donated books are piling up on the tables and floor, moreover no one has checked to see if we have multiple copies of some titles.
3. The theater has already given out over one hundred complimentary tickets, in addition they have given discount certificates for many of their concession stand items.
4. We do not have any record of your having received the required immunizations, notwithstanding, you may still register but you will continue to receive notices until your medical records are up to date.
5. The police began to crack down on teenage loitering along Main St., nevertheless every Saturday scores of high schoolers pack the street with cars and foot traffic.

E. Provide full form–function trees for the following sentences.

1. Jack and Jill went up the hill.
2. We danced and sang in the play.
3. The big and terrifying rollercoaster has been taken down.
4. An angry alligator and a friendly antelope walk into a bar and order a drink.
5. The students have written and will perform their play next year.
6. We hid eggs under the sofa and next to the television.
7. The builders added an additional room and expanded the size of the living room.
8. I ran out of paper, but Esme bought some for me.

Adverbial Clauses

Adverbial clauses, as the name implies, are subordinate clauses that fulfill adverbial functions in a sentence. Since we are talking here about clauses, adverbial clauses will have a subject and a finite verb. It is usual to divide adverbial clauses by the type of adverbial notion they convey. Thus, adverbial clauses express time, place, concession, adverseness, cause, result, purpose, and condition. Generally, adverbial clauses may be placed before or after the main clause. When they precede the main clause, the clauses are usually separated by a comma.

> *I will order the pizza **after you get here**.*
> ***After you get here**, I will order a pizza.*

Adverbial clauses, like other types of adverbials, are quite flexible in their position; they can even occur in the middle of the main clause, as a parenthetical addition:

> *The decision will, **because you have requested so**, be announced by tomorrow.*

This sort of parenthetical adverbial clause probably works best in speech, where it is clearly indicated as parenthetical by pausing and intonation; it adds a level of preponderance to an idea. In writing, such interruptions are more likely to break the flow of the reader. Should these kinds of parenthetical adverbial clauses be used in writing, it would be normal to separate them with at least commas, as in the above example, or parentheses:

> *The decision will **(because you have requested so)** be announced by tomorrow.*

Or dashes (usually so-called "emdashes"):

> The decision will—**because you have requested so**—be announced by tomorrow.

TYPES OF ADVERBIAL CLAUSES

Adverbial clauses are introduced by a word that sets up the adverbial notion. In traditional grammar, this word is called a **subordinating conjunction**. In modern grammatical theories, it is frequently called a **complementizer**. We will return to the structure of adverbial clauses and the complementizer later in this chapter, but first let's consider the different types of adverbial clauses. One thing to keep in mind is that some complementizers may introduce several different types of adverbial clauses. For example, *since* may indicate time, as in *Since he left, I haven't had anyone to hunt with*, or it may indicate reason, as in *Since you won't change your mind, I will resign from the project*.

CLAUSES OF TIME

As suggested by the name, adverbial clauses of time express temporal notions. The complementizers used to introduce an adverbial clause of time include the following:

> when / whenever
> while (British: whilst)
> since
> before
> after
> until / till
> as
> as soon as
> as long as
> now (that)
> once

> I will let the dogs out **when I get home**.
> **Before he took the job as manager**, he worked as a horse jockey.
> Siblings will love you **as long as they live**.
> **Once we have the parts**, we can finish the work in less than a day.

CLAUSES OF PLACE

As the name suggests, adverbial clauses of place express location. The complementizers used to introduce an adverbial clause of place are usually *where* or *wherever*:

> **Wherever you go**, I will follow.

Additionally, a number of other words may be used as complementizers to refer to place, some of which are quite informal. They are optionally followed by *that*:

anywhere
nowhere
everywhere
any place (or anyplace)
no place
every place

Everywhere (that) we stopped, *people were very nice.*
Anyplace (that) you want, *I will meet you there!*

CLAUSES OF CONCESSION

Adverbial clauses of concession express a contrast that does not negate or present information that is completely opposite from that in the main clause. Instead, they give information that contrasts somewhat with that in the main clause or presents "surprising information" given the main clause. The complementizers used to introduce an adverbial clause of concession include these:

although
though
even though

Although he attended the meeting only once, *he became an avid follower of the cult's teachings.*
*I love you **even though you drive me crazy most of the time**.*

CLAUSES OF ADVERSENESS

Adverbial clauses of adverseness, or more euphonically **adversative clauses**, are those that express a strong contrast with the main clause, sometimes even reversing the sense completely. The complementizers typically used to express adverseness include

while
whereas
where

While Jack has never held down a job for longer than a week, *his sister is a highly successful CEO of a Fortune-500 company.*
*Cats meow **whereas dogs bark**.*

CLAUSES OF CAUSE

Adverbial clauses of cause give the cause of the predication expressed in the main clause. The complementizers used to introduce an adverbial clause of cause include the following:

because
since
as
now (that)
whereas
inasmuch as
as long as
so long as

*I came here **because I need to talk**.*
*Household furnishings are much cheaper **now that they are made almost exclusively in locations outside of the US**.*
***Since he broke those rules**, he will be suspended from the game for a set number of matches.*

CLAUSES OF RESULT

Adverbial clauses of result give the outcome set up by the main clause. The complementizer *that* is generally used after the degree of an adjective (with *so*) or the expanse/amount of a noun (with *such*, *so much*, or *so many*) has been established:

*They kept so many lamps burning every night **that their electric bill was three-times that of their neighbors**.*
*The tree was **so tall that it towered over the five-story building next to it**.*
*There was **so much garbage in the yard that the neighbors complained to the city council**.*
*Oscar was **such a grouch that his friends eventually stopped inviting him to parties**.*

The complementizer *that* is optionally left out and replaced by a comma:

*There was **so much garbage in the yard, the neighbors complained to the city council**.*

CLAUSES OF PURPOSE

As the name implies, adverbial clauses of purpose state the goal of the predication set up by the main clause. The complementizers used to express purpose include these:

that
in order that
so (that)

We left the blocks outside **so that you can pick them up at your convenience**.
I read the appendix **in order that I might understand the method used to arrive at such results**.

CLAUSES OF SIMILARITY

These clauses are introduced by *as* or *like* and state a similarity to the situation or event set up in the main clause.

Fatima drummed her fingers on the table **like her mother used to do**.

CLAUSES OF COMMENTARY

Comment clauses give the speaker's/writer's opinion or stance within the statement they are making.

The problem, **I believe**, is that parents are too permissive these days.

Comment clauses are thus a kind of attitudinal adjunct, which was presented in Chapter 7 as one of the uses of prepositional phrases.

CLAUSES OF CONDITION

Adverbial clauses of condition often make up a rather extended section of any grammatical treatment of English because they invoke special uses of verb forms or introduce special forms. In Chapter 9, we referred to these forms as "the second subjunctive." The forms and uses of the second subjunctive are taken up in this chapter. For now, we can note that adverbial clauses of condition set up a situation under which the main clause is conditionally true, and at other times supposed or imagined. The complementizers used to introduce conditional adverbial clauses include the following:

if
even if
if only
unless
in case
provided

If you build it, they will come.
I will wait for you at the train station **unless you send word of your refusal**.
Provided they finish all of the work, they will earn a hefty amount for their labor.

THE STRUCTURE OF COMPLEMENTIZERS

Throughout this book we have been using form–function trees in order to visualize the syntactic structure of English and to link form with syntactic function (although the latter enterprise often takes us also into semantics). In this way of representing structure, complementizers are generated by an adverbial clause (written Adv. Cl.), which will have a subordinate clause (written as a small s) as its sister (the node next to it). The complementizer (C) is the head of the Adv. Cl. its function as well as the function of the entire Adv. Cl. is (almost always) "adverbial adjunct."[1] The function of the subordinate clause, the little s, is to complement the complementizer. The labels for all other major noun functions (subj, do, io, etc.) and the predicate (pred) are also written in lower case in subordinate clauses. Consider the tree containing Adv. Cl. in Figure 14.1.

FIGURE 14.1

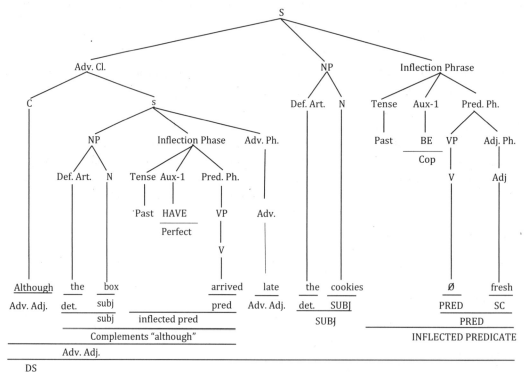

Although the box had arrived late, the cookies were fresh.

---

1 One instance in which an adverbial clause might be analyzed as complement is following certain verbal expressions that would be odd without the adverbial clause, e.g., *The party will start when they get here*. Note the oddity of *?The party will start*. Once again we are reminded that the concepts of complement and adjunct are scalar.

Note, too, that the adverbial clause in Figure 14.1 occurs outside the core of the sentence. In this instance, the adverbial clause occurs before the main clause. It is also possible for the adverbial clause to appear outside the core but after the main clause, as in Figure 14.2.

FIGURE 14.2

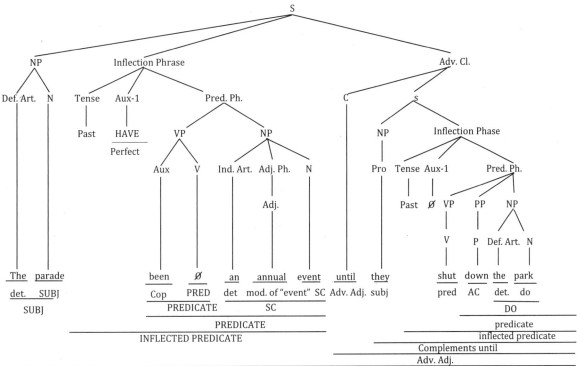

THE SECOND SUBJUNCTIVE

In the section above on adverbial clauses of condition, it was stated that often such clauses invoked the use of subjunctive verb forms, second subjunctive verb forms to be exact.[1]

To understand the use of verb forms in conditional clauses, it is usual to separate them into factual

---

1 In fact, only the verb *be* has a special verb form, as discussed later. The subjunctive forms for all other verbs are identical to forms used in the simple past or in compound past forms. I will discuss them as second subjunctive "forms" here. A longer discussion on the status of those forms appears later in the chapter.

and contrary-to-fact types. As the names imply, factual conditions express conditions under which the predication in the main clause is thought sure or likely by the speaker/writer:[1]

If we work hard, *we will finish by noon.*
If it rained, *they stayed inside.*
If Simon sings, *the show is a hit.*

In the first sentence, the speaker is fairly certain that if we work hard, then the result will be completed by noon. In the second, on every occasion in the past when it rained, they stayed inside. In the third sentence, the speaker is stating the fact that if Simon sings, then the show is habitually a hit. In factual conditions, indicative verb forms are used, such as the ones we saw in Chapter 8.

Contrary-to-fact conditional clauses express a condition that sets up a main clause predication by the speaker/writer that is known not to be true or not likely to be true:

If I were a butterfly, *I would look for nectar.*
If you hadn't told everyone, *we would have been better off.*

In these examples, the predication in the *if*-clause (also called the **protasis**) is known to be non-factual, so the predication in the main clause is mere imagination, fantasy, or supposition. The fact is, I am not a butterfly. The fact is, you DID tell everyone. The second subjunctive verb form is used in contrary-to-fact conditional clauses.

The second subjunctive in English is achieved by a formal verb shift in which past forms take on present subjunctive meanings and past perfect forms take on past subjunctive meanings. For example, in a contrary-to-fact adverbial clause, the simple past form is used to state present time, habitual activity, or other types of time and aspect contours usually expressed by the present tense form. The past perfect form, which in the indicative expresses past before past, is used to express past time and various other aspects usually signaled by the simple past form. The situation is slightly more complex, because progressivity may be added to these forms as well (see Table 14.1).

The main clause in contrary-to-fact conditional sentences (also called the **apodosis**) takes a conditional verb form. Usually the conditional verb form is made up of *would* + the base form for present or future time reference, and *would* + *have* + the simple passive participle for past time reference. However, any modal verb may be used in place of *would* in the case that the speaker/writer wants to apply various shades of certainty to the sentence. Progressive forms, too, may be used in the main clause. Table 14.1 summarizes the use of the verb forms in conditional clauses.

---

[1] One rhetorical use of this type of conditional is to state a disbelief in exaggerated terms:

If he's talented, then I'm Picasso!

TABLE 14.1: VERB FORMS IN CONDITIONAL CLAUSES

if-clause (protasis)	main clause (apodasis)
present time	
If I had help,	*I would finish faster.*
If I were hurrying,	*I would be finishing faster.*
	(or *could, might, should*, etc.)
past time	
If I had checked the facts,	*I would have reported on it.*
If I had been hurrying,	*I would have been done by now.*
	(or *could, might, should have been*, etc.)

Whether we can say that English actually has a subjunctive is a difficult question—and certainly not one with a definitive answer. From a focus purely on form, we might say that English does not have a subjunctive since it does not involve a whole set of unique forms (except perhaps one form, *were*, discussed in the next section). In this sense, contrary-to-fact meanings would simply be further semantic areas covered by a given verb form. On the other hand, subjunctive is often spoken of as a notional concept, that is, having to do with meaning or intent. Most such approaches characterize the subjunctive as a verbal mood in which the information is contrary-to-fact, supposed, or imagined. Given that the notional domains of subjunctivity are expressed through regular patterning of form (i.e., verb form time shift), there are good reasons to talk about a subjunctive in English grammar in view of the grammatical approach taken here.

The present and past meanings of the *if*-clause and main clause may be mixed. For example, if I refer to something contrary-to-fact in the past, the result of the condition may still be true:

If I had gotten it, I would be a lot happier now.

Sometimes the conditional verb forms *would have* + simple passive participle are heard in the *if*-clause as well as the main clause:

If he would have told me, I would have helped him out.

Such uses probably arise from the attracting effects of form harmony (the subconscious urge to have the same form in both clauses), but the use is not standard and is avoided in formal contexts.

Finally, note that second subjunctive forms also appear in contexts outside of *if*-clauses if the general sense is counterfactual or not realized as true at the time of speaking:

It's time you grew up.
Suppose you had fallen off the ladder!

SUBJUNCTIVE VERB FORMS IN OTHER ADVERBIAL CLAUSES

Sometimes in older English or in very formal English, like legal English, the first subjunctive (see again Chapter 9) can be heard in certain adverbial clauses:

*I will fight him wherever he **be**!*
*Although he **be** of sound body and mind, there is no legal precedent for him to bequeath his fortune to a sickly parakeet—especially a parakeet with no heirs apparent!*

In Modern English, one is more likely to use a modal or the indicative:

*I will fight him wherever he **may be** (or wherever he is).*

One final point about the verb form in adverbial clauses is that the future modal *will* rarely occurs in conditional clauses, even if the meaning is clearly future:

*I will see you when you will be here.

Sometimes, however, the future is used in conditional clauses to make an offer:

If you will wash the dishes, I will dry them.

IF I WERE OR IF I WAS?

The grammar student of English will have no trouble finding someone to argue the correctness of *if I were* or *if I was* (and the related *if he/she/it were~if he/she/it was*). Here again, a responsible grammar cannot offer a definitive response; people use both, and neither is absolutely more correct than the other.

*If I **were** a millionaire, I would buy an amusement park.*
*If I **was** a millionaire, I would buy an amusement park.*

In traditional terms, grammarians have over the years generally decided on the side of *were*, since the contrary-to-fact conditional clause seemingly called for a special subjunctive form. However, *was* has become so common in this use that often *were* sounds overly pedantic. Advice for the twenty-first century is to use the one that fits your purpose and desire for self-presentation best: if you wish to sound formal and traditional, you should use *were*; if you prefer to sound more casual and grammatically effortless, you might well use *was*. Remember that "sounding grammatically effortless" is not effortless. Determining the appropriate grammatical forms for self-presentation and effective communication with an audience, in speech or writing, requires thought about and selection of the "correct" forms for the situation—casual, colloquial, formal, etc.

EXERCISES

A. For each of the sentences below, identify the adverbial clause and say what type of clause it is (e.g., time, place, concession, etc.).

1. Until he arrives, we will continue to prepare the minutes from our last meeting.
2. The garden really should be tended to before you plant anything else.
3. The young girl saw life everywhere she looked.
4. My cats will sleep anyplace there is a ray of sun and a soft cushion.
5. Although the forecast called for rain, the sun was shining the entire time.
6. I won't be able to join you even though I really want to.
7. While roses are red, violets are generally blue.
8. I say "tomato" whereas you say "tomahto."
9. Since Alicia moved in with her piano, we now have a pretty good trio ensemble.
10. We went there so that you would have some support in the audience.
11. If you don't know the answer, ask me and I will help you.

B. Conditionals. Identify the type of condition in the following sentences as factual or contrary-to-fact.

1. If you go, take a sweater with you.
2. If Jackson had more time, he could do much better.
3. If the IRS had turned over the documents, the scandal would have dissolved.
4. If he missed the bus, Hideki just rode his bike.
5. If they had made better plans, this wouldn't have happened.
6. If my mom took lessons, she would be a great artist.
7. If you were here, I could deceive you.
8. If the students had contacted the principal, she would have intervened on their behalf.

C. Change the following factual conditions into contrary-to-fact conditions. Pay special attention to the verb. Remember, to make the condition contrary-to-fact, you simply shift the tense of the inflection phrase back in the *if*-clause.

Examples: *If you come to my house, I will give you diamonds.* → *If you came to my house, I would give you diamonds.*

If you are trying to understand, the book will help. → *If you were trying to understand, the book would help.*

1. If the delivery van takes a right, they will get here sooner.
2. If it rained, we carried umbrellas.

3. If the documents contain information about the applicant, we cannot see them before the interview.
4. If we are taking a test, we will study hard.
5. If the trees bloom early in the spring, my allergies are worse.
6. If you sleep all day, you will not be tired tonight.
7. If the bell rang, we went to class.

D. Make full form–function trees for the following sentences.

1. While the band was playing their set, I was setting up my equipment on the lawn.
2. You should have told me the news before I made the flyers for the show.
3. If the soldiers had been in the area, they could have prevented the attack.
4. The workers do not have to arrive until the contract has been settled.
5. Although an alert was sent to listserve, we were deceived by this scam because we did not get the message.

Relative Clauses

Relative clauses are sometimes called adjective clauses in traditional grammar because their function is to modify nouns in ways not unlike adjectives. A preliminary and crucial matter to understand about relative clauses is that they do not have complementizers as adverbial clauses do; instead, they are introduced by a **relative pronoun**.[1] Whereas complementizers stand outside of the subordinate clause structure, relative pronouns have a function *within* the subordinate or dependent clause. Thus relative pronouns actually have a dual function. On the one hand, they refer to a noun phrase in the main clause in ways not unlike the personal pronoun *he* might refer to *Mike* in the compound sentence *Mike saw the accident and **he** reported it to the police*. On the other hand, relative pronouns also serve a function in their own clause, like that of subject, direct object, object of a preposition, and so on.

Consider this sentence:

The student who finishes last should close the door and turn off the lights.

In this sentence, the main clause is *The student should close the door and turn off the lights*. The relative clause is *who finishes last*. The word *who* is the relative pronoun. *Who* refers to the noun phrase *the student* (as *he* referred to *Mike* in the example above). In other words, *the student* is the **antecedent** of the relative pronoun *who*; but in the relative clause itself, the relative pronoun *who* is the subject of the verb *finishes*.

---

[1] In some grammatical treatments, in fact, some of what are called relative pronouns are better treated as "relative complementizers." The matter need not concern us here, and certainly traditional grammars have considered all relative pronouns to be of the same structure, as we will here.

Here are the relative pronouns in English:

who (whom)
that
which

There are several rules (and misunderstood rules) governing the use of relative pronouns, and those rules depend on an important difference between two types of relative clauses: restrictive and non-restrictive types.

RESTRICTIVE VERSUS NON-RESTRICTIVE RELATIVE CLAUSES

A restrictive relative clause is one that restricts or identifies the reference of a noun. A non-restrictive relative clause does not do so. Consider for instance the following three images:

Book 1

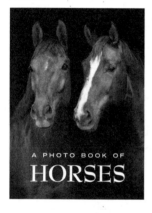

Book 2

Book 3

If I were to utter the sentence

*Please pass me **the book**.*

the listener would not know which of the three books I was referring to; there are three equally likely choices, given the unmodified noun *book*. Now consider the following sentence:

*Please pass me **the book that has the cat on the cover**.*

In this sentence I have added the clause *that has the cat on the cover*, which modifies the noun *book*. (Note that, like prepositional phrases, relative clauses follow the nouns they modify in English.) With the added clause, there is no question which of the nouns I am referring to. In other words, the relative clause *that has a cat on the cover* restricted the possible referents; it is a **restrictive** relative clause.

Now consider the following image:

In our environment at the moment, only a single book is visible, and it happens to have a mouse on it. Therefore, if I issue the following request—

*Please pass me **the book**.*

—there is no question which book I am referring to. There's just one in front of us. Therefore, if I said

*Please pass me **the book, which has a mouse on the cover**.*

the relative clause *which has a mouse on the cover* does nothing in this case to restrict the reference; the reference was already restricted. In this instance, the information in the relative clause is unnecessary for the identity of the noun; it is **non-restrictive**. Be careful to note that by "unnecessary" we do not mean that the non-restrictive clause isn't important in some sense. If a speaker or writer included the information, they must have thought that it is necessary or important for some reason. Restrictive versus non-restrictive refers instead to noun identification in the ways just discussed.

Since non-restrictive relative clauses do not function to identify a noun out of many possible nouns, it then also makes sense that proper nouns, nouns that refer to names of specific things, people, and places, are a category that may be, and often are, followed by non-restrictive relative clauses:

Thomas Edison, who resided in Menlo Park, New Jersey, mass-produced the first incandescent light bulb.

In this sentence, the information given by the relative clause *who resided in Menlo Park, New Jersey* gives no identifying information about the noun *Thomas Edison*; we already know exactly who that refers to before reading/hearing the relative clause.

Again, the difference between restrictive and non-restrictive relative clauses is important because the rules governing the selection and use of relative pronouns (and of punctuation) depends on whether a given clause is restrictive or non-restrictive.

RESTRICTIVE RELATIVE CLAUSES

The following are true of restrictive relative clauses:

1. The relative pronoun *who* is used to refer to human antecedents.

   *We tipped the server **who** brought us a free round of drinks.*

2. The relative pronoun *that* is used to refer to both non-human and human antecedents.

   *I left my wallet on the chair **that** you took back into the other room.*
   *We tipped the server **that** brought us a free round of drinks.*

Sometimes one will find the "rule" that it is only correct for *who* to be used in reference to people and that using the relative pronoun *that* for such reference is incorrect. This is not justifiable by practice or history. Along with the injunction of not ending a sentence with a preposition, that rule is a great example of a facile, and highly uninformed, grammatical pronouncement (see Chapter 18).

Who *and* That *as Subjects and Direct Objects*

As with certain *wh*-questions, it can be difficult to identify the syntactic function of a relative pronoun in certain situations because they always appear at the front of their clause. One trick to seeing the "underlying" structure of a relative clause is to "unpack" it. Unpacking involves taking a complex sentence and setting it into two independent clauses.

For example, the sentence *We tipped the server who brought us a free round of drinks* consists of two predications:

1. *We tipped the server.*
2. *The server brought us a free round of drinks.*

In unpacking the sentence, I replace the relative pronoun, *who*, with its antecedent and place that antecedent in its normal position. Note that when I do so, it results in two grammatically stand-alone sentences. Unpacking a complex sentence with a relative clause makes it easier to see what that function of the original relative pronoun is. If we consider the function of the noun phrase *the server* in the unpacked relative clause (sentence #2 above), it should be a fairly straightforward matter to know that *the server* is the subject. By stating this, I can also know that the relative pronoun in the original complex sentence was the subject in its own clause. Figure 15.1 shows the form–function tree diagram for the complex sentence with the relative clause.

RELATIVE CLAUSES

FIGURE 15.1

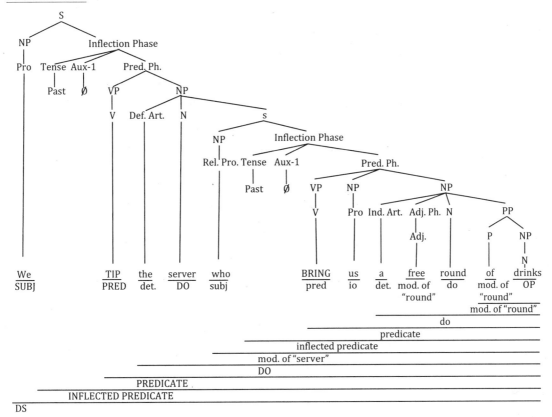

Now let's consider another sentence:

Mary identified the suspect who police were holding in custody.

In "unpacking" this complex sentence, I would first isolate the main clause:

Mary identified the suspect.

Then I am left with the relative clause *who police were holding in custody*. Next, I replace the relative pronoun with its antecedent. This leaves me with

the suspect police were holding in custody

However, the point of unpacking is to get back to two well-formed, independent clauses—two full sentences that could stand alone. *The suspect police were holding in custody* is not a well-formed, independent clause. The normal syntax would be this:

Police were holding the suspect in custody.

Now it should start becoming more obvious how we can determine the function of the relative pronoun in the original complex sentence. Note how in the unpacked relative clause *police were holding the suspect in custody*, the noun phrase repeated from the main clause, *the suspect*, is the direct object; one can extrapolate that information onto the complex sentence and know that the function of the relative pronoun in the original sentence, *who*, was that of direct object as well. Figure 15.2 shows the form–function tree diagram for this complex sentence with the relative clause.

FIGURE 15.2

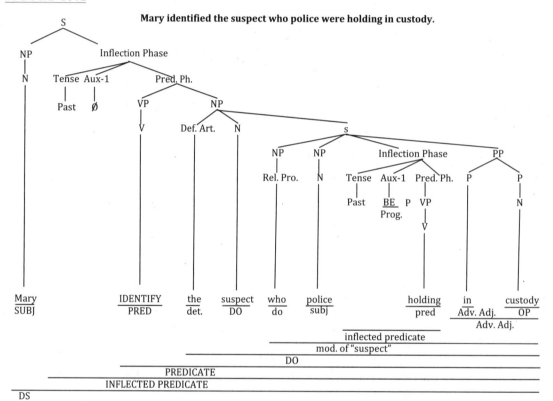

Recall from Chapter 10 that when the *wh*-question word *who* was functioning as the object, it was possible to use *whom*, although the use was a little stiff and archaic-sounding. *Whom* may also be used for the relative pronoun in sentences like the one we have been considering, since it is functioning as the object:

*Mary identified the suspect **whom** police were holding in custody.*

Let's now consider some further examples with the relative pronoun *that* as subject and as direct object:

*The builders finished the house **that** sits on Sycamore St.*
*The builders finished the house **that** the Ramirezes bought last month.*

Again, unpacking will help us to uncover the syntactic function of the relative pronouns in each sentence. Remember that to unpack a sentence, you should do the following:

1. Isolate the main clause.
2. Replace the relative pronoun with its antecedent.
3. Make adjustments in order to put the antecedent in the unpacked relative clause back into its normal position so that it constitutes a grammatical sentence.

Thus for the first sentence, we would do this:

1. Isolate the main clause: *The builders finished the house.*
2. Replace the relative pronoun with its antecedent: *The house sits on Sycamore St.*
3. Make adjustments in order to put the antecedent in the unpacked relative clause back into its normal position: not applicable in this sentence.

After performing these three steps, we would be able to identify that *the house* in the unpacked relative clause, *The house sits on Sycamore St.*, is a subject, so the relative pronoun in the original complex clause was also a subject. Figure 15.3 shows the form-function tree diagram for this sentence.

FIGURE 15.3

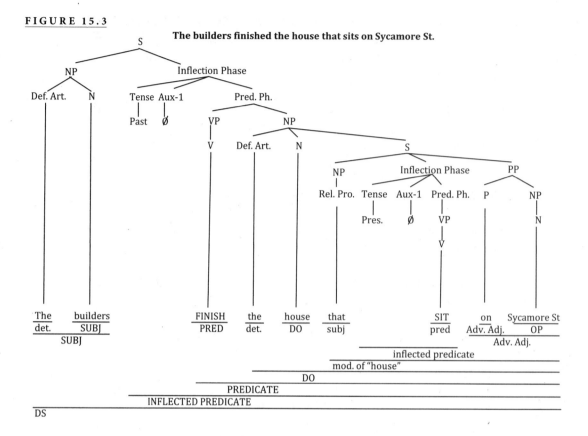

For the second sentence:

1. Isolate the main clause: *The builders finished the house.*
2. Replace the relative pronoun with its antecedent: *The house the Ramirezes bought last month.*
3. Make adjustments in order to put the antecedent in the unpacked relative clause back into its normal position: *The Ramirezes bought the house last month.*

The house in the unpacked relative clause *The Ramirezes bought the house last month* is a direct object, so the relative pronoun in the original complex clause was also a direct object. Figure 15.4 shows the form-function tree diagram for this sentence.

FIGURE 15.4

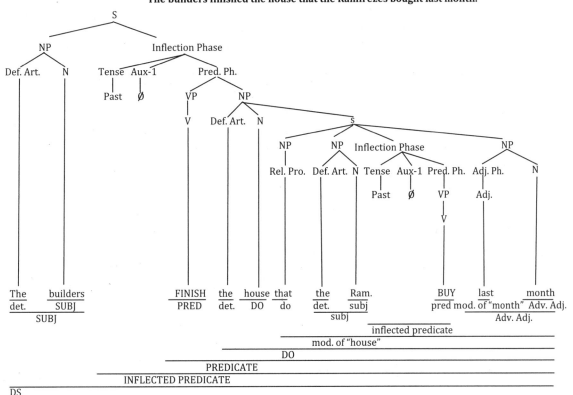

Ø-Relative

Consider the two sentences that we have been analyzing:

> *Mary identified the suspect who(m) police were holding in custody.*
> *The builders finished the house that the Ramirezes bought last month.*

For these two sentences, we identified that the relative pronouns *who* (or *whom* if you prefer) and *that* were direct objects in their own relative clauses. Note now that it is possible to omit the relative pronouns in these two sentences:

> *Mary identified the suspect Ø police were holding in custody.*
> *The builders finished the house Ø the Ramirezes bought last month.*

The rule for this omission is that the relative pronoun may be omitted in restrictive relative clauses when it is the direct object.

That kind of omission is not possible when the relative pronoun is the subject, although it is allowed in certain dialects, such as the southern American Midlands English and Irish English.

?We tipped the server Ø brought us a round of free drinks.

When the relative pronoun is omitted, it still appears in a tree diagram as Ø, and its function is labeled, in this case as a DO, as we see in Figure 15.5.

FIGURE 15.5

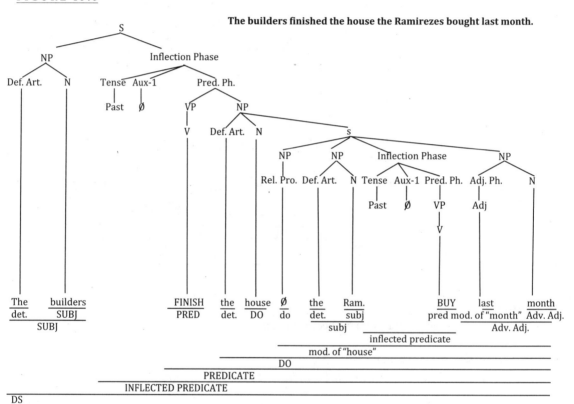

Relative Pronouns as Object of the Preposition
Now consider this sentence:

Charlotte saved the pen with which Cher signed her autograph.

If we perform the unpacking function on this complex sentence, we arrive at these two sentences:

1. *Charlotte saved the pen.*
2. *Cher signed her autograph with the pen.*

In the second sentence, we can see that the reinstated full noun phrase, *the pen*, is the object of the preposition (op) *with*. By applying that analysis to the relative clause in the original complex sentence, we can conclude that the relative pronoun *which* was the object of the preposition *with* as well. Figure 15.6 shows the form-function tree diagram for this sentence.

FIGURE 15.6

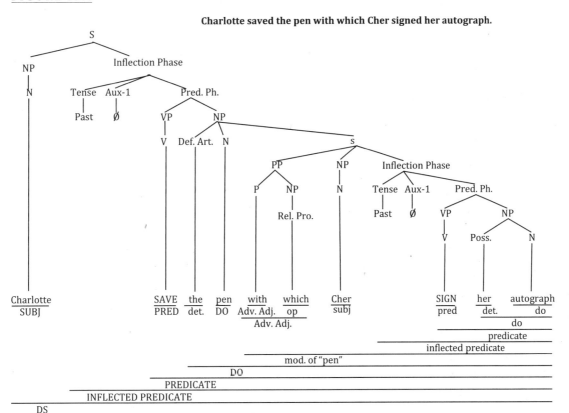

Pied-Piping versus Preposition Stranding

In Chapter 12, we saw that when a *wh*-word was the object of a preposition, it was possible to bring the *wh*-word to the front of the sentence and strand the preposition, or to bring the preposition along with the *wh*-word, a process referred to as pied-piping. The same stylistic choices occur with relative pronouns when they are the object of a preposition:

*Charlotte saved the pen **that** Cher signed her autograph **with**.*
*Charlotte saved the pen **with which** Cher signed her autograph.*

First, it should be said that again some language purists and certain manuals of style reject the first sentence, the one with the stranded preposition (and see also Chapter 18). However, the form is completely regular in speech and non-objectionable in most writing styles.

Second, note that if the preposition is pied-piped, the relative pronoun must be *which*, never *that*:

*Charlotte saved the pen with that Cher signed her autograph.

Third, if the preposition is stranded in a restrictive relative clause, the Ø-relative is a possible alternative:

Charlotte saved the pen Ø Cher signed her autograph with.

Fourth, if the relative pronoun is *who*, *who* or *whom* may be used when the preposition is stranded:

*I admire the doctor **who/whom** the biography was written about.*

However, if the preposition is pied-piped, only *whom* may be used:

*I admire the doctor about **whom** the biography was written.*

This syntactic position is in fact the only place where *whom* is still obligatory for most speakers of English.

Note, then, that in a restrictive relative clause when the relative pronoun is the object of a preposition and it refers to a non-human noun, there are three possible syntactic and stylistic configurations for the relative clause:

*Charlotte saved the pen **that** Cher signed her autograph **with**.*
*Charlotte saved the pen Ø Cher signed her autograph **with**.*
*Charlotte saved the pen **with which** Cher signed her autograph.*

In a restrictive relative clause when the relative pronoun is the object of a preposition and refers to the human noun, there are five possible syntactic configurations:

*I admire the doctor **who** the biography was written **about**.*
*I admire the doctor **whom** the biography was written **about**.*
*I admire the doctor **that** the biography was written **about**.*
*I admire the doctor Ø the biography was written **about**.*
*I admire the doctor **about whom** the biography was written.*

Remember that the difference in these alternatives is not about absolute right versus wrong, but about style, choice of formality or informality, and rhetorical impact. Figure 15.6 shows a form-function tree of a pied-piped preposition, and 15.7 shows an example of a stranded preposition.

FIGURE 15.7

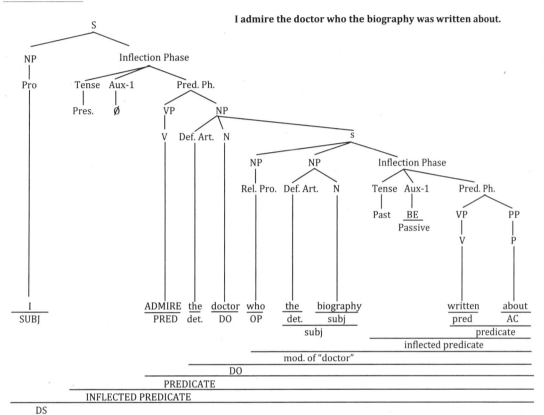

NON-RESTRICTIVE RELATIVE CLAUSES

In non-restrictive relative clauses, the choices for relative pronouns are fewer. In non-restrictive relative clauses, a relative pronoun with a human antecedent is always *who/whom*, and it is always *which* for a non-human antecedent.

> I ran up to my mother, **who** was just getting off the train.
> Jack visited the White House, **which** was undergoing repairs.

Again note that these are non-restrictive because in neither case is the relative clause necessary for identification of the noun it modifies; there aren't multiple White Houses, one undergoing repairs and the rest not. Likewise, I don't have multiple mothers, one being identified as having just gotten off a train.

One important difference between restrictive and non-restrictive relative clauses is that the non-restrictive type is separated from the main clause by one or more commas, whereas the restrictive type is not. In speech, a non-restrictive relative clause is often separated from the main clause by one or more pauses and a lower pitch.

The relative pronoun in non-restrictive relative clauses may be a subject, direct object, or object of a preposition. In the two sentences above, the relative pronouns, *which* and *who*, were subjects. In the following examples, the relative pronouns are direct objects:

The Taj Mahal, **which** *we visited last summer, was built in the seventeenth century.*
President Obama, **who** *I liked very much, was the first African American president of the US.*

As in restrictive relative clauses, when the relative pronoun **who** is an object in a non-restrictive relative clause, it may be expressed as **whom**.

President Obama, **whom** *I liked very much, was the first African American president of the US.*

Note that the relative pronoun cannot be omitted in non-restrictive relative clauses.

When the relative pronoun is the object of a preposition, the preposition may be stranded (remember only *which* may be used in non-restrictive clauses):

The Second Amendment, **which** *lawmakers continue to disagree* **on***, is usually interpreted as the right of individual citizens to own ballistic weaponry.*

Or the preposition may be pied-piped:

The Second Amendment, **on which** *lawmakers continue to disagree, is usually interpreted as the right of individual citizens to own ballistic weaponry.*

If the preposition is pied-piped with the relative pronoun *who*, *whom* must be used.

The President of the University, **with whom** *I had a meeting, will be giving a public announcement concerning pension funds next week.*

RELATIVE DETERMINER *WHOSE*

When the antecedent for a relative is a possessive structure, the relative determiner *whose* is used:

The police arrested the man **whose** *accomplice confessed everything.*

RELATIVE CLAUSES 271

If we unpack this complex sentence, we would find that the antecedent of *whose* is *the man* but we would have to express it in possessive form:

The police arrested the man.
The man's accomplice confessed everything.

Since *whose* is a determiner, it appears in the normal determiner position in the noun phrase, as shown in Figure 15.8.

FIGURE 15.8

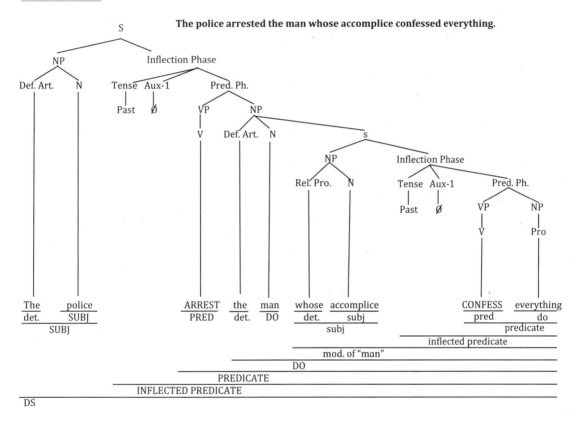

A RECAP OF RELATIVE PRONOUN USAGE

TABLE 15.1: RELATIVE PRONOUNS

Restrictive Relative Clauses

	Subject	Object	Object of a Stranded Preposition	Object of a Pied-Piped Preposition
Human Antecedent	who	who/whom/Ø	who/whom/Ø	whom
Non-Human Antecedent	that	that/Ø	that/Ø	which

Non-Restrictive Relative Clauses

	Subject	Object	Object of a Stranded Preposition	Object of a Pied-Piped Preposition
Human Antecedent	who	who/whom	who/whom	whom
Non-Human Antecedent	which[1]	which	which	which

EXERCISES

A. The following sentences are written completely without punctuation. Rewrite each of the sentences, identifying the relative clause in each sentence. Be sure that your punctuation indicates whether the relative clause is a restrictive or non-restrictive clause.

    Examples: *The sign that they tore down had valuable information* → *The sign that they tore down had valuable information.*

    "that they tore down" is a restrictive relative clause and commas are not necessary to separate it from the main clause.

    The President and his family reside at the White House which stands at 1600 Pennsylvania Ave. in Washington DC → *The President and his family reside at the White House, which stands at 1600 Pennsylvania Ave. in Washington DC.*

---

1 *Which* could formerly be used for human antecedents, as in certain versions of the Lord's Prayer: *Our father, which art in heaven....*

"which stands at 1600 Pennsylvania Ave. in Washington DC." is a non-restrictive clause and it is separated from the main clause by commas.

1. The proposal that we accepted will not be effective until next year.
2. Cher who starred in *Moonstruck* in the early 1980s has had a career spanning more than three decades.
3. We have contacted the officer who you gave the report to.
4. My students who asked for extra work have been doing very well on the exams. (in this sentence, all of "my students" asked for extra work)
5. My students who asked for extra work have been doing very well on the exams. (in this sentence, only a portion of "my students" asked for extra work and they are the ones who have been doing well)
6. The Brooklyn Bridge which was built in 1883 spans the East River between Manhattan and Brooklyn.
7. The journal editor asked me to review an article that was written about the German language.
8. The tabloid story focused on Kate Middleton who married Prince William a few years ago.
9. During our vacation we will visit Montreal which is in the province of Quebec.
10. The tour guide who the company recognized with an award will become the new director of visitor education.

B. An important skill for understanding the syntax of relative clauses is the availability to conceive of the relative clause as an independent clause. As described in this chapter, that skill can be learned by "unpacking" relative clauses. Unpack the following sentences into two full, independent clauses.

Example: *The font that you chose for the poster is difficult to read.*

        a. The font is difficult to read.
        b. You chose the font for the poster.

1. We ordered the coffee that the café had been advertising.

    a. _____
    b. _____

2. The cardigan that was hanging on the clearance rack isn't there any longer.

    a. _____
    b. _____

3. The Normal Post Office, in which you can find boxes, packaging, and tape, will be closed on Sunday.

   a. _____
   b. _____

4. The frozen yogurt stand that opened downtown closed within three months of business.

   a. _____
   b. _____

5. The worker placed the merchandise on the shelf that stood next to the window.

   a. _____
   b. _____

6. Maria, whom you met in my office last week, has just recorded an album of her guitar solos.

   a. _____
   b. _____

7. I really never have liked the hat that you wore to the party.

   a. _____
   b. _____

8. New Mexico, which is located in the desert Southwest, has an official law admitting English and Spanish both as official languages.

   a. _____
   b. _____

9. They have just installed the program on my computer that I bought last month.

   a. _____
   b. _____

10. Jimmy Carter, who won the Nobel Peace Prize in 2002, was the governor of Georgia from 1971 to 1975.

   a. _____
   b. _____

C. Basing your answer on the grammatical function of the antecedent in the "unpacked" relative clauses in B, identity the relative pronoun in each sentence and determine the function of the relative pronoun in the original complex sentence.

   Rel. Pro.   Function

   1. _____
   2. _____
   3. _____
   4. _____
   5. _____
   6. _____
   7. _____
   8. _____
   9. _____
   10. _____

D. Make full form–function trees for the following sentences.

   1. The student who answered the question was reading the textbook before class.
   2. I would prefer the software that you described in our last meeting.
   3. The circumstances around which the confusion arose was unfortunate but comical.
   4. The trainer Molly recommended to me was showing off a new routine for leg muscles.
   5. Disappointingly, Amos has never received the promotion he has been counting on since December.
   6. Morrissey, whom we saw in concert last May, is coming back to The Arena in the fall.
   7. We invited the author whose book became a best-selling hit, but he declined our offer.
   8. The folder that contains this secret formula must be kept under lock and key at all times.
   9. The nervous spy had to give the familiar sign to the agent, who was waiting for him in the restaurant around the corner.
   10. At this point, I will not support any referendum the county commissioner puts up.

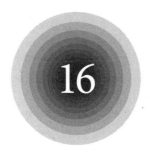

Noun Clauses

Noun clauses are so called because they serve various syntactic functions that are regularly filled by nouns. Thus a noun clause can be a subject, a direct object, an object of a preposition, or a subject complement. They do not commonly fulfill indirect object or object complement functions, although it is not impossible for them to do so.

By way of introduction to the concept of noun clauses, consider the following pair of sentences:

All students would be excused early.
The principal declared this.

If we focus for the moment on the second of these two sentences, we might ask what the relative pronoun *this* refers to. In answering that question, one would normally say that *this* refers to the entire sentence (proposition) *All students would be excused early*. We can then create a complex sentence by turning the first sentence into a noun clause and placing it "inside" the main clause:

*The principal declared **that all students would be excused early**.*

This is the essence of a noun clause: the placing of one proposition into a noun position within a larger proposition. So in the sentence above, the principal declared *something* and the *something* he declared was the entire proposition that all students would be excused early.

Recall that with both adverb and relative clauses, removal of the dependent clause left a fully grammatical sentence. For instance, if the adverbial clause in the following sentence is removed,

After the new parts are delivered, I will fix the mower.

a grammatically complete sentence remains:

I will fix the mower.

Similarly, if the relative clause is removed from the following sentence,

The cat that you found in the tree belongs to my neighbor.

a grammatically complete sentence remains:

The cat belongs to my neighbor.

Thus, the grammatically complete parts of those sentences that contain an adverbial or relative clause were referred to as "main clauses." But notice that when dealing with noun clauses, the removal of a noun clause does not leave a grammatically complete sentence. If the noun clause is removed from the sentence

The principal declared that all students would be dismissed early.

the remaining part of the sentence does not constitute a complete sentence:

*The principal declared.

Therefore, typically the part of the sentence that provides the base for the embedded noun clause is sometimes called the matrix clause. (The term "matrix clause" actually has a broader use than the base clause for an embedded noun clause.) There are three types of noun clauses that we will study in this chapter. Each is treated in turn below.[1]

TYPE I NOUN CLAUSES

A type I noun clause is one that makes a declaration; for the purposes of understanding the grammar of a type I noun clause, we can think of them as being "derived" from a declarative statement, like

---

1 The typology presented here is not exhaustive, and more advanced grammatical study would reveal more types, such as, for example, appositive noun clauses. Contrast the meaning between these two sentences:

*The idea **that reporters are not allowed in the hearing** is shameful.*
*The idea **that she presented in the meeting** was well-received.*

In the first sentence, the clause *that reporters not be allowed in the hearing* elaborates on what the *idea* is, while in the second sentence, the clause *that she presented in the meeting* tells us which *idea* is being referred to. The first is another type of noun clause, an appositive clause, since it gives information about a noun in the sentence, while the second is a relative clause (see Chapter 15) since it restricts or defines which idea is meant.

the example we saw in the last section. Let's consider another example:

The lock on the door had been broken.
Mary saw this.

As in the example before, if we ask what *this* in the second sentence refers to, we would understand that it refers to the entire proposition *the lock on the door had been broken*. Thus we can subsume the entire structure of the first sentence into the second sentence by making it a noun clause:

Mary saw **that the lock on the door had been broken**.

The problem that presents itself regularly when analyzing noun clauses is its function within the sentence. The sentence-combining approach taken so far in this chapter provides a straightforward way of determining that function. Consider again the demonstrative pronoun *this* in the sentence *Mary saw this*. It is fairly easy to recognize that *this* is the direct object of the verb *saw*, as in Figure 16.1.

FIGURE 16.1

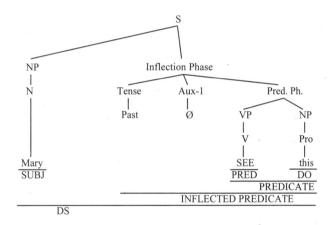

Since noun clauses have noun functions, it is logical to conclude, then, that when the demonstrative pronoun *this* is replaced by an entire clause, a noun clause, that noun clause will have *the same function* as the demonstrative pronoun that it replaced, as in Figure 16.2.

FIGURE 16.2

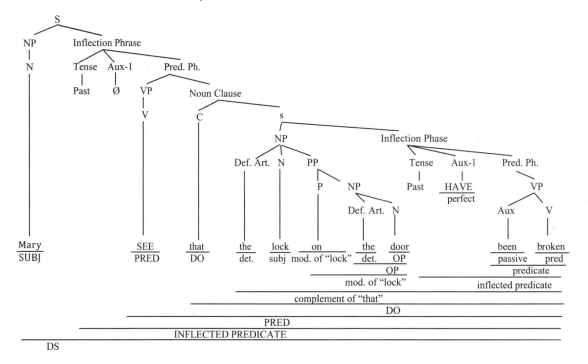

From the tree in Figure 16.2, we can see that the noun clause *that the lock on the door had been broken* is the direct object within the matrix clause *Mary saw*.

While the example above shows a type I noun clause as a direct object, type I noun clauses can be subjects as well (see Figure 16.3):

The plants thrived in the heat.
***This** produced an unusually large yield.*

***That the plants thrived in the heat** produced an unusually large yield.*

FIGURE 16.3

That the plants thrived in the heat produced an unusually large yield.

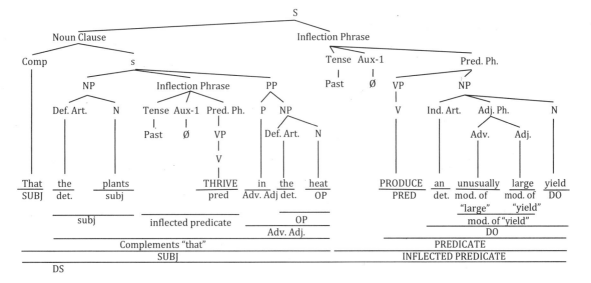

Notice that type I noun clauses are introduced by the complementizer *that* when they serve as the subject or as the direct object.

> ***That*** *the plants thrived in the heat produced an unusually large yield.*
> *Mary saw **that** the lock on the door had been broken.*

When a type I noun clause serves as the direct object, however, *that* is often omitted—what we understand to be a Ø-complementizer (and see Chapter 14 on adverbial clauses for the general structure of complementizers):

> *Anyone could see **that** he needed help.*
> *Anyone could see Ø he needed help.*

When the type I noun clause functions as a direct object with an omitted complementizer, the complementizer position is maintained and filled by Ø, as in Figure 16.4.

FIGURE 16.4

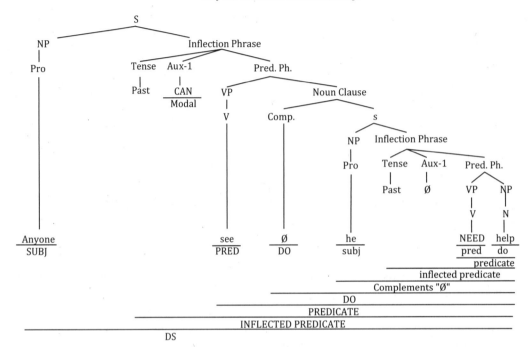

When a type I noun clause functions as the object of a preposition, we cannot use *that* as the complementizer; instead, the compound complementizer *the fact that* is used:

We needed a new sink in the bathroom.
*My husband and I talked about **this**.*

*My husband and I talked about **the fact that** we needed a new sink in the bathroom.*

The fact that is treated like a single complementizer, as seen in Figure 16.5.

NOUN CLAUSES 283

FIGURE 16.5

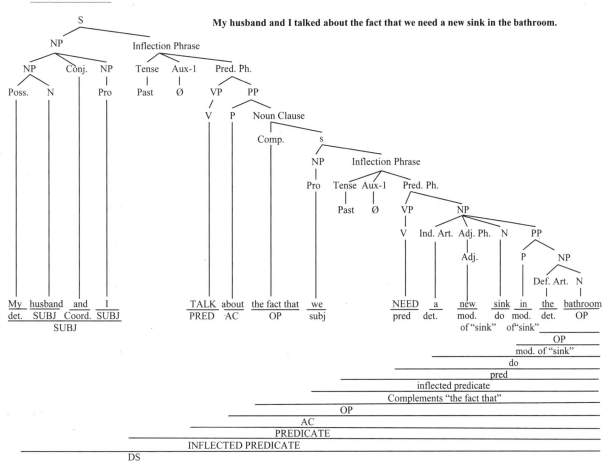

In fact, in Modern English it seems that a number of speakers/writers reject the type I noun clause as a subject, finding sentences such as *That the books were removed angered the faculty* odd-sounding. Often speakers/writers prefer to use the compound complementizer *the fact that* for such uses of the type I noun clause:

The fact that the books were removed angered the faculty.

The reason that a noun clause as subject is awkward to many English writers/speakers likely has to do with their propensity to avoid "heavy" constructions at the beginning of the sentence. *The fact that*, although now best analyzed as a single complementizer, clearly has its origin in the noun *the fact* followed by a clause, *that*.... Thus, at least originally, *the fact* as a simple noun phrase could be analyzed as the subject of *angered*.

However, in avoidance of heavy subjects, such as noun clauses, speakers/writers may also use a variation known as the **anticipatory-*it* construction** (Chapter 6). The anticipatory-*it* construction moves the type I noun clause to the position in the sentence following the main clause and puts a meaningless (or "dummy") *it* as the grammatical subject; the function of *it* is to anticipate the noun clause subject:

*It angered the faculty **that the books were removed**.*

It may be said that the type I noun clause is not fully integrated into the grammatical system of English. As presented in Chapter 12, yes/no questions are formed by inverting the subject and Aux-1, and this is true even when the subject is very "heavy":

***The very heavy snowfall that occurred on Monday morning** is still creating problems for drivers two days later.*
*Is **the very heavy snowfall that occurred on Monday morning** still creating problems for drivers two days later?*

In the first of these examples, the subject is an NP with an Adj. Ph. modifier and a relative clause modifier, thus making it a relatively "heavy" NP. However, it still inverts Aux-1 in question formation, as seen in the second of these examples.

However, noun-clause subjects do not invert in the same way:

That the civic parade has been canceled is indicative of the shortage of funds available for public events.
*Is that the civic parade has been canceled indicative of the shortage of funds available for public events?

Note the ungrammaticality of the inverted noun-clause subject in the second of these examples. In such cases, anticipatory *it* is required:

Is it indicative of the shortage of funds available for public events that the civic parade has been canceled?

Finally, type I noun clauses can also be subject complements:

Alex cheated on the exam.
*The problem was **this**.*

*The problem was **that Alex cheated on the exam**.*

When a type I noun clause functions as a subject complement, the complementizer is either expressed as *that* or left out as Ø (see Figure 16.6).

The problem was Ø Alex cheated on the exam.[1]

FIGURE 16.6

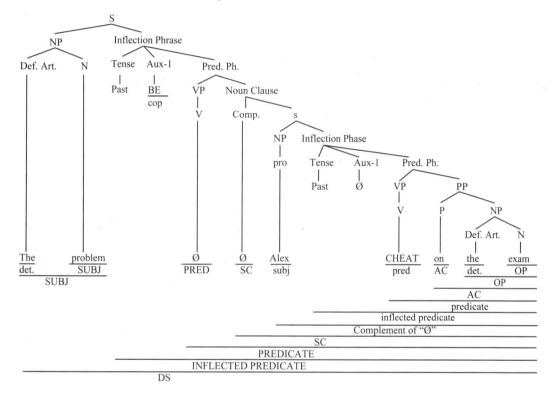

The problem was Alex cheated on the exam.

TYPE II NOUN CLAUSES

Type II noun clauses can be thought of as being derived from yes/no questions. For example:

Was Alex attending the class?
*We wondered **this**.*[2]

---

1 Note that the prepositional phrase "on the exam" is an adverbial complement, not an adverbial adjunct. If it were an adverbial it would mean that Alex's body was somehow located on the exam, i.e., the place where the subject does the predicate. In this case, however, *on the exam* is the location of the cheating only and thus completes the sense of the predicate.
2 In some grammars, these are also called "indirect questions."

In the same combining strategy that we used above, if we ask what *this* in the second sentence refers to, we would acknowledge that it refers to the entire proposition expressed in the first sentence, *Was Alex attending the class?*, which is a yes/no question. Thus, we could combine the two sentences by subsuming the entire first question into the second sentence (see Figure 16.7):

We wondered whether Alex was attending the class.

And, again, we can note that the function of the demonstrative *this* in the original sentence is the function of the newly created noun clause; both function as direct objects.

FIGURE 16.7

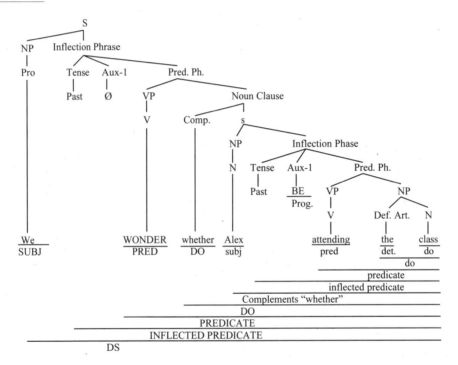

When a type II noun clause functions as a direct object, it may be introduced by the complementizer *whether*, as in the example above; however, the complementizer *if* may also be used:

*We wondered **if** Alan won the prize.*

Like type I noun clauses, type II noun clauses may also function as subjects in a sentence (see Figure 16.8).

Do you know the murderer?
This intrigues me.

Whether you know the murderer intrigues me.

FIGURE 16.8

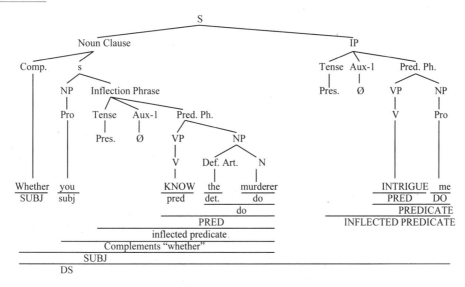

Note, however, that when the type II noun clause serves as the subject of a sentence, *whether* is preferred for formal registers of English. However, some speakers accept *if* as a complementizer in such sentences:

?If you know the murderer intrigues me.

If as a complementizer for a type II noun clause functioning as a subject is to be avoided in formal language use.

A type II noun clause can also be the object of a preposition, as in Figure 16.9.

Did Virgil intend a satirical allegory of Imperial Rome?
*We argued about **this**.*

*We argued about **whether Virgil intended a satirical allegory of Imperial Rome**.*[1]

FIGURE 16.9

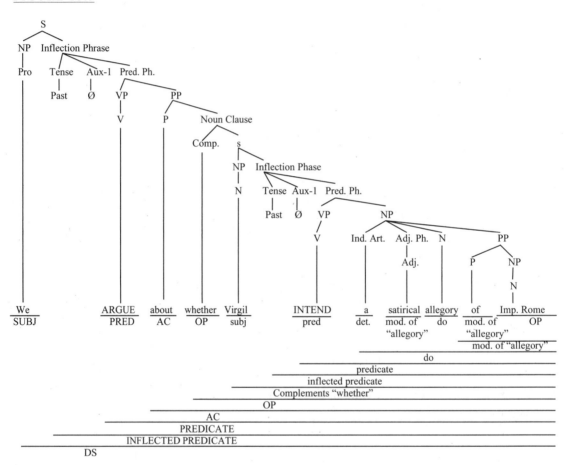

Only the complementizer *whether* may be used when the type II noun clause is the object of a preposition.

---

1 Note that in the tree diagram for this sentence, I have treated "Imperial Rome" as a single proper noun.

TYPE III NOUN CLAUSES[1]

Using the same derivation model as we have for the type I and type II noun clauses above, we can say that type III noun clauses are derived from *wh*-questions. On the one hand, this means that the kinds of words that can introduce a type III noun clause are many because they include all of the *wh*-words and *wh*-expressions that we use to make *wh*-questions (see Chapter 12). However, unlike the type I and II noun clauses, the *wh*-word in the type III noun clause is not a complementizer. Instead, the *wh*-word, like *wh*-words in *wh*-questions or like relative pronouns in relative clauses, has a grammatical function inside its clause. Consider the following examples of *wh*-questions turned into type III noun clauses, functioning as subject, DO, and OP, respectively (for tree diagrams of the first two, see Figures 16.10–16.11).

Where do they live?
***This** is a mystery.*

= ***Where they live** is a mystery.*[2]

FIGURE 16.10

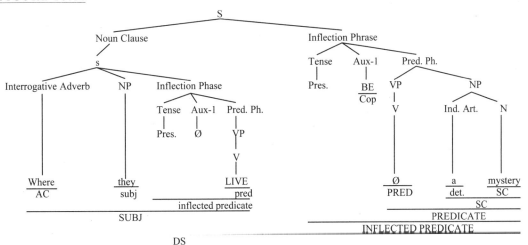

---

1 The scheme presented in this book concerning Type III noun clauses simplifies the topic a bit. Some of the noun clauses treated under this type would include what some call "headless relative clauses," as in *We didn't like what he said*. The idea is that there is a noun-idea, something like *We didn't like the thing that he said*. In that analysis the noun head *thing* and the relative pronoun are said to be merged as *what*. Others also consider certain noun clauses treated under this type as indirect or embedded questions, as in *They asked what he said*, and the chapter does not treat subordinated exclamatives: *We were surprised by **what a good dancer he was***. Certainly greater distinction in analysis is possible at more advanced levels of grammatical study.

2 Note that in Figure 16.10, the *wh*-word, *where*, has been labeled as an adverbial complement in its clause. This analysis is due to the fact that the verb *live* takes on a somewhat different meaning between senses such as *He lives* and *He lives in a brick house*. In the first sentence, *live* means something like "exist," while in the second sentence it means "reside." Given that the location makes such a difference in the meaning of the verb, it is analyzed to have a more integral syntactic relationship with it, thus a complement (as opposed to an adjunct).

How did he do it?
*I asked **this**.*

= *I asked **how he did it**.*

Why are they fighting?
*We wonder about **this**.*

= *We wonder about **why they are fighting**.*

FIGURE 16.11

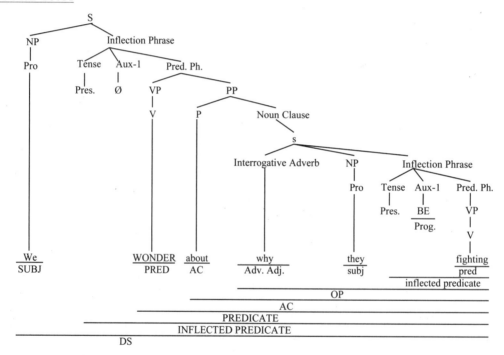

As in *wh*-questions, *why*, *when*, *how*, and *where* have an adverbial adjunct or adverbial complement function (see again Chapter 12). *Who* and *what*, however, will have a noun function. Consider the following:

Who called?
*We asked **this**.*

If we make the *wh*-question into a type III noun clause, it will replace *this* in the second sentence, a process we have done many times. Since *this* is a DO in the second sentence, it stands to reason that the converted noun clause will also have the function of a DO.

*We asked **who called**.*

However, when we want to determine the function of *who* inside of the noun clause, we have to rely on the tests that we used for determining the function of *who* and *what* in *wh*-questions that we learned in Chapter 10. Consider again the original question: *Who called?* If we answer that question, then the function of the NP that answers the question will also be the function of the word *who*. *Who called? Raymond called. Raymond* is the subject of the answer, so *who* was the subject of the original question as well, and therefore, by extrapolation, we know that *who* is also the subject in the noun clause (see Figure 16.12).

FIGURE 16.12

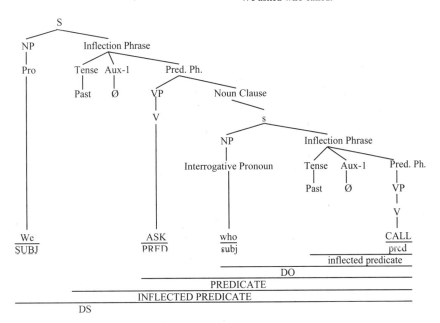

Let's consider one more example:

What was he eating?
*We asked **this**.*

*We asked **what he was eating**.*

There are two questions to solve here before I can make a diagram: (1) What is the function of the *wh*-word *what*? (2) What is the function of the noun clause? The first question can be answered by providing an answer to the original *wh*-question: *What was he eating? He was eating soup.* Since the answer to the *wh*-question, *soup*, is a direct object, we know that *what* in the original question was the direct object; it will remain a direct object throughout the noun-clause derivation. In order to answer the second question, we will note that the demonstrative pronoun *this* (which the whole noun clause will substitute for) is also a direct object; therefore, the noun clause, after it is derived and put into the second sentence, is also a direct object. Don't be confused at this point: *what* is the direct object inside the noun clause, but the entire noun clause is the direct object of the whole sentence—those facts are unrelated (for the diagram, see Figure 16.13).

FIGURE 16.13

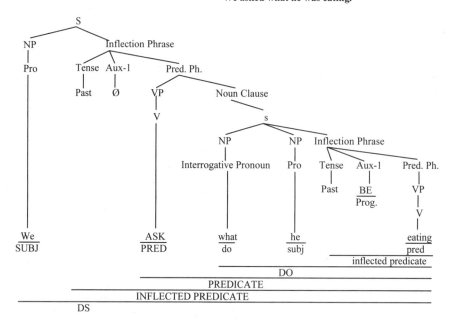

REPORTED SPEECH AND TENSE SHIFTING

Noun clauses are closely related to the topic of reported speech; in fact, traditional grammarians often consider reported speech clauses to be noun clauses. In direct speech reporting, a person attempts to capture exactly what another says, said, asks, asked, inquires, inquired, exclaims, exclaimed, and so forth:

She said, "I am late."

In this case, *I am late* is exactly what *she said*. Note the use of *I*, referring to the person who made the original statement, and the use of the simple present *am*, the tense in which the statement was originally made. However, if I report what she said, then the statement becomes subsumed within the matrix of the *she said* portion of the sentence. In that world, the speaker of the statement is referred to in the third person and the time is shifted into the past. That will cause some very specific changes in the form of the report:

She said that she was late.

I is converted to *she* since now I am talking about her, and *am* is converted to *was*. Since the verb of reporting, *asked*, is in the past tense, it shifts the entire statement into the past time as well. A rather lost art of grammatical style, such shifting shows superb control over verb choice and lends an air of authority to one's writing. Table 16.1 shows the relationship between the verb in the matrix and the verb in the reported speech clause.

TABLE 16.1: VERBS IN REPORTED SPEECH

Verb in Matrix	Verb in Original Statement		Verb in Reported Speech
Any present verb form	Present	→	Present
	Present Progressive	→	Present Progressive
	Present Perfect	→	Present Perfect
	Present-Perfect Progressive	→	Present-Perfect Progressive
	Present Modal	→	Present Modal
	Past	→	Past
	Past Progressive	→	Past Progressive
	Past Perfect	→	Past Perfect
	Past-Perfect Progressive	→	Past-Perfect Progressive
	Present Modal	→	Present Modal
	Past Modal	→	Past Modal
Any past verb form	Present	→	Past
	Present Progressive	→	Past Progressive
	Present Perfect	→	Past Perfect
	Present-Perfect Progressive	→	Past-Perfect Progressive
	Past Progressive	→	Past-Perfect Progressive
	Past-Perfect	→	Past Perfect
	Past Perfect Progressive	→	Past-Perfect Progressive
	Present Modal	→	Past Modal
	Past Modal	→	Perfective Modal

Thus, for example, in the direct quote

Mary was saying, "I have forgotten my keys!" over and over.

the matrix verb is past progressive and the verb in the speech to be reported is in the present perfect. Thus, the present perfect verb form will be shifted to past perfect in reporting (along with the expected shifting of pronominal reference):

*Mary was saying that **she had forgotten** her keys over and over.*

In the case that the verb in the reported speech is thought to still be true at the time of utterance or writing, the verb may not be shifted, as in the case of general/scientific truths:

*The teacher explained that the Earth **moves** around the sun.*

EXERCISES

A. Type I Noun Clauses. Combine the following sentences, making the first sentence into a noun clause by replacing *this*. Take special notice of the grammatical function of the noun clause after the sentences are combined and state what that function is.

1. The certificate was hung on the wall next to the window.
   Luckily, the visitors noticed this.

   _____
   _____

   Function of the noun clause: _____

2. Louis's panoramic photograph of the city appeared in the magazine.
   This surprised everyone.

   _____
   _____

   Function of the noun clause: _____

3. Faisal was smirking triumphantly at the other team.
   The judges of the tournament had a discussion about this.

   _____

Function of the noun clause: _____

4. Laurent was wearing a dark corduroy jacket.
   We knew this.

   _____
   _____

   Function of the noun clause: _____

5. His friends arrived safely at the airport in Rome.
   This was good news.

   _____
   _____

   Function of the noun clause: _____

6. That mix of colors was hurting her eyes.
   This seemed unlikely.

   _____
   _____

   Function of the noun clause: _____

7. The mountain cabin must be rented for a minimum of a week.
   The couple had not planned on this.

   _____
   _____

   Function of the noun clause: _____

B. Make full form–function trees for the combined sentences in exercise A.

C. Type II Noun Clauses. Combine the following sentences, making the first sentence into a noun clause. Take special notice of the grammatical function of the noun clause after the sentences are combined, and state what that function is.

1. Did he leave because he was angry?
   We asked this.

   _____
   _____

   Function of the noun clause: _____

2. Were the most expensive items saved from the fire?
   This is still not determined.

   _____
   _____

   Function of the noun clause: _____

3. Did the gardener create those wonderful topiaries?
   The host had not mentioned this.

   _____
   _____

   Function of the noun clause: _____

4. Has the new series debuted on television?
   The announcement was unclear about this.

   _____
   _____

   Function of the noun clause: _____

5. Should they get a new tattoo?
   They couldn't decide on this.

   _____
   _____

   Function of the noun clause: _____

6. Is my painting bigger than the size that was stipulated in the announcement?
   The panel will disregard this.

   _____
   _____

   Function of the noun clause: _____

7. Does Armin regret his decision now?
   This will never be told to Maya.

   _____
   _____

   Function of the noun clause: _____

D. Make full form–function trees for the combined sentences in Exercise C.

E. Type III Noun Clauses. Combine the following sentences, making the first sentence into a noun clause. Take special notice of the grammatical function of the noun clause after the sentences are combined, and state what that function is.

1. What is the model of that car?
   Genesis is going to ask this.

   _____
   _____

   Function of the noun clause: _____

2. Where did Alegra find the cologne?
   This was the topic of her exchange with Diedre.

   _____
   _____

   Function of the noun clause: _____

3. Why did the brave knight stand on the back of his horse?
   Historians have been debating this for decades.

   _____

_____

Function of the noun clause: _____

4. Who left these tennis shoes in the locker room?
   The custodian asked Jose about this. (Note that in the answer, you probably will omit the word *about*.)

_____
_____

Function of the noun clause: _____

5. What did you buy him for his birthday?
   This will remain a secret until June.

_____
_____

Function of the noun clause: _____

6. Who did Stacy give the program to?
   I do not know this.

_____
_____

Function of the noun clause: _____

7. When did Vince unchain the bike from the tree?
   I am not sure about this. (Note that in the answer, you probably will omit the word *about*.)

_____
_____

Function of the noun clause: _____

F. Make full form–function trees for the combined sentences in Exercise E.

Infinitive and Participle Phrases

INFINITIVES

In Chapter 8, we saw that the infinitive was made by combining *to* and the base form of the verb. In fact, however, that was the **simple infinitive**, and in this chapter we will learn the forms and uses of that infinitive as well as the several periphrastic infinitives that are possible in English.

FORMS OF THE INFINITIVE

By definition, infinitives cannot show tense since they are non-finite. However, they can show aspect through their various forms. Additionally, infinitives can be in the active or passive voice, as seen in Table 17.1.

TABLE 17.1: FORMS OF THE INFINITIVE

Active

Simple	*Progressive*	*Perfect*	*Perfect-Progressive*
to write	to be writing	to have written	to have been writing

Passive

Simple	*Progressive*	*Perfect*	*Perfect-Progressive*
to be written	X	to have been written	X

One can imagine what the forms of the passive progressive and passive perfect progressive would be: *to be being written* and *to have been being written*. But the forms, while not entirely impossible, are not at all common and would likely be rejected by most as bad style.

Aspect among infinitive forms is a matter of the relation between the main verb, the infinitive form, and adverbials that may appear in the sentence. The simple infinitive, both passive and active, commonly signals a habitual action that coincides with the main verb:

> Jack hates **to write** memos.

In this sentence, the action of writing memos is habitual in so far as each time that Jack must do so, he hates doing it (and since *hate* is a stative verb of emotion, we may also say that he hates writing memos even during those times he is not actively engaged in writing one).

The progressive infinitive expresses progressive aspect, that is, an action ongoing at some reference time (see again Chapter 8). That point of reference is established by the main verb together with various other temporal expressions in the sentence:

> Jack wanted **to be finishing up** his dissertation by now.

The infinitive *to be finishing up* occurs (or would occur) at a point in the past delineated by the past tense time of the main verb and the adverbial expression *by now*. However, since the specific point of reference is established by a sometimes-complex set of time relations, the ongoing reference can easily be set up in any time frame:

> He really **hopes to be feeling** better tomorrow.

In this sentence, the time orientation is future, and the progressive infinitive is happening at a specific future reference point, namely tomorrow.

The perfect infinitive is used when the action, state, or event happens (and is completed) before another point of reference. That point of reference will be expressed in the collusion of time expressions in the sentence such that the relationship between the perfect infinitive and the reference point may be past-before-past:

> (said on Wednesday following the Monday referred to in the sentence): *Mr. Markum planned to have finished before Monday.*

Or the reference point may be future, as in the following example:

> Jackie will claim to have bought everything.

In this case, Jackie's claim will be preceded by her buying everything, whether it is true or not.

The perfect-progressive infinitives, not unlike the perfect-progressive finite verbs forms (see Chapter 8), are used to show that an action, event, or situation begins prior to some reference point and continues up until that reference point, usually uninterrupted:

The CEO was reported to have been embezzling funds from the company for more than 10 years.

In this case, the CEO's embezzling began at some point in the past and continued on for some ten years afterwards.

FORMS OF THE PARTICIPLE

In Chapter 8, we learned the forms of the simple active and the simple passive participles. In that chapter, we saw the use of those participles in creating compound verb forms. The participles, however, have a number of periphrastic forms and uses. They may be used as a modifying structure in an adverbial or adjectival function, and the simple active participle also has a special noun function traditionally referred to as a **gerund**. The active and passive participles have the forms shown in Table 17.2.

TABLE 17.2: FORMS OF THE PARTICIPLE

Active Participle

Simple	*Progressive*	*Perfect*	*Perfect-Progressive*
writing	X	having written	having been writing

Passive Participle

Simple	*Progressive*	*Perfect*	*Perfect-progressive*
written	being written	having been written	having been being written

The active progressive form of the participle does not exist for most English speakers. However it is not impossible to find instances of active progressive participle uses, such as *being going*. The passive perfect-progressive participle is also rare, and while it is a more likely form than the active progressive participle form, its use may be regarded as bad style by some.

Aspect among the participles is similar to aspect among infinitives. The simple active and passive participles generally show that the action, situation, or event expressed in the participle is contemporaneous with the time of the main verb, most frequently as a habitual or gnomic[1] situation:

> **Memorizing** 10 new words a day, Alia prepared for the GRE in the several weeks leading up to the exam.
> **Displayed** at every science fair, the diagram of the atom shows a nucleus of protons and neutrons with several orbiting electrons.

---

[1] The term "gnomic" means that the action, situation or event is always true, such as statements of science, such as *The Earth is round*.

In many cases, however, the simple passive participle shows that the action, situation, or event expressed by the participle occurred before the situation set up by the main verb and is sometimes the cause for the later situation.

> **Acquired** by more than 400 million people as a native language, Spanish is the second most spoken language in the world.

In this example, the acquisition of Spanish has occurred (several times) in order to make it the second most spoken language in the world. The meaning of the passive participle in these situations is thus similar to the finite perfect forms which we saw to express perfective aspect, discussed in Chapter 7. In fact, some grammars refer to the passive participle as the "perfect" participle.

From the chart on participle forms it can be seen that there is no specific progressive active participle. Most frequently, the simple active form covers the progressive meaning:

> Seemingly **flipping** through a magazine, the spy kept track of her target's every purchase.

As the spy kept track of her target's purchases, she *was flipping* through a magazine. In other words, the simple active participle in this sentence denotes a progressive activity. If one wishes to highlight the progressive aspect with a passive participle, one may use the progressive passive participle:

> While **being held** prisoner for over 30 years, the political dissident was subjected to regular interrogations by the secret police.

Although the progressive passive participle can be quite useful in foregrounding progressivity, as in the example above, it should be used cautiously because often the simple passive participle is adequate for expressing the meaning when there is no progressive meaning involved:

> **Being elected** by more than 70 percent of the voters, the candidate won the election by attracting a majority from every demographic group.

In this case, *elected* is sufficient since the meaning of the sentence is to report on a past and completed event without reason to "zero in" on the moment of election.

The perfect forms of both the active and passive participles are used to emphasize the completedness of the action, situation, or event expressed in the participle:

> **Having been charged** with a felony, the released prisoner found it difficult to find gainful employment.
> **Having enjoyed** the evening with her friends, Valerie returned home in high spirits.

The perfect-progressive active participle is used to focus on the ongoing nature and completedness of the action, situation, or event expressed by the verb in the participle:

> **Having been studying** for more than four hours, Jackson took a break and played his favorite video game.

In this sentence, Jackson was studying continuously before he stopped and began a different activity. Again, while the perfect-progressive passive participle can be quite useful stylistically, it is probably best to use it with a "less is more" aesthetic, that is, only if the focus on the verb activity is really desirable.

THE PHRASE-CLAUSE BOUNDARY

The traditional concept of a sentence is not always useful in linguistics since it depends too much on notions of prescription, notions which, like most prescriptions, are often unprincipled, capricious, and ultimately somewhat random.

Instead, in linguistics we tend to be interested in predication as the core of clausal meaning. In simplest terms, a predication is the linguistic act of saying something about something. In the following sentence, we have one predication:

Jack slept.

In the next sentence, however, we have two predications:

Jack clapped while the clowns danced.

In this case, we have said something about Jack (i.e., that he clapped) and something about the clowns (i.e., that they danced). Each of those predications is expressed in its own clause through finite verb forms.

It should not be assumed, however, that only finite verb forms (or finite clauses as is sometimes said) can make a predication; indeed, infinitives (and as we will see soon, participles as well) can make predications. For example:

Jack wanted to leave.

The sentence makes two predications: Jack wanted and Jack [leave]. (Note that I have placed *leave* in brackets to refer to a more abstract level of predication that is made between the infinitive verb and the subject of the sentence.) In this sentence, however, there is only one noun, so it serves as the "subject" of both predications, [want] and [leave].

However, in other cases the infinitive may have its own "subject." (Note carefully that subject here is in quotations because it is not the grammatical subject—it is the logical subject; grammatical subjects trigger agreement, which logical "subjects" of non-finite verb forms do not in English.)

Jack wanted Mary to leave.

Again, we have two predications; *wanting*, which is predicated of Jack, and *leaving*, which is predicated of Mary.

In traditional grammar, the sentence above is analyzed as *Jack* = Subject, *wanted* = Predicate, *Mary* = DO, and *to leave* is called an infinitival complement. In non-traditional grammatical theory, or linguistic theory, the analysis is that *Mary to leave* constitutes its own "clause" because it makes a predication. In this book we take a sort of middle ground between these two approaches: on the one hand we will accept the predication of the entire string *Mary to leave* and on the other hand we will also accept Mary as the logical "subject." Thus, we will acknowledge that its status as clause is special because it does not contain a finite verb, which was our earlier definition (see Chapter 3). We will also recognize its status as a phrase. So in our analysis, *Mary to leave* is an infinitive phrase coming off the main predicate phrase. The infinitive phrase is immediately identified as an S, so that we can account for its clause-like aspects. Inside of the S, we have an NP and a small predicate phrase; the NP is realized as the noun *Mary*, the function of which is "subject" (in quotation marks). Coming off the other side of S is a predicate phrase. Note carefully that there is no inflection phrase, since infinitives are non-finite. From that predicate phrase is a verb phrase, made up in turn of the particle *to*, and the base form *leave*. The word *to*, which marks the infinitive (and is labeled as "infinitival marker") is an aux(iliary) off of the VP. While it may seem odd to consider "to" an auxiliary, it is a common treatment in many theoretical grammars, the reasons for which we will not review here. The entire infinitive phrase has the function of DO of the main predicate in the sentence, *wanted*. A form–function tree of this sort is shown in Figure 17.1.

FIGURE 17.1

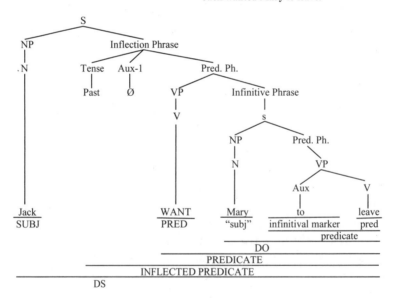

The analysis for the sentence *Jack wanted to leave* is essentially the same. However, we say that the "subject" of the infinitive is omitted because it is the same as the subject of the finite verb. Therefore, an NP position is placed in the infinitive phrase, but it is realized as Ø, as shown in Figure 17.2.

FIGURE 17.2

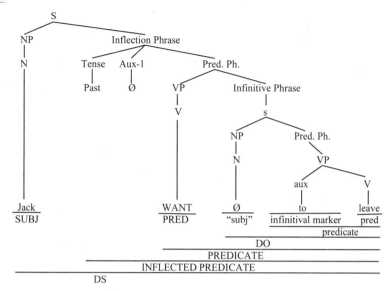

It is important to remember that since the "subject" of the infinitive is not a grammatical subject, because again only finite verbs have grammatical subjects, it appears in the object case when it is a pronoun (see Figure 17.3):

*Annette told **him** to wait.*

FIGURE 17.3

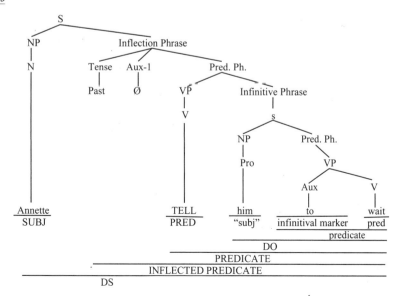

Because infinitives are essentially verbs, they have the ability to take complements of their own, like direct and indirect objects, subject complements, and adverbial complements. They can also take adverbial modifiers, like adverbial adjuncts. Thus in the sentence

Brian asked Gerald to sign the paper.

the paper is the direct object of the verb *sign*. In our analysis of the infinitive phrase, there is a layer of predicate phrase, and as in finite clauses, the complements extend from that layer of structure. The tree structure for *Brian asked Gerald to sign the paper* is shown in Figure 17.4.

FIGURE 17.4

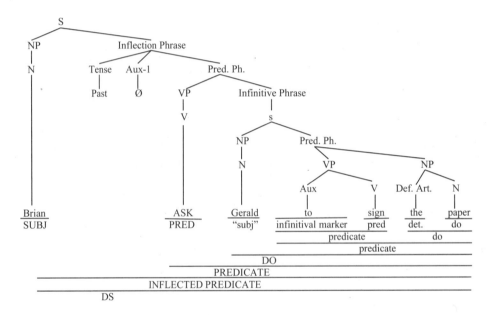

In the examples above, all of the infinitive phrases have been direct objects of the main predicate. However, it is possible for an infinitive phrase to be the subject in the main clause, sometimes without an expressed "subject" (mind the quotation marks!):

To love is a great joy.

At other times, the infinitive phrase will have an expressed "subject." In that case, the "subject" appears with the preposition *for*:

For Arno to sleep is a rare event.

In traditional grammar, *for Arno* is a prepositional phrase, the function of which is "subject." At first it may seem odd to have the function of a prepositional phrase as a subject of any kind, but it may be recalled from Chapter 6 that in fact it does happen. When we have a sentence like

In the cave is scary.

in the cave is a prepositional phrase and is the subject. While a PP as a grammatical subject, as in this sentence, is not generally found in formal language use, it is not wholly uncommon in spoken English. The tree diagram for *For Arno to sleep is a rare event* is seen in Figure 17.5.

FIGURE 17.5

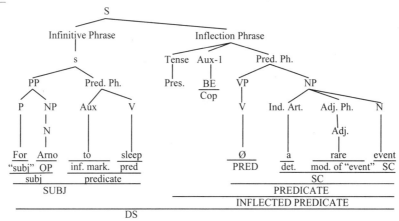

In the earlier example, *To love is a great joy*, there was no "subject" of the infinitive to love. We assume the subject would be "someone," "everyone," etc. However, as we have already seen in Figure 17.2, even when the subject is not expressed we include a branch for it, filled with Ø and still labeled as "subject." This is also true for infinitive phrases in subject position (see Figure 17.6).

FIGURE 17.6

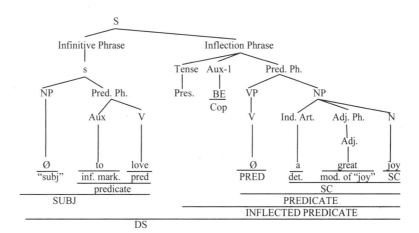

PARTICIPLE PHRASES AND GERUNDS

In the section above, we saw the infinitive phrase in the role of noun, either as direct object or subject. Participles also constitute phrases, and in this section we will look at participle phrases in their role of fulfilling noun functions. In terms of participle phrases fulfilling noun functions, we often encounter the term "gerund." "Gerund" is used with different definitions in grammatical treatments of English (and also other languages) and often not even consistently under the definition provided!

Here we will adopt what is probably the most typical definition for a gerund. A gerund is the simple active participle in the function typically fulfilled by an NP. In other words, it is the *-ing* form of the verb functioning as subject, direct object, object of a preposition, or subject complement. The following are examples of what we may consider gerunds in various syntactic funtions.

As a subject:

Writing is an important skill in college.

As a direct object:

I enjoy writing.

As a subject complement:

The problem is writing.

As the object of a preposition:

We talked about writing.

In the grammatical approach taken here, we will consider gerunds to be a participle phrase, thus maintaining a parallel status between infinitive phrases and participle phrases. In the same way that an infinitive phrase can be made up of a simple infinitive, as in Figure 17.2 or 17.6, so too can the simple active participle. Furthermore, just as we treated infinitives as a full predication with space allotted for a "subject," we will do so for (nearly all) participle phrases also. A diagram of a participle phrase containing only a simple active participle is given in Figure 17.7.

FIGURE 17.7

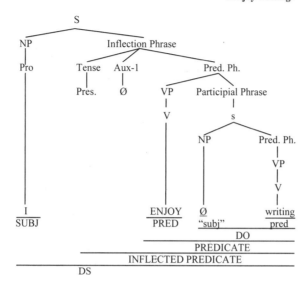

From the analysis you will find many things in common with the infinitive phrase. For example, the predicate phrase inside the gerund phrase is a non-finite verb phrase. Also notice that we have left a place for an NP as "subject" inside the participle phrase. This empty "subject" slot was also seen in infinitive phrases, and obviously it is there to accommodate a possible noun phrase structure to function as the "subject."

The "subject" of a gerund phrase is a contested area of grammar, by which I mean that what people actually do and what formal prescriptive grammarians say we should do are not aligned.

We enjoy John visiting.

In speech, this type of sentence creates no problem; we understand that what is enjoyed is the predication [John visit]. If one asked "What is it that you enjoy?" The answer would be "John visiting," not merely "John," which tells us that the whole predication is the direct object. The analysis of such a sentence is pretty straightforward. Note again that the "subject" of the participle appears in quotes since by definition a non-finite verb form such as a participle cannot have a grammatical subject in English (see Figure 17.8).

FIGURE 17.8

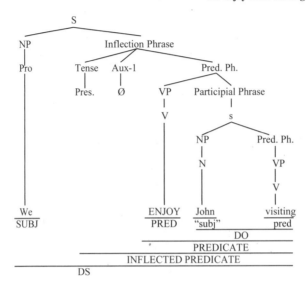

One problem is that prescriptive grammars require the "subject" of a participle phrase in a noun function to be in the possessive form. The reasoning behind that requirement is, however, faulty. The reasoning goes that since the gerund is a noun, it should be modified by a possessive form:

We enjoy John's visiting.

However, the participle phrase is not a noun. It is a non-finite verb form functioning as a subject, direct object, object of a preposition, etc. In other words, the confusion on the part of grammarians has been form–function conflation. The problem is especially acute in cases where the "subject" is a pronoun. The object form of the pronoun sounds quite normal to most speakers of English:

I resented him smoking.

The analysis for such gerund phrases is again quite straightforward, as seen in Figure 17.9.

FIGURE 17.9

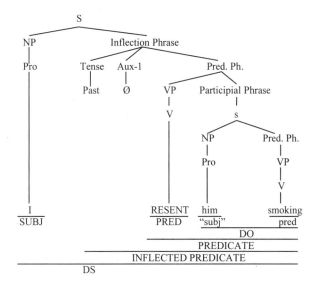

The prescribed form with the possessive determiner is likely to sound overly formal to many modern-day users of English:

I resented his smoking.

Perhaps, however, one can discern a difference in meaning in so far as *I resented him smoking* seems to focus on the person, while *I resented his smoking* focuses on the activity, so both can be considered acceptable.

THE PARTICIPLE-NOUN CONTINUUM

Some participles become highly conventionalized and thus become nouns in their own right, as for example *reading*. To say that a participle has become conventionalized as a noun means that it takes the fuller set of nominal morphology and syntactic possibilities. While it is arguable that *reading* has become more conventionalized as a noun, *skiing* probably has not, at least not to the same degree. Note, for instance, that *reading* can appear with the indefinite article *a*, but *skiing* cannot:

A reading of Thoreau
*A skiing of the Alps

Also, *reading* can be plural and appear with a quantifier, whereas *skiing* cannot:

Several original readings of that text
*Several dangerous skiings of that slope

However, all participles can be less or more noun-like. In the previous section, we saw examples of the participle as it formed predications, together with a "subject." However, participles can also appear in phrases along with the definite article. In that use it is generally followed by an *of*-phrase. That *of*-phrase may express the logical "subject" or an object of the gerund:

The running of the bulls. (*bulls* is the logical "subject" of run)
The lighting of the lamps. (*lamps* is the logical "direct object" of light)

The greater "nouniness," if you will, of the *the* + participle construction may be sensed by comparing the following:

Jim's ringing the bell every morning was a town ritual.
The ringing of the bell every morning by Jim was a town ritual.

In fact, since the focus has become the action of the ringing and not who is doing the action, the second sentence is most likely to omit the agent phrase *by Jim*:

The ringing of the bell every morning was a town ritual.

COMPLEMENTS AND ADJUNCTS IN INFINITIVE AND PARTICIPLE PHRASES

In our investigation of infinitive and participle phrases, we have noted that they may contain a "subject" (again mind the quotes). However, as mentioned in passing earlier, participles and infinitives can also take complements like DOs, IOs, SCs, and ACs, as well as adjuncts.

Consider the following sentence:

Buying gifts during the holidays can become quite expensive.

In this sentence, the predicate is *can become quite expensive*. If we were to ask what that phrase is being predicated upon, we would conclude that it is *buying gifts during the holidays*. In other words, *buying gifts during the holidays* is the subject of the entire sentence. The general structure of the sentence is that given in Figure 17.10.

INFINITIVE AND PARTICIPLE PHRASES   313

FIGURE 17.10

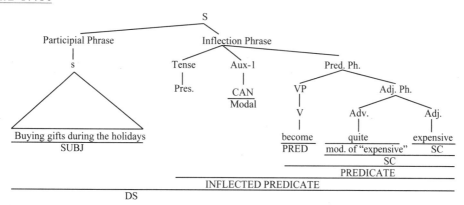

But what about the internal structure of the participle phrase? Actually, nothing about the phrase is different from the kinds of analyses we have been doing all along. *Gifts* is the direct object of *buying* and *during holidays* is an adverbial adjunct, modifying the entire participle phrase. The structure of the entire sentence is given in detail in Figure 17.11.

FIGURE 17.11

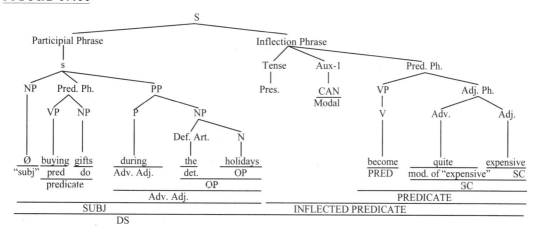

In fact the only difference between the internal structure of the participle phrase and predicates in simple sentences that we diagrammed much earlier is that the predicate phrase in the participle phrases is uninflected. The following examples illustrate further complements and adjuncts in participle and infinitive phrases (see Figures 17.12–17.14).

For us to give you this bad news hurts deeply.

FIGURE 17.12

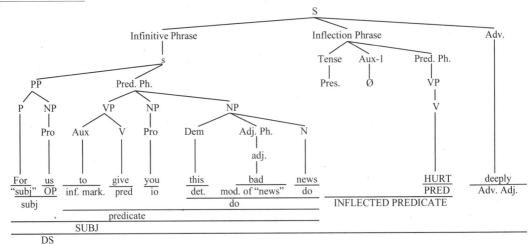

We do not approve of Gianni's bragging about his success.

FIGURE 17.13

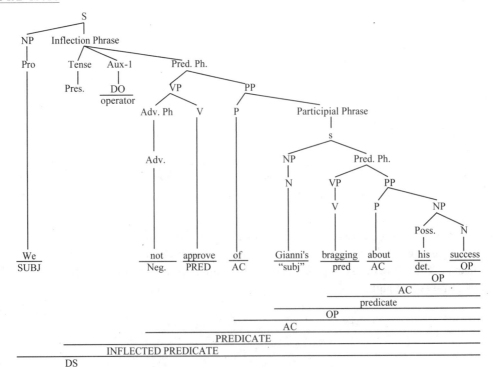

Andy refused to pick up his dirty clothes off the floor.

FIGURE 17.14

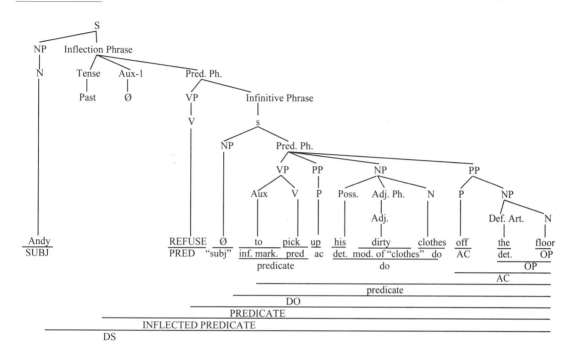

COMPOUND INFINITIVES AND PARTICIPLES

From the charts earlier in this chapter on infinitives and participles, we can see that compound aspectual forms are possible:

having seen
to be traveling
being viewed
having been convinced

Compound infinitives and participles have the same basic structure as other verb phrases. In each, we can identify a main or lexical verb, and the other components are auxiliary verbs. Since participle and infinitive phrases do not contain inflection phrases, all auxiliaries come from the predicate phrase, as shown in Figure 17.15.

FIGURE 17.15

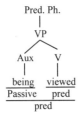
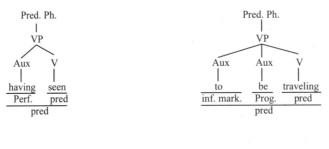
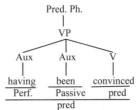

INFINITIVES AND PARTICIPLES IN MODIFYING FUNCTIONS

In this section we will look at participle and infinitive constructions that modify other parts of the sentence. First let's consider the modification of nouns.

The simple forms of the active and passive participles may modify a noun in the regular pre-noun position:

*the **walking** man*
*a **forgotten** song*

Infinitives, however, always follow the noun they modify:

*The thing **to do** was obvious to everyone.*
*A good person **to know** is Greg; he can fix anything.*

In the case that a simple active or a simple passive participle modifies the noun, we will follow the most straightforward kind of analysis, as shown in Figure 17.16. In that diagram, the participle is simply labeled as such and its function is to modify the noun. This analysis seems motivated in the sense that indeed nothing else may occur with a simple modifying participle in that position.[1]

---

[1] Note that the N in Figure 17.16 is simply labeled X since the NP is not contextualized within a larger syntactic setting.

FIGURE 17.16

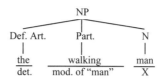

For infinitives, the situation is more complex, and we need to indicate that even a simple infinitive makes up a non-finite clause, as shown in Figure 17.17. That non-finite clause, then, is said to modify the noun it follows, in this case *person*. Again, this is motivated because the infinitive may have a "subject," as in Figure 17.18.

FIGURE 17.17

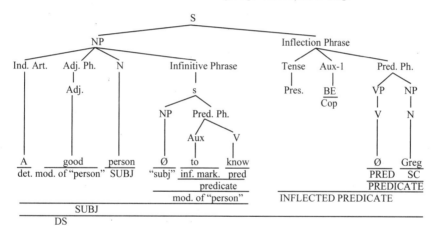

FIGURE 17.18

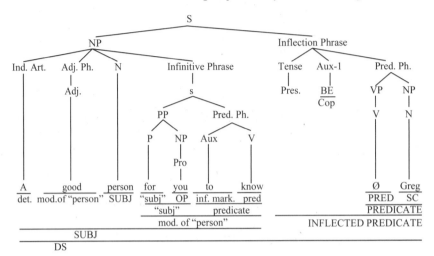

Even in a modifying function, participles and infinitives retain their ability to take complements and modifiers of their own, thus sometimes creating complex participle and infinitival phrases. For example, consider this sentence:

We saw Haley carrying a blue flag.

Here, *carrying* is a simple active participle, but since it is still a verb, it has its own direct object, *a blue flag*. Note carefully that when a participle has complements or adjuncts, it must follow the noun. These more complex participle phrases also have more elaborated analyses in form–function diagrams, as we will see below.

Similarly, the infinitive in the following sentence has a complement structure:

The woman to put in the race tomorrow is Breunta.

To put, while an infinitive modifying the noun *woman*, also has its own adverbial complement, *in the race*. It also has its own adverbial adjunct, *tomorrow*.

Diagramming such participle and infinitive phrases is similar to those seen earlier in this chapter; they lack an inflection phrase, as shown in Figures 17.19 and 17.20. In the case of participle phrases, the logical "subject" is understood to be the same noun it modifies, but we will continue to include a place for the "subject" for consistency's sake. Thus, in a sentence like *We saw Haley carrying a blue flag*, the logical "subject" of *carrying* is *Haley*.

INFINITIVE AND PARTICIPLE PHRASES 319

FIGURE 17.19

We saw Haley carrying a blue flag.

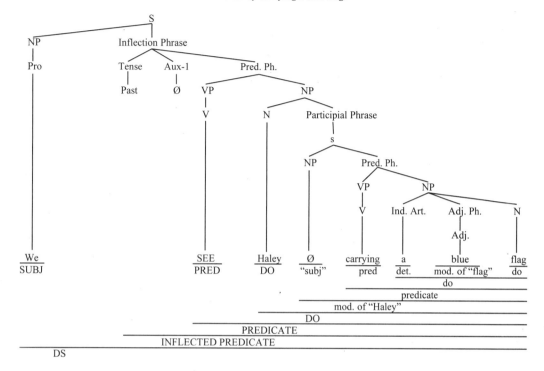

FIGURE 17.20

The woman to put in the race tomorrow is Breunta.

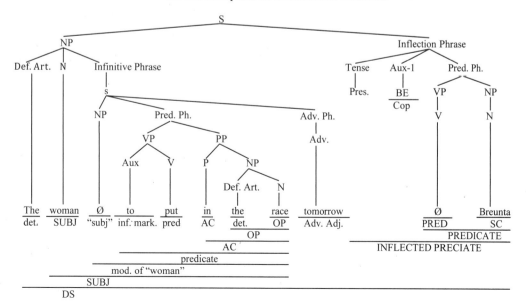

ADVERBIAL FUNCTION OF INFINITIVES AND PARTICIPLES

Participles and infinitives can also function as adverbials. In that function they are generally placed at the beginning or end of the sentence (although, as with all adverbials, there is some flexibility). They are often set apart from the rest of the sentence by commas, particularly if they come first in the sentence.

To make it to the movie on time, Maria took a taxi.
Frank called his brother to invite him to his party.
Having been fired from his job, Richard avoided his former colleagues out of embarrassment.
The barista took the rest of the day off, having spilled hot coffee on his leg.

One important rule about these kinds of modifiers is that the subject of the main clause must be their logical "subject." In the following examples, the subject of the main clause is not the logical "subject" of the infinitive or participle, and therefore it is said to be **dangling**:

*Not **paying** attention, the books were left on the counter by the students.*
***To compile** their tax records, hundreds of receipts were strewn around the couple's living room.*

In order to align the participle and infinitive with the grammatical subject of the main clause, these sentences might be changed as follows:

*Not **paying** attention, **the students** left their books on the counter.*
***To compile** their tax records, **the couple** had strewn hundreds of receipts around their living room.*

Diagramming infinitive and participle phrases is a straightforward matter; they will be non-finite clauses with no inflection phrase. Their function will always be that of "adverbial adjunct," as shown in Figures 17.21 and 17.22. And again, even though the logical "subject" in such participle phrases is co-referential with the grammatical subject of the main clause, we will keep an NP line for the subject of the participle for consistency, stemming from the S containing the participle in a tree diagram.

INFINITIVE AND PARTICIPLE PHRASES 321

FIGURE 17.21

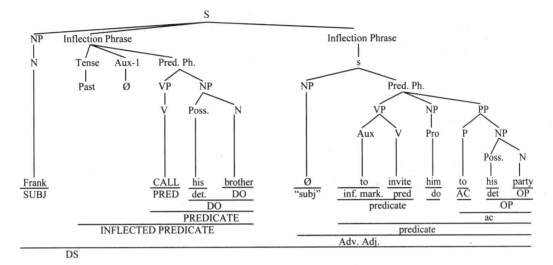

FIGURE 17.22

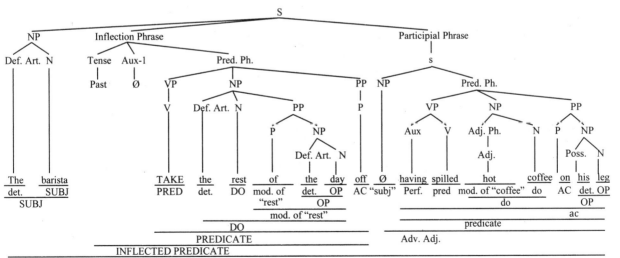

Participle phrases in the function of adverbial adjunct may sometimes occur with a complementizer to sharpen the meaning of the adjunct:

After having finished her test, Lauren called her brother for a ride.
We advise writing down the information when listening to the lecturer.

In the form–function trees for such sentences, the complementizer is simply included, as in Figure 17.23, but remember that the complementizer, as you learned in Chapters 14 and 16, stands outside of the S.

FIGURE 17.23

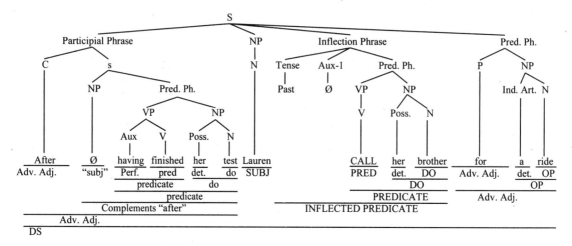

After having finished her test, Lauren called her brother for a ride.

A FINAL NOTE ON FORM–FUNCTION TREES

Students often become very enthusiastic about grammar and about drawing form–function trees to show that grammar. It should be remembered that trees, as used in this book, are heuristic—that is, tools to aid in the analysis of grammar. The trees have no predictive power of their own. For example, the trees cannot tell us whether the form of the noun functioning as "subject" of the participle will be in the plain or possessive form. The trees are thus product-oriented. They don't create structure per se; they represent structure post facto.

Any introductory book on grammar must be selective in what points of elementary grammar will be covered, and to be sure, there is much, much, much more about grammar to be known than what has been covered in this and the preceding chapters. And while it is hoped that the form–function trees have been helpful in the learning of these basic grammatical notions, we have probably reached the limit at which such diagrams can be useful for understanding the grammatical structure of a language.

EXERCISES

A. Turn the bolded part of each sentence into an infinitive phrase. Note that such changes will often involve the loss of modal verbs, the meanings for which are "included" in the infinitive form. Try, however, to maintain other auxiliaries by using the compound infinitive forms found in the chapter.

Examples: *We knew **that Jeff had lied to the detective on several occasions**. → We knew Jeff **to have lied to the detective on several occasions**.*

*The soldiers stacked sandbags **so that they could stop the flood waters from advancing any further**. → The soldiers stacked the sandbags **to stop the flood waters from advancing any further**.*

1. Students are never quite sure **whether they should be attending class in the lab or the classroom** since that information is not included on the syllabus.
2. Morihiro's parents preferred **that he drive to Chicago rather than take the train**.
3. The news outlet reported **that the suspect had been traveling west on I-80 at 3:15pm**.
4. The technicians believed **that the remaining supplies were exhausted**, but in fact the lab manager had recently purchased new materials.
5. I will expect **that the new client will have been contacted before the end of the week**.
6. I wouldn't be surprised **if I were to be traveling to Washington DC next month** given our new contract with the federal government.
7. The only people **that have seen the rare book collection** are those who were able to obtain passes before the online lottery expired.
8. Our neighbors have been wanting **that we might extend our fence a few more feet toward the back portion of our property**.

B. Turn the bolded part of each sentence into a participle phrase. Take special care to note whether the meaning is active or passive and try to maintain other auxiliaries by using the compound participle forms found in the chapter. Remember, too, that the "subject" of the participle may be expressed in the possessive form.

Example: *Carlo didn't mind **that Hannah had destroyed the upholstery**. → Carlo didn't mind **Hannah's having destroyed the upholstery**.*

1. The coffee **that was bought at the café** had a richer taste than the grocery store variety.
2. The landlady reported **that the tenants kept late hours**, but otherwise she also said that she had seen no suspicious activity.
3. We don't deny **that the customer purchased the item from us**, we simply don't believe that it was defective.

4. The issue, **which has been wholly resolved**, will not prohibit you from being allowed to make a claim at a later date.
5. Alvin encouraged **that Sammy play tennis at the club** even though he didn't think he was the same caliber of player as the other members.
6. Selena has understood **that Matt has made an error on the form,** but she couldn't understand why he didn't fix it.
7. The servers in the restaurant asked that the garbage can **that was placed next to the back door** be moved.

C. Determine whether the following sentences contain a dangling participle modifier. If the sentence does have such a dangling modifier, suggest an edit that would eliminate the dangling structure.

1. Finishing in last place, the judges gave Marty a medal of honorary mention.

2. Heard from as far as five miles away, the residents of the small town couldn't imagine what would cause such an explosion.

3. Carl knew he had won the game, having placed the last card down.

4. Furtively walking through the door, an unexpected surprise awaited the black-clad burglar.

5. Having been selected to help local economies, the cities in which the finals will be held are all located along the Colplacege River.

6. Flaquito was suspicious of the stranger's words of admiration, never having experienced such flattery before.

7. Taken in small doses, patients rarely experience any side effects from the drug.

8. When running the machine, a small stream of hot milk should be added during the blending process.

9. Emotions among the travelers ran high, after having arrived in the strange land.

10. Whether drunk or not, there is no loitering outside the liquor store after dark.

D. Make full form–function trees for the following sentences.

1. Alain did not call you to talk about the bill.
2. Roaming around the neighborhood, the stray cat hunts for food during the night.
3. We had wanted the manufacturers to build a wall around the patio in the back of the house.
4. Julen's taking courses in summer means that he will graduate early.
5. The brochure suggested taking a tour and not walking around the dangerous streets.
6. Her friends had defended her writing a complaint to the manager, but they did not expect that she would receive a free meal.

Grammar Myths

While linguists view grammar (and language generally) as a system with patterns discoverable through scientific inquiry requiring the analysis of examples and data, popular views of grammar are rife with "grammar myths," which I will define here as unfounded claims about the nature of language, founded in misconceived notions of prescriptivism and proscriptivism, and revealing of ideologies, convinced of human turpitude, sure of propensity toward laziness, and confident of the abdication of good morality and even citizenship. In this chapter, we will look at some of those myths and learn why they are myths and not facts about language.

GRAMMAR MYTH #1: DON'T END A SENTENCE WITH A PREPOSITION

When I begin teaching a grammar class, I start with two questions. The first is this: Who claims that they have never been taught grammar? A conservative measure is that about 75 percent of the class will raise a hand. My next question is this: Finish this sentence: "Don't end a sentence with _____." To this prompt, about 90 percent of any given class will answer "a preposition." So some large number of the 75 percent who claim never to have learned grammar feel secure enough to answer the grammar question eliciting the grammar myth *Don't end a sentence in a preposition*. The numbers reveal that the rule prohibiting sentence-final prepositions is not one necessarily learned in school but one that resides in many different places of our public discourse.

One of the very earliest grammar books to state the rule against sentence-final prepositions was Robert Lowth's 1762 *A Short Grammar of English*. We should look closely at what Lowth wrote:

> The Preposition is often separated from the Relative which it governs, and joined to the Verb at the end of the sentence, or of some member of it: as, "Horace is an author, whom I am much delighted with."... This is an Idiom which our language is much inclined to;[1] it prevails in common conversation, and suits very well with the familiar style in writing; but the placing of the Preposition before the Relative is more graceful, as well as more perspicuous, and it agrees much better with the solemn and elevated style.[2]

There are many interesting points to be made. First, we have to note that Lowth does not prohibit the sentence-final preposition absolutely but distinguishes "common conversation" and "solemn and elevated style." In other words, Lowth's stricture is about style, not about grammar. Second, we can also note that Lowth doesn't really offer a sound reason why sentence-final prepositions are less desirable in "elevated style" other than to claim that non–sentence-final prepositions are more "graceful" and "perspicuous." Neither gracefulness nor perspicuity is measurable in evaluating language use, and such notions have more to do with personal taste. I think it is healthy to ask why anyone's taste in language should dictate someone else's.

The fact is that prepositions play a very important syntactic role in English, both in terms of relating nouns to other parts of the sentence and in certain verbal constructions (e.g., phrasal verbs). Sooner or later a preposition ends up at the end of a sentence. Consider the sentence *Find a good financial advisor you can confidently hand your money over to*. Wouldn't the sentence sound a bit absurd to say instead, "Find a good financial advisor over to whom you can confidently hand your money"? In some other cases involving phrasal verbs, there simply is no alternative other than to change the idiom completely: *The laboratory blew up!* versus *The laboratory exploded*. However, it could be argued that the idiom *blew up* is more expressive or attention grabbing—which may be desirable.

Furthermore, even the merest browsing of texts of all types, from formal to less formal, will reveal many instances of sentence-final prepositions. For example, in P. Hume Brown's *Scotland: A Short History*, we can read, "The Government was greatly alarmed, for it seemed that the rebellion that had long been dreaded had at last broken out" (p. 264). Hume's *History* is hardly intended to be written in the style of "common conversation." Again, such examples are easy to find.

Finally, to return to the point that in my classes 90 percent "know" the rule not to end a sentence with a preposition, although 75 percent claim never to have learned grammar, it seems highly unlikely that many readers would recognize a sentence that did end in a preposition! In my own experience of publishing my writing, I can say that never, not once, has any editor ever mentioned amending a sentence-final preposition. It just isn't a rule.

---

1 Note Lowth's use of a clause-final preposition.
2 Robert Lowth, *A Short Grammar of English* (1762), p. 139.

GRAMMAR MYTH #2: DON'T START A SENTENCE WITH A CONJUNCTION

I would classify "Don't end a sentence with a preposition" as the most commonly uttered myth, but coming in a close second would be that which states that one should not start a sentence with a conjunction. Let's begin by noting that many, many good writers, writing in academic styles, begin sentences with a conjunction. Again taken from Hume's *Scotland: A Short History*, the following sentence offers an example: "And it was not only near Edinburgh that fighting went on, but in other parts of the country" (p. 204). Where, then, does this grammar rule come from?

I believe it has its roots in teaching young children to write. Conjunctions, at least in traditional grammar, are either coordinating conjunctions (*and, but, or, nor, for, yet, so*) or subordinating (*because, when, after, since,* etc.). The latter group constitutes what we call complementizers in more modern grammatical theory. The problem stems from the fact that subordinating conjunctions link subordinate clauses to independent clauses; a subordinate clause cannot be a sentence on its own. So when young children are learning to write in English, they might create a pair of sentences like: *I like chocolate. Because it tastes good.* Identifying *because* as a conjunction, and telling a student simply not to begin a sentence with it, would be an effective way to avoid the kind of grammar error that results in an incomplete sentence.

Of course, writers begin sentences with *because* all of the time, as well as with the coordinating conjunctions as we saw earlier. Unfortunately, this grammar rule got stuck in our public mind and has become "self-evidently true." But, again, given the atrophied knowledge of grammar as a result of our cultural/educational avoidance of it in school curricula, it is not very likely that many would be able to identify a sentence that begins with a conjunction of the subordinating or coordinating type in the first place. And, again, it just isn't a rule.

GRAMMAR MYTH #3: PEOPLE WHO DON'T SPEAK CORRECTLY ARE LAZY

It is not difficult to find instances in which a person or a group of people using non-standard English are accused of being "lazy" or using "lazy" speech. I suppose that the charge stems from the misconception that those speakers know standard English but lack the industrious spirit to recall and use it. That's not really what is going on.

There has never been a language, past or present, that all people speak (or write) the same way as everyone else using the language. In other words, it is the very nature of human language to vary, by geographical location, social group, and so on. But those variations of the language, which you might think of as dialects or sociolects, are not simply random. All varieties of all languages are structured in terms of their grammatical forms and vocabulary. As incredible as it may sound to some, a sentence like *Jason ain't never said no such thing* has definable structure. We must also acknowledge that different varieties of a language are appropriate for different situations; a scholar writing a textbook for mass consumption would use a different variety of English than two good ol' friends meeting up for a beer in a rural Tennessee bar! A person speaking in a non-standard variety is accessing a grammar in their mind (albeit not the grammar of Standard English) and may well be using the most socially appropriate variety.

The idea that non-standard grammar forms are merely lazy "work-arounds" for standard English is easily challenged. For example, consider the grammar of a well-studied and old dialect of American English, African American English.[1] In that variety of English, we note that the copulative verb *be* may not be inflected as it is in some other varieties of English, so speakers of African American English generate forms like *I be, you be, he/she/it be, we be, you be, they be*. Such forms are good candidates to confirm the "laziness" of African American English since they appear, on the surface of things, to simplify the varied forms of *be* in Standard English: *I am, you are, he/she/it is*, etc. But is the fact that African American English does not inflect the verb *be* a sign of sloth?

In answer to that question, let's consider Japanese, where the verb for *be* is *desu*. Here are the forms of *desu* with different pronouns:

Watashi-wa **desu** (I am) Watashitachi-wa **desu** (we are)
Anata-wa **desu** (you are)
Kare-wa **desu** (he is)   Karera-wa **desu** (they are)
Kanajo-wa **desu** (she is)

You will notice that the form for *be*, *desu*, never changes in Japanese, just like in African American English, and yet people do not accuse the Japanese of being lazy for speaking Japanese! One reason that African American English speakers are judged differently from the Japanese on this point may be the mistaken idea that African American English speakers somehow "work through" standard English before generating African American English forms. That simply is not so. An African American English speaker (or any speaker of any variety of English) does not access standard English in their mind in order to speak their variety of English; the grammar of that variety is present independently of other varieties of English that the speaker may know and is accessed as such. In other words, a speaker of a variety of English like African American English no more accesses standard English first in order to speak their variety of English than a Spanish speaker does in order to speak Spanish!

GRAMMAR MYTH #4: PEOPLE WHO DON'T SPEAK CORRECTLY ARE STUPID

Related to Myth #3 regarding the perception of non-standard English speakers as being lazy is the myth that such speakers are stupid. It is not difficult to find instances of the country bumpkin character underscoring his stupidity by violating every grammar rule known to English.

---

1 African American English refers to several related dialects that have their roots in the speech-ways of enslaved Africans and their descendants of the American South; thus the name "African American English" is meant to recognize and respect the historical source of those varieties of English. Like all languages and language varieties, it is culturally learned and there is no assumption that all African Americans speak African Americans English or that only African Americans speak African American English. For more on African American English see Lisa Green's book *African American English: A Linguistic Introduction* (Cambridge UP, 2002).

The fact is that intelligence and language variation are unrelated. Obviously, many of our cultural measures of "smartness," like college entrance tests, are set up to disadvantage speakers of non-standard English, since the verbal sections of such tests are largely assessments of the kind of vocabulary one learns in an academic setting—so yes, there is a correlation between success on such tests and access to education, socio-economic status, motivation to learn academic English, etc. But that is not a measure of intelligence, per se.

Often the non-standard forms of a person's dialect may be invoked as evidence for the assumed "lack" of intelligence. However, some may be surprised to learn that there are frequently areas of grammar in dialects of English showing linguistic complexity not found in standard English. For example, contrast these two sentences in African American English:

Simone be watchin' TV.
Simone watchin' TV.

The two sentences show what some may assume to be "simpler" structures than standard English in so far as the first sentence shows uninflected *be* (see Myth #3) and the second sentence shows no auxiliary verb at all. However, the two sentences actually reveal a subtle complexity in that the first sentence has the aspectual meaning of habituality—that is, Simone customarily watches TV—while the second is progressive—Simone is watching TV now. Looked at in a certain way, the sentences do not present simplified forms of standard English but instead a new formal marking of a discursively relevant distinction.

Another example of emerging grammatical complexity from African American English involves the marking of future time. In addition to the auxiliary *will* and *to be going to* (sometimes reduced to *-a*, as in *Ima call you later*), African American English offers two more ways of expressing future. One involves a reduced variant of the Southern American English periphrastic form *to be fixing to*, in the form of *finna*, as in the following example in which *finna* could be substituted with *gonna*, "I feel like I'm going to die," although that would change the meaning slightly:

… but as another convicted man who has not received a death sentence told *The Root*: "I feel like I'm finna die."[1]

And, more recently, the future auxiliary *tryna* has emerged. While *tryna* has its roots in the fuller expression *trying to*, it shows instances in which it is not about attempt but about prediction of the future. For example, in the passage below, the writer is not talking about attempting to pay college athletes but about the future willingness of the colleges to do so.

If they not tryna pay these college athletes then the nba should let them come straight outta HS.[2]

---

1 Retrieved from https://www.theroot.com/i-feel-like-im-finna-die-why-everyone-in-alabamas-pris-1845985484.
2 Isaiah Thomas, draftee for the Denver Nuggets, February 2019; retrieved from https://hoopshype.com/rumor/1240396/.

We might paraphrase *tryna* with *going to*: "If they are not going to pay these...." Thus, in African American English, there are subtle differences among and between future expressions of the following type:

He'll call you.
He('s) gonna call you.
He('s) finna call you.
He('s) tryna call you.

If more people knew where to look for the complexity in non-standard dialects instead of merely noting apparent deficiencies, the more impressed they would be with the intricacies of the variety and less likely to think people speaking it were "stupid."

GRAMMAR MYTH #5: DON'T USE THE PASSIVE

In my first year as a professor, I attended a grant-writing workshop to which a venerable and distinguished faculty member of the English Department had been invited to give some general writing advice. His suggestion was, "Don't use the passive voice." Needless to say, I was very disappointed because his proscriptive counsel was in fact nothing more than facile grammatical pronouncement. I should not really have been all that surprised; it is easy to find similar statements of prohibition of the passive from many "authorities" on writing.

Most simply put, the passive wouldn't exist in the language if it didn't have some purpose and usefulness. The proscription probably stems from the fact that some young writers, who might be insecure in their own voice, use the passive in a way that mitigates their writerly authority and control over the text. Consider the following passage:

> It came the time for Pouya and Reda to write the conclusion to the paper they had been working on together. At first, Reda volunteered to make a draft, but she soon discovered she didn't have many ideas. She finally admitted her writer's block and Reda was helped by Pouya.

It is likely that you might find the passive part of the sentence *Reda was helped by Pouya* a bit odd-sounding. That is because the passage has both Reda and Pouya as actors (and topics), so there is good reason to make Pouya the subject of the last sentence with an active verb, "...and Pouya helped her."

Otherwise, the passive is a natural choice in situations when the subject is unknown, obvious, or undesirable to mention:

Corn is grown in most of the counties in Illinois. (subject is obvious)
My wallet was stolen! (subject is unknown)
All of the chocolate was eaten. (subject may be known but for politeness reasons not desirable to expose)

The passive is also frequent in certain kinds of writing, like scientific and linguistic writing, in which the process is more important than the actors:

The passive is formed by using the auxiliary be *and the simple passive participle of the verb.*

So simply to say "don't use the passive" may allow the person giving such advice to feel authoritative, but it is also simply wrong in many instances.

GRAMMAR MYTH #6: SINGULAR *THEY* IS WRONG

In Chapter 5, I broached the topic of using *they/them/their* for singular reference in the case that the gender of the antecedent was unknown, as in this example:

Anyone can join. They only need to fill out the membership application.

As I discussed in that chapter, the use of *they/them/their* for singular reference is not new in English, but it has over the years been met with some disapproval since, in the example above, *anyone* is singular and *they/them/their* is plural, at least according to some very traditional grammatical views.

More recently, *they/them/their* has been adopted and encouraged as a way to refer to singular individuals whose gender identities do not fit into the binary suggested by *she/her* on the one hand and *he/him/his* on the other, as exemplified in the following sentence:

My roommate is at home this weekend visiting **their** *parents.*

While objections to singular *they/them/their* are certainly becoming fewer, they are still raised from time to time by some purists. However, when considering this problem, I think it is important to remember that the pronoun *you* used to be plural. In Early Modern English, the second-person pronoun system was like this:

	subject form	**object form**
singular	*thou*	*thee*
plural	*ye*	*you*

Based on the French system, plural forms began to be used as respect forms, even in reference to singular addressees (like *vous* in French, *usted* in Spanish, etc.). For reasons that are not entirely clear, *you* became the only form of second person address, singular or plural, and *thou/thee* fell into disuse. So what was once a plural pronoun is now used for singular reference. Interestingly, to my knowledge there is little record of objection in this case, probably because the change took place within the realm of hierarchical social relationships and politeness.

So we have to ask, what is really bothering people about the use of singular *they*? I would suggest that it has to do with the apparent obfuscation of a person's binary gender, information which may be expected, an expectation that the language for a long time has obliged. In other words, this language change—or, more appropriately put, acceptance of language change—also challenges very old beliefs about how humans should be categorized in the world; it is bound to cause anxieties.

GRAMMAR MYTH #7: USE OF SINGULAR *THEY* ACHIEVES GENDER "NEUTRALITY"

The expression "gender neutral" is heard a lot these days in reference to uses of singular *they/them/their* as a means of avoiding the gender binary suggested by *he/him/his* and *she/her*, as in the sentence we saw in Myth #6:

> *My roommate is at home this weekend visiting **their** parents.*

But I will suggest that such terminology isn't really accurate in terms of what the language is doing or in terms of what we would like to achieve with such uses of *they/them/their*.

You are probably familiar with the fact that some languages have gender systems in which nouns in the language are assigned masculine, feminine, and sometimes neuter status, often in seemingly arbitrary ways. So in Spanish a table, *la mesa*, is feminine, but in German the word for the same referent, *der Tisch*, is masculine. In those languages, if I refer back to the noun "table," I have to call it the equivalent of "she" in Spanish and "he" in German. Of course, these systems are merely classificatory, and neither Spanish speakers nor German speakers have any sense that a table is female-like or male-like.

English used to have a gender system like that of Spanish or German but, during the Middle English period (1100–1500), that system was changed into one in which animacy was the central organizing principle, with biological gender a secondary principle. Thus, inanimate things belong to one category and are referred to in the singular with the neuter pronoun *it*. Animate entities are in another category and then further divided into male (masculine) and female (feminine) and referred to through the pronouns *he/him/his* and *she/her*, respectively. (Animals vary in their assignment; those for which biological gender is known and important, like cows, are classed as animate, but lizards are generally classed as inanimate, unless they are a pet.)

The third-person plural pronoun forms *they/them/their* continued to cover both animate and inanimate referents:

> *The students have finished **their** work. **They** can now take a vacation.*
> *Here are the boards for the subfloor. Please carry **them** to the back of the house.*

Thus, *they/them/their* is a natural choice for animate reference in the case that binary gender is to be avoided. But is that really "gender neutral"?

Note that in the singular, there is a gender-neutral pronoun, "it." But notice, too, that we cannot use it to refer to people unless we are attempting to be jocular or insulting:

*My roommate is at home this weekend visiting **its** parents.*

The unavailability of *it* for human, animate reference suggests that the larger concern here is not really gender neutrality but instead gender non-specification. In this way, singular *they/them/their* is an acceptable linguistic strategy to achieve gender non-specifying reference but still maintain the animate status of the referent—probably a good thing to do.

GRAMMAR MYTH #8: TWO NEGATIVES MAKE A POSITIVE

In Chapter 10, I addressed the topic of double negatives and made the point that two negatives do not make a positive meaning. It is easy to understand where the idea that two negatives cancel one another comes from; after all, it is true in math and many logical systems. It just isn't always true in language. An early instance of justifying the injunction against double negation by claiming it results in a positive meaning is again Lowth, who in his *Short Grammar of English* (p. 139), says,

> Two negatives, in English, destroy one another, or are equivalent to an affirmative; as, "*Nor* did they *not* perceive the evil plight in which they were."

Lowth chose his example carefully because the two negatives there do indeed cancel each other, something still possible in Modern English as well:

Well, I'm not not *having a good time.*

However, while such reversals in meaning are possible (depending on what parts of the sentence the first negative has dominion over), it is not usually the case. Thus in the following sentence, a positive meaning is not intended:

Axel didn't bring nobody with him.

The sentence does not mean Axel *did* bring someone with him. In fact, the term double negation is not really accurate for what is happening in varieties of English that allow such negation. The phenomenon is better known as "negative concord," and essentially in varieties of English in which negative concord operates, all possible targets in a sentence will be made negative:

He didn't never tell nobody nothing.

What may be surprising to learn, however, is that multiple negation was the norm in English until the modern period. We find, for example, in Chaucer's *Canterbury Tales* (c. 1390) the following:

> He nolde noght disconforten hem alle. (lit. "He didn't not want to discomfort them all"; "The Knight's Tale," line 2704)

Scholars have shown that use of multiple negation began to dwindle in many types of writing even before strictures against it began to show up in grammars. It is clear that multiple negation is not accepted in written standard English, but not because two negatives make a positive meaning—but because it's company policy, and like many company policies, it's a bit arbitrary.

GRAMMAR MYTH #9: PEOPLE USED BETTER LANGUAGE IN THE PAST

When I am out and about in public places, like the gym, a bar, the line at the grocery store, and I start to exchange small talk with someone, I'm a bit reluctant to say that I am a professor of linguistics who teaches grammar, because almost always the conversation then turns to the person accusing younger people of using worse English "nowadays." Sigh.

I don't believe that it is empirically possible to show that young people today use language any less perfectly than in the past—and what would it mean to "use language better or worse" anyway? By some measure against standard English? And in what domain? Speaking? Writing?

It should be remembered that standard English, in so far as it is a definable entity, is meant to regulate mostly writing, and the fact is that young people have always developed their own way of speaking as a means of asserting their identities as separate from their parents, and even their contemporaries, within a couple of years' age range. Just think about how different the slang you used in high school was from that of your parents, and even that of older and younger siblings! So whether it's saying "twenty-three skiddoo" in 1925, "daddy-o" in 1963, "gag me with a spoon" in 1984, or whatever the kids are saying these days, the impression on the part of older generations is that young people are speaking the language worse.

But what about writing? Is there evidence that young people wrote better in the past? Consider this letter written in 1943 by a GI in World War II to his family back home:[1]

---

[1] Taken from Dan Lamothe, "Brothers in Arms," *The Washington Post*, 6 Dec. 2017, https://www.washingtonpost.com/graphics/2017/national/world-war-two-letters/.

IMAGE 18.1

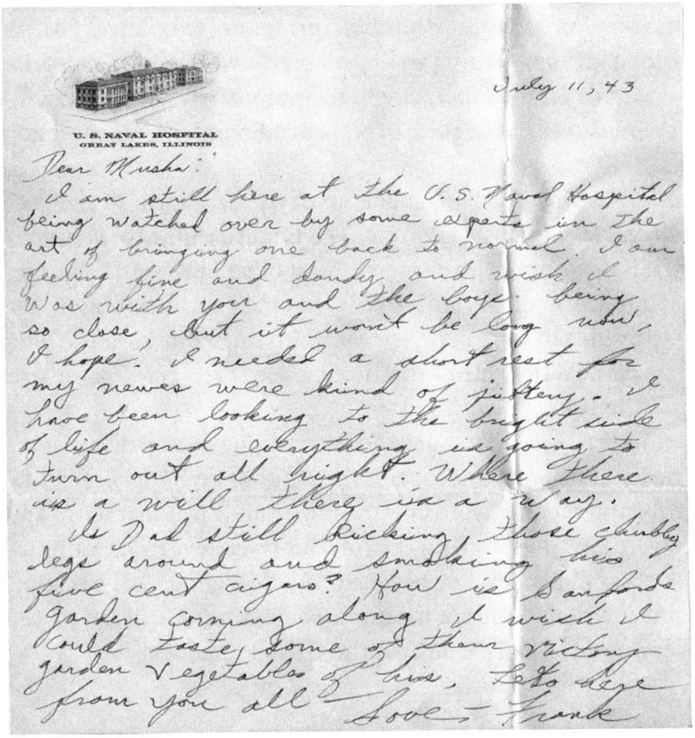

U. S. NAVAL HOSPITAL
GREAT LAKES, ILLINOIS

July 11, 43

Dear Musha:

I am still here at the U.S. Naval Hospital being watched over by some experts in the art of bringing one back to normal. I am feeling fine and dandy and wish I was with you and the boys being so close, but it won't be long now, I hope. I needed a short rest for my nerves were kind of jittery. I have been looking to the bright side of life and everything is going to turn out all right. Where there is a will there is a way.

Is Dad still kicking those chubby legs around and smoking his five cent cigars? How is Sanfords garden coming along I wish I could taste some of them victory garden vegetables of his. Lets hear from you all—

Love—Frank

As you can see, the letter is wonderfully engaging and lucid, but it can hardly be said to adhere to standard English to any greater degree than would a letter a written by a 19-year-old today. The possessive form "Sanfords" doesn't have an apostrophe; the writer says he would like to "taste some of **them** victory garden vegetables"; there is no period between certain sentences.

While we certainly can't make conclusions based on a single letter sample from 1943 about the state of writing then or now, we do know that writing has always varied in terms of adherence to standard English depending on how formal or informal the writing is. The sample above is a letter, a pretty "chatty" genre; it is not an academic paper. Academic papers in the past, just like now, reflect more standard English practices because they are written in a genre that expects those conventions. However, more personal writing can flout those conventions, whether it be letter writing in 1943 or social media posts in the 2020s.

Perhaps I should ask those condemning young people's use of English how many academic papers written by young people they have read. But people spouting language myths and ideologies aren't really looking to be schooled. It's probably best to smile politely and look for a way to end the conversation as quickly as possible.

GRAMMAR MYTH #10: DON'T SPLIT INFINITIVES

Classic *Star Trek* fans know well that the mission of the Starship *Enterprise* was "to boldly go where no man has gone before." While the public sat rapt waiting to see what new worlds the Enterprise would enter (and by the way there were women on the *Enterprise* too!), grammarians were less willing to let Captain Kirk violate one of the most venerable rules of standard English—the injunction against split infinitives.

The infinitive in English, as discussed in Chapter 17, is made up of the base form of the verb preceded by *to*; hence we get *to have, to see, to talk, to gesture,* etc. The English infinitive is unique among most European languages in that it is made up of two elements. Most other European languages express the infinitive in a single form. So in German the infinitive is the single form ending in *-en*, as in *lernen* 'to learn'; the Spanish infinitive ends in *-er*, *-ir*, or *-ar*: *comer* 'to eat,' *venir* 'to come,' and *hablar* 'to speak'; and perhaps most importantly, the Latin infinitive ends in *-āre, -ēre, -ere,* or *-īre*: *navigāre* 'to sail', *monēre* 'to warn,' *ducere* 'to lead,' *audīre* 'to listen.'

Since the infinitival marker is part of the word, obviously no intervening material can come between the verb stem and the infinitival ending. It may well be this fact, as observed from Latin, that has led English grammarians to proscribe intervening words between the infinitival marker *to* and the base form of the verb, as in *to boldly go*. Some reflection on the rule, however, reveals its arbitrary nature; I do not see that there is better or worse understanding between "to boldly go" or "to go boldly."

In fact, it may be argued that to achieve certain kinds of meaning, some words are better placed in the split infinitive position, such as degree adverbials. Consider these two sentences:

Leticia really wanted to win the game.
Leticia wanted to really win the game.

The first sentence is about Leticia's strong desire, but the second is about the degree to which she wanted to win—a lot, perhaps by a lot of points.[1] In summary, I think we have to recognize that the syntactic position between the infinitival marker *to* and the base form of the verb is a fairly open syntactic position in which modifying structure can and sometimes even should occur.

GRAMMAR MYTH #11: *AIN'T* AIN'T A WORD

Every school child has heard the refrain "Ain't ain't a word because it ain't in the dictionary." Question: If *ain't* ain't a word, why can I understand the sentence above? Because if, in fact, *ain't* weren't a word, then any use of it should be nonsense to the listener. *Splurg* isn't a word in English, and if I say, "Go *splurg* the window!" you don't know what I mean precisely because *splurg* isn't a word.

---

1 In fact, the alternative choices without splitting the infinitive sound odd, "Leticia wanted to win really the game," or they don't mean the same thing, "Leticia wanted really to win the game."

So what exactly makes a word a word? The answer is usage! If I utter a word and you understand that word in the sense that I intended it, it's a word. It's just that simple. When teachers say "*ain't* ain't a word," what they mean is it isn't accepted as standard English. Fair enough. But how did the word come to have such a beleaguered existence?

The truth is, no one is quite sure why the word is so hated. The origin of *ain't* is also uncertain, although it most likely stems from a contraction of either *am + not* or *are + not*. In earlier English, the form seemed to have some currency even among speakers/writers of the affluent and literate classes. The *Oxford English Dictionary* gives an example of its use in a letter written by the English essayist and poet Charles Lamb in 1829:

> An't [presumably a variant spelling for *ain't*] you glad about Burke's case? (Lamb, *Life and Letters*, Letter 472, cited in the *OED*, s.v. *ain't*)

And just in case you missed it, the example above is from a dictionary, so *ain't* is in the dictionary after all.

A point I made earlier is that all languages vary; they have done so in the past, do so now, and will continue to do so in the future. *Ain't* is a wonderful example of the diversity of the English language, offering forms that allow us to adjust our idiom for different situations. How monotonous it would be if we all wore the same uniform, sported the same hair style, had the same color of skin, practiced the same cultural activities, shared the same beliefs—or spoke the same language and language variety all the time.

Appendix A   Prepositions

SINGLE-WORD PREPOSITIONS

aboard
about
above
across
after
against
along
alongside
amid
among
around
as
at
barring
before
behind
below
beneath
beside
besides
between
beyond
but
by

concerning
despite
down
during
except
excepting
excluding
following
for
from
in
into
like
minus
near
notwithstanding
of
off
on
onto
opposite
outside
over
past

pending
per
plus
regarding
save
since
than
through
throughout
till
to
toward
towards
under
underneath
unlike
until
up
upon
via
with
within
without
worth

MULTI-WORD PREPOSITIONS

according to	in between	opposite to
across from	in favor of	other than
apart from	in front of	out of
aside from	in lieu of	outside of
as for	inside of	owing to
aside from	in spite of	prior to
away from	instead of	regardless of
because of	irrespective of	thanks to
by means of	next to	together with
contrary to	on account of	up against
depending on	on board	up to
except for	on top of	up until

Several prepositions have variant forms that end in -st/-xt. For example, many American English speakers say "acrosst" instead of across. It is stigmatized as non-Standard, however, as is the form betwixt. In the UK, amidst instead of amid and amongst instead of among are preferred, while the latter of each pair is more usual in the US.

In addition, there are a number of archaic or foreign prepositions that one finds in certain types of texts in English:

anent (meaning 'about/concerning')
anti
pace (meaning 'with the exception of')
per
pro
sans (meaning 'without')

Appendix B   List of Phrasal Verbs

The following is a list of some common phrasal verbs and their idiomatic meanings. "NS" indicates that the phrasal verb is non-separable. This list is hardly exhaustive and could be expanded by many, many pages.

bring about (NS): "cause"

His complaint brought about changes in the company.

bring on: "initiate/cause"

The hot weather is sure to bring on some afternoon thunderstorms.

bring up: "raise (as in children)/introduce a topic"

The teacher brought the student's poor test performance up during a meeting with his parents. Alex and Jonathan brought up three very exceptional children.

call off: "cancel"

The game was called off because of rain.

call up: "telephone"

We can call the police up to find out if anyone turned in a missing wallet.

come out: "reveal one's sexual orientation, usually as same-sex-attracted"

Emma came out to her parents during the Winter Break.

come to (NS): "to total/become conscious again"

> The bill came to 200 dollars.
> The patient came to shortly after surgery.

come up (NS): "appeared"

> A new twist in the case has suddenly come up.

draw out: "extend (with a sense of too long)"

> The plot was drawn out and, frankly, unbelievable.

get over (NS): "recover"

> The economy still has not gotten over the blow it received during the international crisis.

get up: "rise (from bed)"

> Sean got up too late to make it to class.

give out: "distribute/fail"

> The office gave out monthly bonuses to the highest sellers.

give up: "surrender"

> The enemy gave up without a fight.

go for: "attempt/try at/believe"

> Akbar is going for his PhD.
> We heard you; we just aren't going for your story.

go over (NS): "review"

> The students went over their notes carefully before class in case of a quiz.

go with: "coordinate in an aesthetic sense/date informally"

> This shirt doesn't go with these pants.
> Is Ally still going with Matteo?

hand in: "submit"

Will you please hand your assignments in to the TA?

hold down: "suppress/keep (a job)"

The Vikings held the opponent down for most of the game.

hold up: "cause delay/rob (a bank)"

Traffic has been held up on the Parkway since noon.

live up to (NS): "meet (someone's expectations)"

They can never live up to their mother's expectations.

look after: "to care for"

Simca looks after her younger siblings after school.

look up: "search for"

You can always look the word up in a dictionary, you know?

make up: "end hostility/invent (usually something false)"

The couple finally made up after having been in an argument for several days. And then we found out he had been making up the entire story all along!

pass out: "lose consciousness/distribute"

The player passed out after practicing for hours in the grueling summer sun. You may begin as soon as I have passed out all of the copies.

pass up: "decline"

You are passing up a very good opportunity.

pick on (NS): "to torment/tease"

The older children constantly picked on the younger ones on the school bus.

pick out: "choose"

Will you pick out an outfit for me for dinner?

pick up: "begin an activity/collect"

Jayson picked up the flute when he was about 10.

put off: "postpone"

We will have to put the poetry reading off this year.

put on: "dress/deceive/tease"

I think I will put on a scarf today.
That can't be true! You're putting me on!

put out: "extinguish"

The diner crudely put his cigarette out in the leftover mashed potatoes on his plate.

run across (NS): "meet by chance"

Gabe ran across an old friend on the quad.

run over: "hit by a car"

The motorist ran over several traffic control devices at full speed.

sleep off: "recuperate"

Syncere tried to sleep off her headache.

take after: "resemble"

Eva takes after her mother in eye color.

take over: "conquer"

The smaller nation was taken over by its hostile neighbor during the last war.

turn down: "reject/lessen volume or strength"

> The voters turned the referendum down.
> Please, turn down the TV!

turn off: "cease power or flow"

> Jack turned the light off.

turn on: "start power or flow"

> Could you turn on the cold water, please?

turn out: "result in/become"

> The weather actually turned out pretty nice today.

turn up: "make louder/stronger"

> The team really turned up their effort in the final quarter.

wear out: "make tired"

> Tyler's new puppy wore him out with its constant need for attention and desire to play.

Index

Note: Page numbers in *italics* denote figures and tables.

Ø-complementizers, 281–82, *282*, 285, *285*
Ø-plural, 82
Ø-relative pronoun, 265–66, *266*

ability, expressed through modals, 179
AC. *See* adverbial complements (AC)
active and passive voice
    diagramming passive sentences, 207–12, *208–12*
    passive verb forms, 206–07
    passivization, described, 204–05
    semantic roles, 203–04
    stative vs. inchoative passive, 207
    when to use the passive, 205–06
    chapter exercises, 212–14
additive conjunctions, 44
Adj. *See* adjectives (Adj.)
adjective clauses, 52
    See also relative clauses
adjective phrases (Adj. Ph.)
    diagramming noun phrases, 69–70, *69–70*
    as subject complements, 104, *105*
adjectives (Adj.)
    characterized, 35–39
    adverbial complements following, 147–48, *148*
    diagramming noun phrases, *69*, 69–70, *70*
Adj. Ph. *See* adjective phrases (Adj. Ph.)

adjuncts
    characterized, 41–42
    attitudinal, 121–23, *122*, *123*
    core clause elements and, 120–21, *121*
    as "extra," 119–20
    in infinitive and participle phrases, 312–15, *313*, *314*, *315*
    See also adverbial adjuncts (Adv. Adj.); adverbial complements (AC)
Adv. *See* adverbs (Adv.)
Adv. Adj. *See* adverbial adjuncts (Adv. Adj.)
Adv. Cl. *See* adverbial clauses (Adv. Cl.)
adverbial adjuncts (Adv. Adj.)
    characterized, 41–42, 123–27, *124*, *125*, *126*
    participle phrases as, 320–22, *321*, *322*
adverbial clauses (Adv. Cl.)
    characterized, 52, 245–46
    of adverseness, 247
    of clause, 248
    of commentary, 249
    of concession, 247
    of condition, 249
    of place, 246–47
    of purpose, 248–49
    of result, 248
    second subjunctive, *250*, *251*, 251–54, *253*
    of similarity, 249
    structure of complementizers, 249–51, *250*, *251*
    of time, 246
    chapter exercises, 255–56

adverbial complements (AC)
    diagramming, 128–32, *129*, *130*, *131*
    following adjectives, 147–48, *148*
    following copulative verbs, 128
    intransitive phrasal verbs, 137–39, *138*
    multiple prepositional phrases, 133–35, *134*, *135*
    prepositional-phrasal verbs, *145*, 145–47, *146*, *147*
    prepositional verbs, 136–37, *137*
    separable and inseparable phrasal verbs, 143–45, *144*
    transitive phrasal verbs, 139–43, *140*, *141*, *142*, *143*
    See also prepositional phrases (PP)
adverbs (Adv.)
    as adverbial complement, 130–31, *131*
    as attitudinal adjuncts, 123, *123*
    conjunctive, 42, 232
adversative clauses, 247
adversative conjunctions, 44
agent (semantic) role, 203–04
agreement patterns, 51
ain't, grammar myth surrounding, 338–39
anaphoric reference, 85
antecedent nouns, 85, 257
anterior-continuing aspect, 161
anticipatory *it*, 100–01, 284
any, 199–201, *200*, *201*
apodosis, 252
aren't I vs. *am I not*, 222–23
aspect vs. tense, 154–55
Att. Adj. *See* attitudinal adjuncts (Att. Adj.)
attitudinal adjuncts (Att. Adj.), 121–23, *122*, *123*, 249
attributive adjectives, 35–36, 69
Aux. *See* auxiliary verbs (Aux)
Aux-1. *See* auxiliary-1 verbs (Aux-1)
auxiliary-1 verbs (Aux-1)
    diagramming modals, 182, *182–90*, 184, 187, 189
    diagramming verbs, 162–67, *163*, *164*, *165*, *166*, *167*
    inflection phrases and, 108–09, *109*
    when *be* is sole verb, 168–70
    See also noun phrases, diagramming
auxiliary verbs (Aux)
    characterized, 43
    diagramming verbs, 162–67, *163*, *164*, *165*, *166*, *167*

negation in predicate phrase, 193–96, *194*, *195*
subject-auxiliary inversion, 216–17, 222
See also auxiliary-1 verbs (Aux-1); modal verbs

base verb form, 155
basic sentences
    adjectives, *69*, 69–70, *70*
    declarative sentences, 53, *53*, *61*, 61–62, 215–17
    determiners, 63–69, *67*, *68*, *69*
    diagramming, *61*, *62*, *73*
    form vs. function, *61*, 61–62
    language as multi-layered, 60
    prepositional phrases, 70–72, *71*, *72*
    question formation vs., 215–17
    subject-predicate split, 59–60
    chapter exercises, 74–75
    See also sentence types
be as sole verb in sentences, 168–70
Brown, Peter Hume, *Scotland*, 328, 329

C. *See* complementizers (C)
Canterbury Tales (Chaucer), 336
case and compound pronouns, 89–90
cataphoric reference, 85
clauses
    defined, 52
    core elements of, 120–21, *121*
    in form-function diagrams, 61, *61*
cleft sentences and dummy subjects, 99–101
closed-class words, 30, 40, 42, 43
collective nouns, 80
common nouns, 77–78
complementation, 62
complementizers (C)
    in adverbial clauses, 246–49
    in noun clauses, 281–83, 286–87
    with participle phrases, 322, *322*
    structure of, 249–51, *250*, *251*
complex sentences, 234
    See also adverbial clauses (Adv. Cl.); noun clauses; relative clauses
compound pronouns and case, 89–90
compound sentences. *See* coordination and compound sentences

compound verb forms, 158
concord, subject-verb, 51
Conj. *See* conjunctions (Conj.)
conjunctions (Conj.)
    defined, 44
    coordinating, 227–30, 235–41, *235–41*
    correlative, 230
    grammar myth surrounding, 329
    subordinating, 246
conjunctive adverbs, 42, 232
constituents, 63
Coord. *See* coordination and compound sentences
coordination and compound sentences (Coord.)
    conjunctive adverbs, 42, 232
    coordinating conjunctions, characterized, 227–28
    coordinating conjunctions, diagramming, 235–41, *235–41*
    correlative conjunctions, 230
    false coordination, 230–32
    lists and the Oxford comma, 228–29
    parallel structure, 229–30
    simple, compound, and complex sentences, 234
    subordination vs. coordination, 233
    chapter exercises, 241–43
Cop. *See* copulative verbs
copulative verbs (Cop.), 104–06, 128, 167, 170
correlative conjunctions, 230
count nouns, 78–80

dangling participles, 320
declarative sentences (DS), 53, *53*, *61*, 61–62, 215–17
    See also basic sentences
Def. Art. *See* definite articles (Def. Art.)
definite articles (Def. Art.), 31–32, 63–64
Dem. *See* demonstratives (Dem)
demonstratives (Dem), 65, *74*, 91
deontic meaning, 178–79
dependent linguistic items, 52, 62–63, 89
descriptive grammar, 17–18, 22–25
det. *See* determiners (det.)
determiners (det.)
    defined, 43–44, 63
    definite articles, 31–32, 63–64
    demonstratives, 65, *74*, 91

    diagramming noun phrases with, *66*, 66–69, *67*, *68*, *69*
    indefinite articles, 64–65
    no, 196–98, *197*
    possessive determiners, 66, *73*, 88–89
    relative determiner *whose*, 270–71, *271*
    review of, within noun phrases, 73–74
diagramming
    basic sentences, *61*, 62, 73
    coordinating conjunctions, 235–41, *235–41*
    modals, 182, *182–90*, 184, 187, 189
    noun phrases as direct objects, 110, *110*, 166
    noun phrases as subjects, 66, *67*, 67–68
    object complements, *114*, 114–15, *115*, 166, *167*
    passive sentences, 207–12, *208–12*
    prepositional phrases, 70–72, *71*, *72*
    subject complements, *112*, 112–13, *113*, 166, *167*
    verbs, 162–67, *163*, *164*, *165*, *166*, *167*
direct objects (DO/do)
    diagramming noun phrases as, 110, *110*, 166
    noun phrases as, 102–04
    that and *who* as, 260–65, *261*, *262*, *264*, *265*, 270
distal demonstratives, 65
ditransitive verbs, 107
DO/do. *See* direct objects (DO/do)
do-support, 193
double negatives, 201, 335–36
DS. *See* declarative sentences (DS)
dummy subjects and cleft sentences, 99–101

echo questions, 221
-en participle, 155–56
epistemicity, 179
exclamative sentences, 56–57
existential constructions, 101
expletive *it*, 100–01
extraposed subjects, 100–01

false coordination, 230–32
finite verbs, 50–51, 155
first subjunctive, 175–77
foreign plural nouns, 83–84
form-function trees, *61*, 61–62, 322
    See also diagramming

form vs. function
    basic sentences and, *61*, 61–62
    forms with different functions, 91
    See also active and passive voice
future time, 179–81

gender and pronouns, 86–87, 93–94, 333–35
general present form, 157
gerunds and participle phrases, 301, 308–11, *309*, *310*, *311*
got-passive, 207
grammar
    descriptive and prescriptive, 17–18, 22–25
    grammar myths, 327–39
    meaning of, 18–20
grammaticalization, 30
grammatical patterns of nouns, 31–32
grammatical word classes
    auxiliary verbs, 43
    conjunctions, 44
    determiners, 43–44
    lexical word classes vs., 28
    pronouns, 42–43
    See also units of grammatical analysis
Greek plural nouns, 84

headwords, 60
Hebrew plural nouns, 84
hortative sentences, 56
hypercorrection, 90

imperative sentences, 55–56
impersonal pronouns and gender, 93–94
i-mutation plurals, 82
inchoative vs. stative passive, 207
Ind. Art. *See* indefinite articles (Ind. Art.)
indefinite articles (Ind. Art.), 64–65, *73*
indefinite pronouns, 92–93, 198–99, *199*
independent clauses, 52
independent possessive pronouns, 89
indirect objects (IO/io)
    diagramming noun phrases as, 111, *111*, *166*
    noun phrases as, 106–07
infinitival markers (inf. mark.), 304, *304*, *305*, *306*, 338

infinitive and participle phrases
    adverbial functions of, 320–22, *321*, *322*
    complements and adjuncts in, 312–15, *313*, *314*, *315*
    compound infinitives and participles, 315–16, *316*
    forms of the infinitive, 155, *299*, 299–301
    forms of the participle, 156, 162, *301*, 301–03
    grammar myth surrounding, 338
    in modifying functions, 316–19, *317*, *318*, *319*
    participle-noun continuum, 311–12
    participle phrases and gerunds, 301, 308–11, *309*, *310*, *311*
    phrase-clause boundaries, 303–07, *304*, *305*, *306*, *307*
    chapter exercises, 323–25
inflection phrases
    characterized, *61*, 61–62, 108–09, *109*
    be as sole verb, 167–70
    diagramming verbs, 162–67, *163*, *164*, *165*, *166*, *167*
    past perfect, 161–62
    past-perfect progressive, 162
    past progressive, 161
    present perfect, 160–61
    present-perfect progressive, 161
    present progressive, 158–60
    synthetic vs. periphrasic verbs, 153
    tense vs. aspect, 154–55
    verb forms, notes on, 155–58
    verb forms, synopsis, 158, *158*
    chapter exercises, 171–73
    See also noun phrases (NP); verb forms
inflection predicate, *61*, 61–62, 108–09, *109*
inf. mark. *See* infinitival markers (inf. mark.)
-ing participle, 155–56
intelligence, grammar myth surrounding, 330–32
interrogative pronouns, 95
interrogative sentences. *See* question formation
interrogative words, 54
intransitive verbs, 104, 137–39, *138*
IO/io. *See* indirect objects (IO/io)
irregular plural nouns, 81–84

Lamb, Charles, 339
language unity, fallacy of, 20–22

Latin plural nouns, 83–84
laziness, grammar myth surrounding, 329–30
lexical entries in diagrams, 67
lexical word classes
    adjectives, 35–39
    adverbs, 39–42
    grammatical word classes vs., 28
    nouns, 30–32
    verbs, 33–34
lists, 228–29
Lowth, Robert, *A Short Grammar of English*, 328–29, 335

matrix clauses, 278
modal verbs
    characterized, 177–78
    ability, 179
    deontic meaning, 178–79
    diagramming, 182, *182–90*, *184*, *187*, *189*
    epistemicity, 179
    future time, 179–81
    with progressive and perfect verb form, 181–82
    quasi-modals, 181
modification, 62
mood, 175

N. *See* nouns (N)
near-negatives, 196
Neg. *See* negation; negator (Neg.)
negation
    any, 199–201, *200*, *201*
    double negatives, 201, 335–36
    near-negatives, 196
    negative indefinite pronouns, 198–99, *199*
    no, 196–98, *197*
    not, 168, 193–96, *194*, *195*
    chapter exercises, 202
negative indefinite pronouns, 198–99, *199*
negator (Neg.), and *not*, 193
NICE (Negation, Inversion, Coding, and Emphasis), 168–70
no, 196–98, *197*
non-count nouns, 78–80
non-finite verbs, 51, 155

non-restrictive clauses, 269–70
not, 168, 193–96, *194*, *195*
noun clauses
    characterized, 277–78
    reported speech and tense shifting, 292–94
    type I, 278–85, *279*, *280*, *281*, *282*, *283*, *285*
    type II, 285–88, *286*, *287*, *288*
    type III, *289*, 289–92, *290*, *291*, *292*
    chapter exercises, 294–98
noun phrases (NP)
    defined, *61*, 61–63
    adjectives, *69*, 69–70, *70*
    appositives, 115–16
    determiners, 63–69, *66*, *67*, *68*, *69*
    as direct object, 102–04
    dummy subjects and cleft sentences, 99–101
    existential constructions, 101
    as indirect object, 106–07
    negation in, 196–201
    as object complement, 107–08
    prepositional phrases, 70–72, *71*, *72*
    review of determiners within, *73–74*
    as subject, 97–99
    as subject complement, 104–06
    transitivity, 104
    chapter exercises, 116–18
    See also inflection phrases
noun phrases, diagramming
    overview, 108–09, *109*
    with determiners, *66*, *67*, 67–69, *68*, *69*
    as direct object, 110, *110*
    as indirect object, 111, *111*
    as object complement, *114*, 114–15, *115*
    as subject complement, *112*, 112–13, *113*
nouns (N)
    collective, 80
    count and non-count nouns, 78–80
    in diagramming noun phrases, *66*, *67*, 67–68
    foreign plurals, 83–84
    older English plurals, 82–83
    participle-noun continuum, 311–12
    pluralia tantum, 81
    proper and common nouns, 77–78
    voicing plurals, 83

chapter exercises, 95–96
See also infinitive and participle phrases; pronouns (Pro)
NP. *See* noun phrases (NP)

object complement (OC)
    diagramming, *114*, 114–15, *115*, *166*, *167*
    noun phrase as, 107–08
object of the preposition (OP)
    diagramming noun phrases as, 72, *72*
    relative pronouns as, 266–69, *267*, *269*
    wh-words as, 220–21
object pronouns, 87–88
OC. *See* object complement (OC)
older English plural nouns, 82–83
OP. *See* object of the preposition (OP)
open-class words, 30, 40
operators, 163, 195
Oxford comma, 229

P. *See* prepositions (P)
parallel structure in coordination, 229–30
participle phrases. *See* infinitive and participle phrases
parts of speech
    adjectives, 35–39
    adverbs, 39–42
    auxiliary verbs, 43
    conjunctions, 44
    determiners, 43–44
    lexical vs. grammatical, 28
    nouns, 30–32
    pronouns, 42–43
    top-level categories, 27
    verbs, 33–34
    word classes and productivity, 29–30
    word classes treated herein, 28–29, *29*
    chapter exercises, 45–48
    See also adjectives (Adj.); adverbs (Adv.); auxiliary verbs (Aux); conjunctions (Conj.); determiners (det.); nouns (N); pronouns (Pro); verbs (V)
passivization
    described, 204–05
    diagramming passive sentences, 207–12, *208–12*

grammar myth surrounding, 332–33
passive verb forms, 206–07
stative vs. inchoative, 207
when to use, 205–06
past participle, 155–56
past perfect, 161–62
past-perfect progressive, 162
past progressive, 161
patient (semantic) role, 203–04
periphrasic verbs, 153
personal pronouns
    compound pronouns and case, 89–90
    gender and, 86–87, 93–94, 333–35
    object pronouns, 87–88
    possessive pronouns, 88–89
    subject pronouns, 85–86
phrasal verbs
    intransitive, 137–39, *138*
    list of common, 343–47
    prepositional-phrasal verbs, *145*, 145–47, *146*, *147*
    separable and inseparable, 143–45, *144*
    transitive, 139–43, *140*, *141*, *142*, *143*
phrase-clause boundaries, 303–07, *304*, *305*, *306*, *307*
phrases, defined, 50–51
pied-piping vs. preposition stranding, 220–21, 267–69, *269*
pluralia tantum nouns, 81
plural markers, 32
plural nouns, irregular, 81–84
polarity, 222
Poss. *See* possessives (Poss.)
possessives (Poss.)
    possessive determiners, 66, *73*, 88–89
    possessive pronouns, 88–89
postcedent noun phrases, 85
postpositive adjectives, 35n1
PP. *See* prepositional phrases (PP)
predicate phrases (Pred. Ph.)
    diagramming modals, *182*, *182–90*, *184*, *187*, *189*
    diagramming verbs, 162–67, *163*, *164*, *165*, *166*, *167*
    inflection phrases and, 108–09, *109*
    negation in, 193–96
    See also noun phrases, diagramming

predicates (PRED/pred), 35–36, 38, 105
Pred. Ph. *See* predicate phrases (Pred. Ph.)
PRED/pred. *See* predicates (PRED/pred)
preposed direct objects, 103
prepositional-phrasal verbs, *145*, 145–47, *146*, *147*
prepositional phrases (PP)
    adjuncts, as "extra," 119–20
    as adverbial adjuncts, 123–27, *124*, *125*, *126*
    as adverbial complements (*See* adverbial complements [AC])
    as attitudinal adjuncts, 121–23, *122*, *123*
    core clause elements and, 120–21, *121*
    diagramming, 70–72, *71*, *72*
    as subject complements, 104, 105
    chapter exercises, 148–51
prepositional verbs, 136–37, *137*
prepositions (P), 44–45, 327–28, 341–42
preposition stranding vs. pied-piping, 220–21, 267–69, *269*
Pres. *See* present forms (Pres.)
prescriptive grammar, 17–18, 22–25
present anterior aspect, 160
present forms (Pres.)
    general present, 157
    present anterior aspect, 160
    present participle, 155–56
    present perfect, 160–61
    present-perfect progressive, 161
    present progressive, 158–60
    third-person singular present, 156
principle verb parts, 157
Pro. *See* pronouns (Pro)
Prog. *See* progressive forms (Prog.)
progressive forms (Prog.)
    defined, 43
    modal verbs with, 181–82
    past-perfect progressive, 162
    past progressive, 161
    present-perfect progressive, 161
    present progressive, 158–60
pronouns (Pro)
    characterized, 42–43, 84–85
    compound pronouns and case, 89–90
    demonstrative, 91
    gender and, 86–87, 93–94, 333–35
    indefinite pronouns, 92–93
    object pronouns, 87–88
    possessive pronouns, 88–89
    quantifier expressions, 95
    reflexive/reciprocal, 94–95
    relative and interrogative, 95
    subject pronouns, 85–86
    chapter exercises, 95–96
    See also nouns (N)
proper nouns, 77–78
protasis, 252
proximal demonstratives, 65

quantifier expressions, 95
quasi-modals, 181
question formation
    declarative sentences vs., 215–17
    echo questions, 221
    tag questions, 56, 169, 222–24
    who/whom, 219–21
    wh-questions, 54–55, *55*, 217–19, 289–92
    wh-words as objects of a preposition, 220–21
    yes/no questions, *53*, 53–54, *54*, 216–17, 285–88
    chapter exercises, 224–25

reflexive/reciprocal pronouns, 94–95
regeneration, of structure, 235
relative clauses
    characterized, 52, 257–58
    Ø-relative, 265–66, *266*
    non-restrictive, 259, 269–70
    relative determiner *whose*, 270–71, *271*
    relative pronouns as objects of the preposition, 266–69, *267*, *269*
    relative pronoun usage recap, 272
    restrictive clauses, defined, 260
    restrictive vs. non-restrictive, 258–60, 272
    who and *that* as subjects and direct objects, 260–65, *261*, *262*, *264*, *265*, 269–70
    chapter exercises, 272–75
relative pronouns (Rel. Pro.)
    Ø-relative, 265–66, *266*
    functions within relative clauses, 95, 257–58

as objects of the preposition, 266–69, *267*, *269*
usage recap, 272
who and *that* as subjects and direct objects, 260–65, *261*, *262*, *264*, *265*
Rel. Pro. *See* relative pronouns (Rel. Pro.)
reported speech and tense shifting, 292–94
resultative aspect, 160

s. *See* subordinate clauses (s)
SC. *See* subject complement (SC)
Scotland (Brown), 328, 329
second subjunctive, 177, 251–54, *253*
semantic roles, 203–04
sentence types
    declarative, 53, *53*, 61, *61*–62, 215–17
    exclamative, 56–57
    imperative, 55–56
    tag questions, 56
    wh-questions, 54–55, *55*, 289–92
    yes/no questions, *53*, 53–54, *54*, 216–17, 285–88
    See also basic sentences; question formation
A Short Grammar of English (Lowth), 328–29, 335
simple active participle, 155–56
simple infinitives, 155, 299
simple past, 157
simple perfect participle, 155–56
simple sentences, 234
    See also basic sentences
singular *they*, grammar myths surrounding, 333–35
speech, parts of. *See* parts of speech
standard English, 18–19, 23
stative vs. inchoative passive, 207
structural definition, 31
suasive verbs, 176
subject-auxiliary inversion, 216–17, 222
subject complement (SC)
    diagramming, *112*, 112–13, *113*, *166*, *167*
    noun phrases as, 104–06
subject-predicate split, 59–60
subject pronouns, 85–86
subjects (SUBJ/subj)
    diagramming noun phrases as, *66*, *67*, 67–68
    form vs. function, 61, *61*
    noun phrases as, 97–99

that and *who* as, 260–65, *261*, *262*, *264*, *265*, 269
SUBJ/subj. *See* subjects (SUBJ/subj)
subjunctive mood, 175
subordinate clauses (s), 52, 233
    See also adverbial clauses (Adv. Cl.)
subordinated exclamatives, 289n2
subordinating conjunctions, 246
synthetic verbs, 153

tag questions, 56, 169, 222–24
tense (inflection phrase branch)
    diagramming modals, 182, *182*–90, *184*, *187*, *189*
    diagramming verbs, 162–67, *163*, *164*, *165*, *166*, *167*
    inflection phrases and, 108–09, *109*
    See also noun phrases, diagramming
tense shifting and reported speech, 292–94
tense vs. aspect, 154–55
that as subject and direct object, 260–65, *261*, *262*, *264*, *265*
there is and *there are*, 223–24
third-person singular present, 156
transitive phrasal verbs, 139–43, *140*, *141*, *142*, *143*
transitivity, 104
type I noun clauses, 278–85, *279*, *280*, *281*, *282*, *283*, *285*
type II noun clauses, 285–88, *286*, *287*, *288*
type III noun clauses, *289*, 289–92, *290*, *291*, *292*

umlaut plurals, 82
units of grammatical analysis
    clauses, 52
    declarative sentences, 53, *53*, 61, *61*–62, 215–17
    exclamative sentences, 56–57
    imperative sentences, 55–56
    phrases, 50–51
    tag questions, 56, 169, 222–24
    wh-questions, 54–55, *55*, 217–19, 289–92
    words, 49–50
    yes/no questions, *53*, 53–54, *54*, 216–17, 285–88
    chapter exercises, 57–58
    See also parts of speech
univerbating, 50

V. *See* verbs (V)
verb forms
    synopsis of, 158, *158*
    ability and, 179
    deontic meaning and, 178–79
    epistemicity and, 179
    first subjunctive, 175–77, 254
    future time and, 179–81
    modal verbs, characterized, 177–78
    modal verbs with progressive and perfect form, 181–82
    notes on, 155–58
    passive verb forms, 206–07
    past perfect, 161–62
    past-perfect progressive, 162
    past progressive, 161
    present perfect, 160–61
    present-perfect progressive, 161
    present progressive, 158–60
    quasi-modals, 181
    reported speech and tense shifting, 292–94
    second subjunctive, 177, *235, 250, 251*, 251–53, *253*
    subjunctive mood, 175
    chapter exercises, 190–91
verb phrases (VP), 109, *109*, 164, *164*
verbs (V)
    introduced, 33–34
    be as sole verb, 167–70
    copulative, 104–06, 128, 167, 170
    diagramming, 162–67, *163, 164, 165, 166, 167*
    ditransitive, 107
    finite, 50–51
    prepositional, 136–37, *137*
    synthetic vs. periphrasic, 153
    transitive and intransitive, 104
    verb trajectory completion and adverbial complements, 132–33
    See also modal verbs; phrasal verbs; verb phrases (VP)
vocatives, 55
voice. *See* active and passive voice
voicing plural nouns, 83
VP. *See* verb phrases (VP)

weak nouns, 82
were vs. *was*, 254
who as subject and direct object, 260–65, *261, 262, 264, 265*
whose as relative determiner, 270–71, *271*
who/whom, 219–21
wh-questions, 54–55, *55*, 217–19, 289–92
wh-words as objects of a preposition, 220–21
word classes. *See* parts of speech
words, defined, 49–50

yes/no questions, *53*, 53–54, *54*, 216–17, 285–88
Yule, George, 21

From the Publisher

A name never says it all, but the word "Broadview" expresses a good deal of the philosophy behind our company. We are open to a broad range of academic approaches and political viewpoints. We pay attention to the broad impact book publishing and book printing has in the wider world; for some years now we have used 100% recycled paper for most titles. Our publishing program is internationally oriented and broad-ranging. Our individual titles often appeal to a broad readership too; many are of interest as much to general readers as to academics and students.

Founded in 1985, Broadview remains a fully independent company owned by its shareholders—not an imprint or subsidiary of a larger multinational.

To order our books or obtain up-to-date information, please visit broadviewpress.com.

broadview press
www.broadviewpress.com

This book is made of paper from well-managed FSC® - certified forests, recycled materials, and other controlled sources.